In Defense of Public Lands

STEVEN DAVIS

In Defense of Public Lands

The Case against Privatization and Transfer

TEMPLE UNIVERSITY PRESS
Philadelphia • Rome • Tokyo

TEMPLE UNIVERSITY PRESS
Philadelphia, Pennsylvania 19122
www.temple.edu/tempress

FRONTISPIECE: Porcupine Mountains Wilderness State Park, Michigan.
(Photo by the author.)

Design by Kate Nichols

Library of Congress Cataloging-in-Publication Data

Names: Davis, Steven, 1964– author.
Title: In defense of public lands : the case against privatization and
  transfer / Steven Davis.
Description: Philadelphia : Temple University Press, 2018. | Includes
  bibliographical references and index.
Identifiers: LCCN 2017051753 (print) | LCCN 2018011721 (ebook) |
  ISBN 9781439915387 (E-book) | ISBN 9781439915363 (hardback :
  alk. paper) | ISBN 9781439915370 (paper : alk. paper)
Subjects: LCSH: Public lands—Government policy—United States. |
  Privatization—United States. | BISAC: POLITICAL SCIENCE /
  Public Policy / Environmental Policy. | NATURE / Environmental
  Conservation & Protection. | BUSINESS & ECONOMICS /
  Environmental Economics.
Classification: LCC HD216 (ebook) | LCC HD216 .D38 2018 (print) |
  DDC 331.1/60973—dc23
LC record available at https://lccn.loc.gov/2017051753

Printed in the United States of America

9 8 7 6 5 4 3 2 1

To Samuel, Julian, and Zola: I hope I have instilled in them a love of our public lands and a fierce dedication to protecting them

And in memory of Bob Marshall (1901–1939), for whom the love of wilderness and the love of equality and social justice were indistinguishable parts of a whole

Contents

Preface

They hang the man and flog the woman
That steal the goose from off the common,
But let the greater villain loose
That steals the common from the goose.

—Eighteenth-century English folk poem, quoted in Bill Wade,
"A New Tragedy for the Commons," *George Wright Forum*

I GREW UP among the vast tracts of postwar suburbia around Chicago. My parents, like their parents, were urban people who grew up in three-flats and apartment blocks in Chicago and Brooklyn. So as a suburban kid with city-bred parents, I did not have much exposure to wild nature or any sort of family tradition in the Great Outdoors. There were no camping trips, no summer camps in the North Woods, no grand tours of the national parks.

How, then, did I come to spend most of my life seeking out, enjoying, longing for, teaching about, reading about, studying, contemplating, and advocating for wild land? A good chunk of the credit must go to the visionary planners and civic leaders who had the bold foresight and civic devotion to establish the Forest Preserve District of Cook County (Illinois) in 1916 (the same year when the National Park Service was created). Growing eventually to 67,000 acres, or roughly 11 percent of the nation's second-most populous county,[1] the Cook County Forest Preserves consist of corridors of wild land along the region's riverways and beyond. Along with the neighboring counties' forest preserve districts, they form a green necklace of forests, wetlands, prairies, and savannas around one of America's most intensely urban metro areas, whose asphalt sprawl stretches across the flatlands of northern Illinois for nearly 7,200 square miles.[2] Today, an appraisal of the real estate on which these preserves sit would likely yield an astronomical sum that would suggest to a free-market advocate that frogs, big bluestem, and bur oaks are not the "best and highest use" of this land. It is something of a small miracle, then, that this wild land, some of which has never seen a plow or saw, remains intact.

As a ten-year-old kid marooned in an ocean of manicured lawns, cul-de-sacs, strip malls, and parking lots, I would seek my escape by jumping on my bike and riding the two miles to Linne Woods, the nearest outpost of the forest preserves along the North Branch of the Chicago River. Despite being little more than 100 acres and surrounded by six-lane arterials and fast-food joints, Linne Woods was, to me at least, a mighty citadel, bursting with mystery, adventure, inspiration, and integrity. In this little refuge, mammoth cottonwoods, which seemed to me as big as Sequoias, lined the bottomlands beside the river and were often full of raucous, roosting crows. In the drier areas, dark old forests of red oaks and sugar maples were carpeted with trillium and mayapples in the spring. Along the western edge, the forest gave way to sunny open prairies and brushy, rabbit-laden meadows that filled the humid summer air with the smell of wild bergamot and Virginia mountain mint, both of which grew profusely. There, the natural world cast its spell on me and led me to become its life-long student. There, I wandered aimlessly for hours and once tried, unsuccessfully of course, to fish with a stick and a string and a safety pin. There, I taught myself to identify trees and once fell through the ice of the river on a 10-degree day and lived to tell about it.

Later, as a teen, when I procured the driver's license that conferred full citizenship on a child of the suburbs, I began to branch out farther, exploring the larger preserves along the Des Plaines River and beyond. By the time I got to college, there was no stopping me. Over the years, I have had the joy and the privilege of trekking and tramping through public lands—from the dark dripping rain forests of Washington's Olympic Peninsula to the

enchanting Sea Islands off Georgia's coast and from the magnifi-
cently austere Canyonlands of the Southwest to the still, clear
lakes and emerald-green forests of the North Woods. Mine has
been a life spent exploring and observing our public lands and
never ceasing to come away inspired and enriched, whether on a
special trip to a far and grand place or, much more frequently, on
a hike close to home in southern Wisconsin's rolling oak woods.
Public wild land, then, has shaped my entire life, both professional and personal.

Those who would privatize public land often scornfully dismiss as *rent seekers* those who hike, hunt, pick mushrooms, or kay-
ak on public land, contending that they want to push the costs of
their personal preferences onto everyone else. This book strongly
challenges that notion, perhaps as a way of engaging in what I
like to think of as *rent paying*, a way of attending to my debt for
this irreplaceable inheritance that I, as an American citizen, have
had bestowed on me.

For those who even vaguely monitor natural resource policy
in this country, it is becoming quite obvious that for public lands
and their supporters, some very dark clouds have gathered over-
head. Hardly a month seems to go by without the emergence of
new threats to our public lands, whether in the guise of radical
state and federal legislation to privatize, declassify, or transfer
public land, or the seizure of public land facilities and threats
against land managers by armed militants. At the subnational
level, state and local public land systems are increasingly beset by
disinvestment, outsourced management, and even mothballing
and outright sell-off.[3] And now, with the change of administration in Washington and the corresponding move from whole-
hearted support of public lands to something far less, the pace
of change promises to accelerate. To those interested in keeping
public land public, our nation has entered an extremely perilous
age (as Chapters 1 and 7 address in greater depth).

I offer this book, then, as something of a "gentle polemic,"
to borrow Charles Goodsell's characterization of his own renowned defense of the federal bureaucracy,[4] but a polemic that
is bolstered by all the empirical evidence that I, as a political

scientist, can muster. Until now, my research on the public lands has always stayed scrupulously in the lane of value-free, empirical description and analysis. For this endeavor, however, I feel a compelling need to place my disciplinary expertise at the service of something I care about passionately. As such, this book is prescriptive as well as descriptive and is aimed as much at the policy maker and citizen as at the scholar.

As anyone even remotely familiar with this topic knows, no shortage of ink has been spilled debating the merits or flaws of public land and whether it should be privatized or at least radically reconfigured in some way. Much of this literature, however, argues from the very narrow perspective of economics, ethics, law, or philosophy—and that leaves some large gaps in the public lands literature. For example, few serious comparative evaluations of the performance of our public and private lands are based on overt biological and ecological measures, a realm that seems utterly incomprehensible to the classical economists and is often brushed over in a fairly superficial way even by philosophers and ethicists. This book sets out to offer, at this pivotal moment in the national debate, a fuller, more comprehensive, and multidisciplinary argument for why public land ought to remain firmly in the public's hands. My intent is to make this argument as broad and encompassing as possible, examining empirically and theoretically issues that touch on various aspects of biology, economics, and politics. As such, the individual arguments in their entirety may not even cohere philosophically or paradigmatically. For example, arguments for why privatization is bad economics are almost always instrumentalist in nature, while political arguments about the legitimacy of society's collective preferences tend to stress the inherent value of nature and the morality embedded in that preference. The fact that these two approaches are not necessarily intellectually compatible in no way diminishes their persuasiveness or relevance to the question of privatization. My goal, then, is not to construct a seamless and unified philosophical treatise but, rather, to explore from as many relevant angles as possible why the privatization of our public lands is a dangerous and misguided policy notion and to consider the issue and make this broader argument by borrowing from the insights of diverse perspectives.

The Plan of the Book

This book, then, unapologetically makes the case for public lands on biological, economic, and political grounds. In Chapter 1, I introduce the reader to the massive infrastructure of public land that accounts for nearly 1 in 3 American acres. I begin by presenting a very brief history and basic characteristics of this system at the local, state, and federal levels. Chapter 1 also introduces the growing but also cyclical movement to privatize and otherwise reshape public, and especially federal, lands.

Chapter 2 lays out the privatizers' arguments in greater detail and examines the numerous variations of their policy visions and prescriptions. Chapter 3 begins to make the case for public lands, exploring the biological and ecological dimensions of this debate. Comparing how environmental health can be measured on public versus private land, it tests the privatizers' central claim that private land is destined to be better cared for.

Chapter 4 turns to economics—the privatizers' home turf. Going beyond the intellectual limitations of classical free-market economics, this chapter offers a more expansive and nuanced examination of questions of markets and valuation. This chapter builds a case for public land on the basis of measures that derive not only from a traditional economics paradigm (such as return on investment and multiplier effects) but also from the newer and broader framework of *ecosystem services*.

Chapter 5 looks at the wide-ranging political dimensions of the issue, including the fundamental tension between collective values and democracy, on the one hand, and individual preferences and markets, on the other. It also explores aggregate public preferences as measured through survey research. Chapter 6 continues to make the political case for public lands, focusing on the nature and performance of bureaucratic management, the legitimacy of interest-group participation, and centralized versus decentralized decision making, as well as how these factors correspond to community input. Chapter 7 concludes by contemplating the future of our public lands in the face of the many existing challenges and promises, both immediate and long term.

Acknowledgments

THIS BOOK has been a more-than-two-year labor of love that would not have been possible without the generosity and support of Edgewood College, where I teach and have made my career in the Social Science Department for nearly a quarter century. In the fall 2015 semester, I was granted a research sabbatical, which was essential to this endeavor. I especially thank my colleagues at Edgewood, faculty and staff, for all their help and encouragement. Specifically, David Wells and the Art Department were incredibly generous in allowing me to hole up and write on occasion at the peaceful and beautiful Painted Forest Studio. Additionally, I acknowledge my students, past and present, whose passion and public-spiritedness leave me hopeful for the future. Gratitude is also due to Aaron Javsicas and the editorial staff at Temple University Press for believing in this project, supporting it, and helping bring it to fruition. I also thank all my colleagues across the country who study public lands, whose work has been invaluable and inspirational to me and from which I have freely borrowed.

I thank Jen Tooley for her love and support, her impressive book savvy, and her boundless enthusiasm for this project of mine. My children, Sam, Julian, and Zola, have also extended to me great love, encouragement, and understanding.

Finally, I thank all the fine and competent public servants in the U.S. Forest Service, National Park Service, U.S. Fish and Wildlife Service, Bureau of Land Management, and state and local agencies—the few I have come into contact with over the years and the vast majority I have not—for working diligently, sometimes under very difficult and hostile conditions, to protect public lands on behalf of us all.

In Defense of Public Lands

1

Public Land and Its Discontents

> Public land policy remains a process of maddening historic
> changeability and contingency, and I think that is one principal
> reason why everyone got so cranky in our times. . . . [T]hings
> were unsettled a hundred years ago and things are unsettled now.
> —Patricia Nelson Limerick, "A History of the Public Lands
>   Debate," in *Challenging Federal Ownership and Management*

The Origins of the Public Lands

IN MANY WAYS, public lands in America are a window
into the larger society and its many contradictions and internal tensions. They are, at once, a quintessentially American
idea—in fact, according to Wallace Stegner,[1] "the best idea we
ever had," and at the same time an unfathomable anomaly in the
most Lockean nation the world has ever known. How could it
possibly be true, critics ask, that in the land where faith in private
property approaches a civic religion, 1 of every 3 acres is collectively held?

   The history of our public lands can be seen as a long tug-of-
war between the disposal and retention of the lands that came
under the government's control. With European settlement, native people's communal, ownerless conception of the land they
wandered across and lived and hunted on came to be supplanted
by a regime of English property law. Royal charters were written
that granted to some of the colonies huge, imprecisely drawn,
and often overlapping territory that extended west all the way to
the wilderness of Appalachia and beyond to Ohio.[2] After the War
of Independence, states that were not granted western claims

in their charters came to argue that their participation in the Revolution earned them the right to some of this land. That argument, the squabbles over disputed and unclear state claims, and the prospect of renewed Indian wars in this unsettled land led the states to eventually agree to let the federal government control the frontier lands.[3] And thus was born the concept and reality of federal land, although the intent was for these lands not to be managed or held for long but to be granted to homesteaders as quickly as possible. This disposal was to be achieved not necessarily for revenue, as much as Alexander Hamilton liked that idea, but for the purposes of nation-building and the fulfillment of Thomas Jefferson's dream of a nation of independent freeholders.[4]

Federal control of lands expanded repeatedly in the decades following the Revolution through ensuing waves of treaties, annexations, purchases, and military conquests, including the Louisiana Purchase (1803), Florida (1819), Oregon Territory (1846), Texas (1846), the Mexican War and the resulting Treaty of Guadalupe Hidalgo (1848), the Gadsden Purchase (1853), Alaska (1867), and Hawaii (1898). Over the course of the nineteenth century, the federal government would acquire an astonishing 1.6 billion acres,[5] or nearly 70 percent, of the land in the United States. As stated previously, the federal government's official policy was to dispose of these lands, and dispose of them it did, giving away at least two-thirds for free.[6] All told, the federal government privatized approximately 1 billion acres through grants to homesteaders, railroads, mining interests, and military veterans. This homesteading effort was helped along, it should be noted, by a harsh federal policy of Indian removal and relocation across much of this range. The federal government also granted land (two, and later four, sections from each thirty-six-section township) to each new state, beginning with Ohio in 1803, for the purposes of supporting public education and sometimes other institutions, such as hospitals, prisons, and universities (hence the term *land grant university*).[7] Paul Frymer chronicles how this entire process, despite seeming like a mad rush, was actually tightly orchestrated by a rather small and constrained federal government to facilitate its national vision on its terms, constitutionally and racially.[8]

From Disposal to Retention

This disposal policy may have continued unabated until every last public acre was divested were it not for the confluence of four interrelated developments in the latter half of the nineteenth century. First, America, and especially the populous Northeast, emerged from the Civil War as an increasingly industrialized and urbanized society, which, in turn, gave rise to an urban middle class with the unheard-of luxury of leisure time and some disposable income with which to enjoy it. Second, word began to trickle back east from explorers and adventurers about the strange and glorious wonders of remote western places, such as Yosemite, Yellowstone, and the Grand Canyon. Magazines began to popularize these marvels with breathlessly exuberant articles, and public interest increased.[9] Demographically, the readership of these stunning travelogues and the ranks of this newly affluent leisure class overlapped enough to create new demand to visit and even protect these natural wonders as a wave of nostalgia swept the land. Americans began to pine for the lost virtues of an older, simpler America of brave cowboys and noble Indians and thundering herds of bison.

Third, the policy of disposal began to come undone by its own rapaciousness. In the popular mind, the process of federal land disposal increasingly came to be seen as a sordid affair marred by waste, corruption, scandal, and environmental ruination.[10] This was, after all, the era of unregulated market hunters, which led to the slaughter of the supposedly limitless passenger pigeon and bison and the plumed birds desired for fashionable ladies' hats. Meanwhile, by 1900, the vast pineries of the Upper Midwest were completely obliterated, replaced by countless square miles of fire-prone slash and stump-filled wastelands.[11] Whitetail deer were reduced to a few hundred thousand nationwide, while beaver and otter, to name just a few species, became nearly extinct.[12] Furthermore, in 1890, the Superintendent of the Census declared the frontier officially closed.[13] All at once, it seemed, the country was jolted into a realization of limits and scarcity, which came to replace the assumptions of unlimited bounty and a magically endless frontier that, up until that point, had been seen as the most durable of American birthrights.

Finally, the late nineteenth century began to see a vigorous clamoring for political reform, embodied most significantly by the Progressive movement. By stressing efficiency and good government and emphasizing the public interest over individual self-interests, the Progressives were exactly the right political actors at exactly the right time to put a new policy of retention into motion.

The Movement for Retention of the Western Lands

The first tender shoots of federal land retention policy actually sprouted decades before the Progressive Era, when Congress set aside specific, particularly alluring, parcels of the federal domain on an ad hoc basis. Yosemite, quickly handed over to California for management in 1864, and Yellowstone, protected as the first national park in 1872, are the two most famous examples. As these haphazard withdrawals continued for the next few decades, what limited management that existed was provided by the U.S. military. As time went on, however, it became increasingly clear that some sort of administrative superstructure was needed to properly manage these reserves. As it was, the areas were vulnerable to timber rustling, illegal grazing and homesteading, and poaching,[14] and their lack of any sort of organized constituency left them vulnerable to constant political attack.[15]

The impetus behind the changing attitudes toward public land was not just a concern over recreation and the protection of scenic wonders. There was a growing sense of revulsion and dismay at the massive scale of deforestation east of the Mississippi, but especially in the Upper Midwest, where loggers left behind a scene of environmental plunder and devastation of absolutely epic proportions. Between 1850 and 1910, the nation's annual timber production rose from 5.4 billion board feet (bbf) to 44.5 bbf,[16] and at the epicenter of this great harvest was Wisconsin, which led the entire world in timber production in 1899.[17] In the wake of this destruction in the North Woods, a cycle of cataclysmic fires repeatedly plagued the logged areas, sterilizing the forest soils and leaving stunted, scrubby brushlands in place of once-lush forests.[18] As the Great Lakes states were stripped of their forests, the industry headed south.

Fears of a future timber famine coincided with a strengthening Progressive reform movement, with its focus on scientific, rational planning; careful management; and the prioritization of the collective national interest over individual interests—what Samuel Hayes famously called the "gospel of efficiency."[19] Faced with this pressure, in 1891, Congress granted President Benjamin Harrison the power to establish a system of forest reserves; by 1897, he and his successor, Grover Cleveland, had authorized 39 million acres of new forest reserves to be transferred from the disposal-oriented General Land Office (GLO).[20] In short order, it became abundantly clear that an entity with the expertise that the Progressive ideal demanded was needed to manage all this land. So in 1905, the U.S. Forest Service (USFS) was created within the Department of Agriculture, and an additional 132 million acres of the federal domain were designated as new national forests.[21] Meanwhile, the 1906 Antiquities Act gave the president executive authority to create national monuments, a power that President Theodore Roosevelt, a Progressive, used with great relish.[22]

Although the advancing preservationist ethic of this era envisioned a pristine, empty wilderness, Mark Spence reminds us that the federal lands not disposed of through homesteading to white settlers were by no means unoccupied. In fact, Native American tribes had lived and hunted on these lands for millennia, and the establishment of forest reserves, monuments, and national parks in this era consequently led to the forced removal of many native communities. For many decades thereafter, federal managers would downplay or diminish this reality because, as Spence points out, "full recognition would make plain that the American preservationist ideal is predicated on Indian dispossession."[23]

One might think that because of Progressivism's role in advocating for federal retention and management of land, the movement's penchant for comprehensive, rational, and efficient planning would have had more of an influence in the creation of a more centralized and streamlined structure for federal management. Instead, as Leigh Raymond and Sally Fairfax argue, it was more of an ad hoc, fragmented, and lurching process that took many decades to unfold.[24] The USFS was created to conserve needed resources, but a very different agency with its own preservation-oriented mandate, the National Park Service (NPS), was created in 1916, after much dogged advocacy by a few determined individuals,[25] to manage the scenic wonders and new monuments that had been so recently popularized.

This flurry of legislative and executive action to permanently secure and manage federal lands was certainly significant, but the majority of federal lands in the momentous year of 1916 were still held by the GLO and slated for eventual disposal. The tide did not fully turn from disposal to retention until the New Deal era and the passage of the Taylor Grazing Act of 1934, which mostly ended the sale of federal grazing land and established Grazing Districts to be managed by the government.[26] In 1946, the Grazing Service and the GLO were merged to create the Bureau of Land Management (BLM), which was tasked with managing these vast tracts of rangeland and desert.[27]

Federal Lands in the East

Unlike in the West, areas east of the Rocky Mountains were either never held by the federal government (New England and the Southeast, for example), or, if they were (as in the case of the Illinois or Minnesota Territory), the land was homesteaded and privatized long before the movement for retention began. Still, the federal government currently owns more than 41.6 million acres in the East, the Great Plains, and the Midwest (excluding the Dakotas).[28] It is a very different story how this land came to be federally owned; for the most part, it occurred through a painstaking process of acquisition from private owners rather than retention of already held land. In 1911, Congress passed the Weeks Act, which gave the federal government the authority to purchase private land. From that point, and especially during the New Deal years, the federal government bought and established national forests and, to a lesser extent, parks and wildlife refuges throughout New England, Southern Appalachia, the Upper Midwest, the Ozarks, the Ohio Valley, and the Deep South. Much of this land was exhausted, cutover stump fields left by the logging rush of earlier decades; federal ownership was intended to provide forest restoration and conservation.[29] More often than not, such land was abandoned and tax delinquent, and so the federal government purchased it from states, counties, and other local governments as the tax forfeitures reverted to public ownership. It should be noted that, in the same era, many eastern state forests and county forests (in the few states where they exist) were also acquired through similar tax forfeitures of abandoned land. In Wisconsin, for example, national forest, state forest, and county forest lands exist side by side in the North Woods and largely share the same origins as public land.[30]

As historian Patricia Limerick asserts, federal land policy has always been dynamic and fluid and, consequently, quite contentious.[31] Randall Wilson argues that rather than a simple titanic, zero-sum struggle of commodity seekers versus preservationists, public land politics has been a complex and nuanced "blending" of these "diametrically opposed ideas."[32] Essentially, three broad objectives have motivated public land management to one extent or another for the past century: (1) the preservation of landscapes, ecosystems, and biodiversity; (2) resource extraction of marketable commodities; and (3) recreational opportunities, passive and active, for the general public.[33] Just as federal land policy has evolved from disposal to retention, so too has the tenor and main thrust of federal land oversight since the decision was made to retain and manage public land. Although fragmented federal agencies have always had different mandates and Organic Acts, one can still discern trends and shifts in federal management as a whole over the years. The earliest phase, from the 1890s until the 1940s, was fairly passive, especially in the USFS, which took a custodial role and produced relatively little timber.[34] Moreover, the cutover lands in the eastern forests saw a great deal of reforestation and restoration during this period.

By the post–World War II era, rapid economic growth, pent-up demand for lumber, and a decline in private timber production, especially in the heavily logged South (which saw a 40 percent decline in production between 1945 and 1970), pushed federal land management into its next phase, with a much more aggressive emphasis on resource extraction.[35] In the national forests, controversial and heretofore rarely used even-age timber harvesting (also known as *clearcutting*) became the norm, as annual timber production on federal land skyrocketed 1,700 percent from an annual average harvest of 0.74 bbf in the years before 1940 to 12.6 bbf by 1988.[36] Similarly, on federal rangelands, ranching interests' political power peaked, and a stable regime of political accommodation developed with Congress and the BLM as grazing pressure increased and the prices of leases were kept attractively low. In fact, some political scientists consider this arrangement in the 1950s and 1960s as perhaps the purest real-world manifestation of the concept of the "iron triangle," connecting congressional committees, agencies, and private interests in a mutually symbiotic relationship.[37] To summarize, in this postwar period of rapid economic expansion, federal rivers were for damming, forests for logging, grass for grazing, and national parks for developing tourist-oriented infrastructure.

From the 1970s to the 1990s, such aggressive resource production had become increasingly untenable, politically and ecologically. Legislation passed in the late 1960s and 1970s (the National Environmental Policy Act, the Federal Land Policy and Management Act [FLPMA], the National Forest Management Act [NFMA], and the Endangered Species Act) increasingly gave environmentalists the legal tools and access necessary to challenge federal agencies' policy outputs.[38] This legal pressure, especially related to the logging of the dwindling remnants of old-growth forests, intensified in the late 1980s and early 1990s, causing no small amount of gridlock.[39] Court injunctions and the routinization of administrative challenges and appeals created a reckoning of sorts, which pushed reluctant USFS personnel into the next management era—one focused on restoring a greater balance between resource production and ecological concerns.[40] This more holistic, landscape-scale approach has become known as *ecosystem management*.[41] Around the same time, the BLM and the U.S. Fish and Wildlife Service (USFWS) made similar philosophical shifts toward incorporating ecosystem management principles. It is important, however, not to exaggerate the effects of this shift, as resource extraction, despite claims to the contrary from critics and some western members of Congress, remains a major element of federal and, even more so, state land management policy. One need only look at the explosive spread of natural-gas production sites using relatively new fracking methods all across BLM lands, national forests, and state forests[42] to see evidence of the limits to the ecosystem management "revolution." These issues are explored in considerably more depth in later chapters.

Public Lands in the United States Today

States and the federal government collectively own approximately 836 million acres of land in a nation of 2.27 billion acres, or 36.8 percent.[43] Figure 1.1 shows the distribution of this public land. About three-quarters of this public land (635 million acres) is federal property. For this reason alone, federal land usually dominates any discussion of public land and privatization. The same holds true in this book, but privatization issues certainly touch state public land as well, albeit in different ways. As we shall see, no public land of any jurisdiction is immune to a philosophy that believes that markets rather than law and the public sector should allocate and manage land.

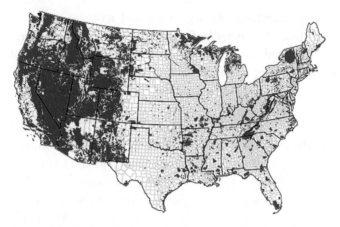

Figure 1.1. State and federal public lands. *(© 2013 Guangqing Chi and Derrick Ho.)*

The Federal Domain

The 635 million acres of federal public land account for more than 1 in 4 acres of land in the United States (27.9 percent).[44] Approximately 609 million acres of this land (or 96 percent) are managed by the four main land management agencies in the federal government: the BLM, the USFS, the NPS, and the USFWS. Control of the remaining 26 million acres is scattered among various federal agencies, including the Department of Defense (16.5 million acres), the Bureau of Reclamation, and the Department of Energy.[45] In addition, 55 million acres of Native American Reservation lands are managed by the Bureau of Indian Affairs in the Department of the Interior, in partnership with individual tribes.[46] These other categories of federal land remain outside the purview of this book, which focuses on public *conservation* lands.

The U.S. Forest Service. The USFS, created in 1905 and housed within the Department of Agriculture, manages 193 million acres, or about a third, of the federal domain. The 155 national forest units constitute most of its land, but the agency also oversees twenty national grasslands. As is the case for all federal land management agencies, the bulk of USFS holdings (85 percent) are in the West; however, the eastern national forests account for one-half of all federal land in the East.[47] It is important to recognize that the origins of the USFS and its mandate are firmly rooted in the utilitarianism of its influential first director, Gifford Pinchot, who believed the agency's lands were to strictly serve the people as "working forests."[48] Thus, the USFS operates under a multiple-use mandate first articulated in the Multiple Use–Sustained Yield Act (MUSYA) of 1960, which directs the agency to manage land for a multiplicity of uses, including resource extraction, recreation, wildlife, and water quality, and does not necessarily bind the agency to the use that has the highest economic returns in the marketplace. The other part of this 1960 mandate instructs the agency to employ *sustained yield* forestry practices, which stipulate that the total volume of timber annually removed from a given national forest unit may not exceed the annual growth in timber volume on that same forest, a practice not necessarily followed on private forest land.

In 1976, the passage of the NFMA expanded and clarified this multiple-use mandate. This law created the framework for long-term planning and decision making regarding the forests, ensured fairly abundant avenues for public participation and input, and spelled out the legitimate uses and purposes of the forests that policy makers had to consider, balance, and weigh.

The National Park Service. The NPS was formed in 1916 with a dual mandate, spelled out in its Organic Act, to provide recreational and aesthetic enjoyment to the public as well as to preserve the integrity of the natural systems under the agency's care. As such, no resource extraction is permitted on NPS lands and, not surprisingly, the agency's organizational culture has always leaned more toward preservation than utility. The agency's portfolio of lands includes 79.7 million acres of national parks, national preserves, national monuments,[49] national recreation areas, national lakeshores, national seashores, national battlefields, and national historic sites. Only Congress can create units in most of these categories, but the Antiquities Act of 1906, as previously mentioned, gives presidents the executive authority to create national monuments, a power that subsequent conservation-minded presidents have relied upon heavily to circumvent Congress for the protection of land and historic sites. Nearly four hundred individual NPS units are scattered across the country and range from enormous preserves with remote backcountry to tiny sites of less than an acre. Two-thirds of the overall acreage, however, is found just in Alaska.[50]

The U.S. Fish and Wildlife Service. Although the first national wildlife refuge was established in 1903, it was not until 1940 that the USFWS was consolidated from several smaller agencies into its present form.[51] Like the NPS, the USFWS oversees a sprawling system of more than 550 refuge units ranging from tiny islands covering a few acres to the nearly 20-million-acre Arctic National Wildlife Refuge.[52] The agency oversees a total of 88.9 million acres, 86 percent of which are in Alaska.[53] Historically, the USFWS has followed a primary-use mandate of preserving fish and wildlife and their habitats. However, secondary recreational and resource extraction objectives do exist on many refuges. In 1997, the refuge system gained a new charter, the National Wildlife Refuge System Improvement Act, to replace its outdated 1966 charter. Significantly, this act adopts an ecosystem management framework rooted in the science of conservation biology and makes it harder to justify any secondary activities on a refuge that conflict with the central mission of wildlife conservation.[54]

The Bureau of Land Management. The BLM controls the single-largest chunk of the federal domain, with 247.9 million acres (or 39 percent) of mostly arid rangeland and desert in the western states.[55] Until they were permanently protected under FLPMA in 1976, these lands were potentially destined for disposal even after the Progressive Era's retention of timberlands and scenic wonders. They are, in the words of Scott Lehmann, "the leftovers," too infertile, too dry, and too isolated to have engendered much interest from previous generations of homesteaders or railroads.[56] The exceptions to the generally arid nature of the lands in the BLM's charge are the 2.4 million lush, timber-rich acres of the so-called *Oregon and California (O&C) Lands*, which were acquired (or, more accurately, reacquired) in 1916 in a rare case of federal confiscation of previously granted railroad land in the state of Oregon. This situation occurred because the O&C Railroad had violated the terms of its land grant with the federal government.[57]

BLM lands make up much of the vast, often desolate landscapes of numerous western states that one sees while zipping down the interstate, yet in recent decades, recreationists and biologists have begun to reappraise the value of some of these BLM lands and have pushed for more stringent protections. As a result, a 35-million-acre subset of BLM lands known as the national conservation lands was created in 2000. Consisting of wilderness areas, wilderness study areas, national monuments, and national conservation areas within the BLM land portfolio, this designation marked a significant turning point in the agency's evolution toward ecosystem management and a focus beyond just commodity production. The BLM is the youngest of the federal land management agencies and was, as previously mentioned, formed in 1946 as the successor to agencies more geared toward homesteading and disposal. Like the USFS, the BLM operates under a multiple-use mandate as laid out in the FLPMA of 1976.

The National Wilderness Preservation System. In 1964, Congress passed the Wilderness Act, which created a new category of land use that strictly prohibited all motorized and extractive activities (save hunting) to preserve the solitude and integrity of primitive landscapes. According to the act:

> A wilderness, in contrast with those areas where man and his own works dominate the landscape, is hereby recognized as an area where the earth and its community of life are untrammeled by man, where man himself is a visitor who does not remain. An area of wilderness is further defined to mean in this chapter an area of undeveloped Federal land retaining its primeval character and influence, without permanent improvements or human habitation, which is protected and managed so as to preserve its natural conditions and which (1) generally appears to have been affected primarily by the forces of nature, with

the imprint of man's work substantially unnoticeable;
[and] (2) has outstanding opportunities for solitude or a
primitive and unconfined type of recreation.[58]

In the half century since the passage of this law, 759 individual
wilderness areas have been designated by Congress, encompassing 109.7 million acres (or about 18 percent of the federal domain).[59] Wilderness is an overlay category that occurs within
existing national parks, national forests, wildlife refuges, and
BLM lands, and so wilderness areas are managed by whichever
agency controls the land in question.

Wilderness acreage is apportioned between national parks
(accounting for 40 percent of all wilderness acreage), national
forests (33 percent), wildlife refuges (19 percent), and BLM lands
(8 percent). Again—not surprisingly—52.4 percent of all wilderness acreage is found in Alaska.[60] It should be noted that the
wilderness designation generally restricts management options
less for the agencies already oriented toward preservation (the
NPS and the USFWS) and more for the multiple-use agencies
(the USFS and the BLM), which must retool their management
of the tracts in question from the wide latitude of multiple use
to single use.

Aside from being a particular land management category mandated by Congress, wilderness represents, to supporters and critics
alike, something far more profound and symbolically important,
and the political battles over it have shaped and influenced the entire realm of public land policy, as James Turner points out:

> Few ideas have been more important than wilderness in
> shaping how Americans have viewed, debated, and man-
> aged the landscape. . . . Debates over wilderness . . . are
> as much about American society and politics as they are
> about the land.[61]

One particularly contentious political debate since the 1970s
has been over the fate of lands, mostly in the national forests,
that have wilderness characteristics (that is to say, are roadless)

and are thus suitable for future designation but are not yet protected. After an initial inventory in 1972, the Roadless Area Review and Evaluation (RARE I), and a court-ordered follow-up (RARE II) in 1977, a question arose as to whether to release the remaining roadless areas to multiple-use-oriented resource development or to hold it in a roadless state, given the potential for future action by Congress.[62] The RARE process was an attempt to not only inventory roadless areas but also establish criteria for what was worth holding in a pristine state. This decision-making process was especially important, because many of the early wilderness designations between 1964 and 1972 were high-altitude alpine tracts with little valuable timber,[63] unlike many of the sites in the RARE inventory. To environmentalists, though, the evaluators—the USFS—had a vested interest in minimizing additions to the wilderness system, given that such designation tended to tie the agency's hands as far as management was concerned.[64]

This perennial issue culminated in a 2001 Executive Order in the very last days of the Bill Clinton administration, the so-called Roadless Rule, which prohibited road construction on most of the remaining roadless inventory in the national forests, some 58.5 million acres.[65] Miraculously surviving a furious administrative and legal counterattack during the George W. Bush years,[66] the Roadless Rule has managed to create a de facto wilderness system parallel to the official one, albeit one that is much more politically vulnerable.

It should be clear from this list of agencies and jurisdictions that the federal domain is fairly fragmented by agency and mandate. In their assessment of the relative power of the federal natural resource agencies, Jeanne Clarke and Daniel McCool find wide disparities between individual agencies, depending on their missions, support from within other government institutions, support from their clients, and how much clout those clients have. On this scale, the USFS stands out as the most powerful and capable, with the NPS "muddling through" significantly behind it, and the BLM and the USFWS seen as being the weakest organizationally.[67]

State Public Lands

In addition to the vast federal estate, the fifty states own another 200 million acres of public land. However, these state lands represent two separate and very distinct systems. Three-quarters of all state-owned land in the United States (149.5 million acres) compose what are known as *trust lands*,[68] which, as described earlier, were granted at statehood by the federal government for the explicit purpose of funding schools and other public institutions. States in the East largely sold, gave away, or otherwise squandered their trust lands in short order, so as a result, Congress eventually imposed tighter regulation on the use of such granted lands; because states in the West generally entered the Union later, after these rules went into effect, they have largely retained their trust lands and thus possess the overwhelming proportion.[69] Again, Alaska leads the pack, with 67 percent (or 99.7 million acres) of all trust lands.

Trust lands differ from all other public lands in that they are managed with a direct fiduciary duty to the trust beneficiaries rather than to the general public; these arrangements are usually stipulated by legislation or sometimes by state constitutional provisions. This duty typically translates into an aggressive and single-minded pursuit of resource extraction, be it logging, grazing, agricultural leasing, energy development, mining, or even commercial development or divestiture, to produce as much revenue as possible for the trust beneficiaries. In fact, so single-minded is such management that the land in question is not even considered truly public (at least in terms of access) by some states; indeed, the public is not guaranteed access to many state-trust parcels. This point is important, as we shall see, because western trust lands are often enthusiastically held up by critics of the federal government as shining models of land management worthy of emulation. Another significant feature of trust lands is that, given their nineteenth-century land-grant origins (two and later four 1-square-mile sections of land per township), they tend to occur as highly fragmented parcels rather than as large contiguous blocks of land.[70]

For the other one-quarter of state land (51.7 million acres), land management objectives and agency jurisdictions are more similar to the federal model—that is, state parks are devoted to recreation and preservation, state forests to multiple uses, refuges to wildlife conservation, and overlay categories to special or high-quality natural areas. Across fifty very different states, there are, of course, wide disparities in the makeup of each state's portfolio of holdings and the extent to which preservation, recreation, and resource extraction are prioritized.[71] Some states, including New York, Wisconsin, Colorado, and North and South Carolina, stand out for stressing preservation goals; others are almost entirely geared toward resource extraction; and still others, mostly in the South and the Great Plains, tend to orient their lands toward high-impact, revenue-generating recreation.[72]

Generally, these nontrust state lands were acquired through a painstaking process of purchase, condemnation, or tax forfeiture. And unlike the federal lands, they are not concentrated in the West. In fact, without their abundant trust lands, Rocky Mountain and Great Plains states have a mean of only around 0.5 percent of their land in state ownership, in contrast with 8.9 percent for northeastern states and nearly 4 percent for midwestern states.[73]

Public Lands at the Local Level

With 19,492 municipal governments, 3,033 counties, and 1,355 special park districts in the United States, there is far too much jurisdictional fragmentation to get any sort of fully accurate accounting of the acreage of public land at the local level.[74] The Trust for Public Land has compiled data on the one hundred largest urban park systems and found 1.08 million acres (subtracting the 490,125-acre Chugach State Park, which is located within Anchorage city limits), but that figure excludes many smaller cities.[75] In the sample, the median percentage of total city land that is composed of public parkland is 8.3 percent.[76] Counties often own public land as well, sometimes in fairly extensive holdings, in proportion to their size. For example, the seven urban counties of northeastern Illinois around Chicago collectively have more than 178,000 acres in their county forest preserve systems, while Maricopa County in Arizona owns 120,000 acres.[77] Numerous other metropolitan counties also have park holdings in the tens of thousands of acres.[78] On the other hand, it is most likely safe to assume that many other counties, especially those in rural areas with low population densities or western areas with abundant federal land, have little to no public land.

Vastly larger than county park systems are the county forests that exist in rural areas of a handful of states. Totaling 5.4 million acres (95 percent of that in just two states—Minnesota and Wisconsin—with the remainder in New York, Michigan, Washington, Oregon, and Pennsylvania), these forests are generally managed according to multiple-use principles, much like the state and national forests that often surround them.[79] Local public lands in metropolitan areas, on the other hand, are almost always managed for some combination of recreation and preservation. All together, one might put forward a best guess that total local public land holdings in the United States are somewhere in the low tens of millions of acres.[80] Yet this low number relative to the massively larger acreage of federal and state lands should not lead anyone to dismiss the significance of local public lands, as this land, scattered in small parcels throughout every corner of the country and concentrated where the population densities are the highest, is probably the land that people most often come into contact with on a daily or weekly basis. While someone might make it to Hawai'i Volcanoes National Park once in a lifetime, or more likely never, that person might frequently visit nearby county or municipal public land.

A Brief History of Privatization

The historian Patricia Limerick reminds us that the debate over the privatization of public lands and the political acrimony that has accompanied it is nothing new. In fact, she identifies numerous rounds of this conflict, starting with the bitter resistance in the nineteenth century to the very idea of creating *any* public reserves. The creation of the forest reserves during the Cleveland administration was, according to critics, "rank imbecility," the "obnoxious measures of Eastern visionaries," and "as nefarious a scheme as ever disgraced the nation."[81] Furthermore, these entities were said to be imposed by "ill-informed bureaucrats," "sentimentalists," "distant dictators," and "people who don't know a ranch from a pink tea party."[82] With attitudes like these afoot, it should not have been a great surprise when President Herbert Hoover in the 1920s made an ultimately unsuccessful attempt to cede federal lands back to the states, an idea that would periodically flare back to life several times over the next century. "The federal government," argued Hoover, "is incapable of the adequate administration of matters which require so large a measure of local understanding."[83]

By 1932, the pendulum swung back to policies broadly supportive of federal control. In this period, the Taylor Grazing Act ended the disposal of rangeland, the national park system expanded, the eastern national forests were established and expanded, and an incredible array of roads, lodges, trails, visitor centers, and other park infrastructure was built as part of an enormous program of New Deal–related public works.

By the 1940s, however, the devolution effort started anew, but this time, driven by ranching interests intent on weakening federal control over grazing, especially by the new BLM. Although these legislative efforts ultimately fell short, they alarmed the journalist and historian Bernard DeVoto to the extent that he described the campaign in 1947 as "only one part of an unceasing, many-sided effort to discredit all conservation bureaus of the government, to discredit conservation itself."[84] "The ultimate objective," he went on, "is to liquidate all public ownership of grazing and forest land in the United States. . . . [T]he plan is to get rid of public lands altogether, turning them over to the states, which can be coerced as the federal government cannot be, and eventually to private ownership."[85]

During the period from the 1960s until President Jimmy Carter left office in 1981, events swung back yet again to what might be thought of as a sort of "golden age" for public lands.

In this era, the MUSYA, the Wilderness Act, the NFMA, the FLPMA, the Endangered Species Act, and the Alaska National Interest Lands Conservation Act (which set aside more than 100 million acres of Alaska as parks, preserves, and refuges) were all passed into law. According to Robert Nelson, this period represented a return to a faith (mistaken, in his opinion) in scientific management as embodied in the original nineteenth-century conservationism.[86]

It did not take long, however, for this exuberant era of federal stewardship to engender a serious backlash, which came in the form of the Sagebrush Rebellion in the late 1970s and early 1980s, as a number of western state legislatures began to pass bills demanding the transfer of federal land into state control. Most significantly, these calls for devolution met a very receptive audience in the newly elected Ronald Reagan administration, with the president himself declaring, "Count me in as a rebel!"[87] While the Sagebrush Rebellion was brewing, so too was a privatization effort, led by libertarian economists inside and outside the administration, to sell parts of the federal domain. The Reagan administration conducted pilot studies and drew up draft proposals identifying federal lands suitable for transfer or divestment. According to Thomas More, more than 35 million acres were earmarked in the initial round for sell-off.[88]

Although many observers conflate these two parallel antifederal land movements, R. McGreggor Cawley argues that they were actually quite distinct in that one originated from western anger and the other from free-market ideological fervor, and, in many ways, they worked at cross-purposes.[89] Both initiatives ultimately ran into the wall of a Democrat-controlled House, but they also engendered opposition from more surprising quarters: ranchers who preferred the secure leases, guaranteed access, and heavily subsidized fees of federal grazing policy to the unpredictability of state or private control. Many wagered that they could find no better deal than what they enjoyed on federal land; why would they want to endure the headache of buying their own land and then paying taxes on it?[90]

The Sagebrush Rebellion eventually fizzled out, but it was replaced in the 1990s by an even more virulent antifederal movement that began to gain currency as the new Clinton administration started to shift federal public land policy to a more traditional conservationist footing after twelve years of relatively unfriendly Republican administrations. Under the loose umbrella term *Wise Use*, this mostly rural, western-based movement drew on antigovernment ideologies, private-property rights activism, and a hodge-podge of county rights, "sovereign citizens," and militia movements.[91] Such developments as the 1991 federal court–ordered injunction on the logging of old growth in northwestern national forests (which eventually led to far smaller USFS harvest volumes), the establishment of new parks and monuments (especially the 1.9-million-acre Grand Staircase–Escalante National Monument in Utah in 1996), and the 2001 Roadless Rule only fueled the fire of rural grassroots anger in the West.

While many Wise Use adherents articulated coherent manifestos of local control and the centrality of private property, the movement has also had a darker side of rejectionism, intimidation, illegal public-land use, and occasional sporadic violence, including firebombings of federal facilities and armed harassment of federal officers.[92] This hyperlocal movement reveled in its bold, if legally dubious, challenges to federal authority, such as the 1991 enactment in Catron County, New Mexico, of a "nullification" of all federal land within its boundaries, a move that was eventually followed by thirty-five additional western counties.[93]

Although this simmering undercurrent of resentment and hostility to federal land management in the West is nothing new at all, this latest manifestation, especially since the Tea Party movement gained prominence during and after the 2010 election cycle, now has the imprimatur of numerous elected officials from county board members to governors to U.S. representatives to presidents. What was previously seen as the intemperate agitation of fringe activists is now the standard stuff of political platforms, floor debates, and campaign speeches.[94] By the time the Republican Party's 2012 platform was written, the goal of privatization was back on its agenda in no uncertain terms:

> Congress should reconsider whether parts of the federal government's enormous landholdings and control of water in the West could be better used for ranching, mining, or forestry through private ownership. . . . The enduring truth is that people best protect what they own.[95]

For evidence of how this fairly extreme orientation toward public land has become normalized, one needs to look no further than the case of Cliven Bundy and his sons. Bundy, a rancher from Clark County, Nevada, had not paid his BLM grazing leases for nearly a quarter century and ignored numerous federal court orders and wildlife protection regulations until the BLM finally made a move to confiscate his cattle in April 2014. In response, armed militias from across the West converged on the area to confront the BLM rangers conducting the roundup, ultimately causing the BLM to back down.[96] Thus emboldened, in January 2016, Bundy's sons and a band of fellow militants staged a forty-one-day-long armed occupation of the Malheur National Wildlife Refuge in eastern Oregon, demanding that all federal land in the area be handed over to private citizens and that two area ranchers convicted of arson on public lands be released from prison.[97]

This cauldron of antigovernment sentiment, locally and nationally, has provided the seedbed for the most recent round of privatization proposals, which began during the George W. Bush administration. For example, in 2002, a proposal was made to adapt the charter-school model to national forests by shifting authority (although not ownership) from the USFS to local trusts consisting of user groups. These so-called charter forests would supposedly reduce conflict and unleash entrepreneurial creativity.[98] In February 2006, President Bush reprised Reagan's outright privatization initiative, albeit on a much smaller scale, with his budget proposal containing provisions for the auctioning of 300,000 acres of national forest land for the express purpose of deficit reduction.[99] Along similar lines, a bill introduced in Congress that same year proposed selling national parks with fewer than ten thousand annual visitors to raise money to pay for federal recovery efforts following Hurricane Katrina.[100]

The rise of the Tea Party faction in the Republican Party and its success in the 2010 and 2014 midterm elections acted as a kind of rocket fuel for efforts at either privatization or the devolution of federal lands. Spearheading the effort, according to Jenny Rowland, has been an "anti-parks caucus" of approximately twenty right- to far-right-leaning Republican legislators, many of whom formally belong to the Federal Land Action Group (FLAG), a congressional working group dedicated to land transfer.[101] The following is a sample of the legislative proposals that were introduced between 2011 and 2017:

- H.R. 1505 (112th Cong.)—would open national parks, national forests, and national wildlife refuges to roads and motorized vehicles and would exempt Border Patrol from compliance with thirty-six separate environmental laws within 100 miles of U.S. borders.
- H.R. 2852 (112th Cong.)—would require the BLM and the USFS to transfer, without sale, 5 percent, or 30 million acres, of their holdings.
- H.R. 1126 (112th Cong.)—would have the BLM sell all lands in the Rocky Mountain states determined to be excess to the highest bidder.
- H.R. 1581 (112th Cong.)—would open all roadless and wilderness study areas on USFS land to roads and resource extraction activities.
- H.R. 638 (113th Cong.)—would prevent the USFWS from establishing any new wildlife refuges.
- H.R. 1021 (113th Cong.)—would allow no further net increase in federal land unless the federal budget was balanced in the year of the purchase.
- H.R. 382 (113th Cong.); H.R. 330, H.R. 2822 Amendment, and S.1 Amendment (114th Cong.); H.R. 3990,

S. 33 and S. 132 (115th Cong.)—would repeal or drastically alter the Antiquities Act of 1906, which gives the president executive authority to designate new national monuments.

- H.R. 1825 (113th Cong.)—would amend the Wilderness Act to allow motorized vehicles, temporary road building, and logging in federal wilderness areas.
- H.R. 1017 (113th Cong.)—would require the BLM and the USFS to annually sell 8 percent of their holdings (approximately 36 million acres) for the next four consecutive years.
- S. Con. Res. 11 Amendment (114th Cong.)—would authorize the sale, transfer, or exchange of federal lands to states, including refuges, wilderness areas, and national forests.
- H.R. 866 and S. 490 (114th Cong.)—would turn over to states leasing and permitting responsibilities for energy production on federal lands.
- H.R. 232 (115th Cong.)—would allow states to select, acquire, and manage up to 2 million acres of national forest in their states.
- H.R. 621 (115th Cong.)—would require the federal government to identify and dispose of 3.3 million acres of "excess" federal land.
- H.R. 622 (115th Cong.)—would prohibit the USFS and the BLM from conducting their own law enforcement and would eliminate all law enforcement rangers.
- H.R. 2936 (115th Cong.)—would shield timber sales from a wide variety of public review, environmental impact assessments, and judicial oversight; turn private easements on public land into outright private ownership; allow USFS timber sales to forgo Endangered Species Act consultations with the USFWS; suspend Sustained Yield Act limitations on BLM timberlands in Oregon; make forest plans advisory rather than binding; and eliminate designation for the Cascade-Siskiyou National Monument.

- H.R. 4299 (115th Cong.)—would allow the military to indefinitely appropriate public land without environmental review.
- H.R. 4558 (115th Cong.)—would codify President Donald Trump's disputed executive action to declassify 862,000 acres of Grand Staircase–Escalante National Monument and place management of the remaining protected land in the hands of the local county governments.[102]

None of this legislation has yet been enacted into law, but such legislation keeps coming in persistent waves; a number of bills have passed the full House, and at least one has passed the Senate as well. State legislation demanding federal land transfer has had greater success, as such groups as the American Lands Council, the Constitutional Sheriffs and Peace Officers Association, and Free The Lands have been organizing in the West and nationally in an attempt to build a critical mass of political support.[103] In Utah, for example, legislation authorizing the transfer of federal lands in the state (and all necessary state lawsuits) was passed into law with the governor's signature in 2012.[104] Similar state legislation is also under review in Idaho, Montana, and Wyoming. Meanwhile, in Arizona, a version of this law also passed in 2012 but was vetoed; a referendum version failed; and then yet another bill passed in 2015 and was also vetoed by the next governor. Devolution efforts in New Mexico and Colorado, meanwhile, have failed to pass the state legislature. If these states' proposals all seem eerily similar that is because most of these initiatives are driven by the corporate-funded American Legislative Exchange Council (ALEC), which developed model legislation for western states to use as a template.[105]

Without a compliant federal government, such legislation, of course, has no chance whatsoever of compelling the change it seeks, as it has no legal ground to stand on—but as a symbolic statement and indicator of the mood of many western policy makers, it is quite telling. Before long, this notion of transferring federal lands to the states gained such currency that the

Republican Party's official position shifted toward this goal over straight privatization, with the 2016 Republican National Committee's platform statement boldly asserting:

> Congress shall immediately pass universal legislation providing for a timely and orderly mechanism requiring the federal government to convey certain federally controlled public lands to states. We call upon all national and state leaders and representatives to exert their utmost power and influence to urge the transfer of those lands, identified in the review process, to all willing states for the benefit of the states and the nation as a whole. The residents of state and local communities know best how to protect the land where they work and live.[106]

Privatization advocates have also focused their attention on state-owned lands, often with much more success than at the federal level. More notes how public parklands of all types went through a period of rapid growth, expansion, and investment from the 1880s until the mid-twentieth century. By the late 1970s, though, incomes and tax revenues became stagnant, and as austerity worked its way down the budgetary chain, park managers increasingly saw a reduced capacity to offer programs, solve problems, or even physically maintain park infrastructure as budget strains mounted.[107] During this period, a *soft privatization* began to take hold in many states. This kinder, gentler form of privatization falls short of outright divestment but rather focuses on funding and operations. The Great Recession of 2008–2010 and the antigovernment and austerity-minded legislatures and governors it empowered in many states only hastened and deepened this trend.

In a funding atmosphere so severely constrained, many state park budgets have come to be seen as a luxury. As a result, park budgets in many states have been severely cut, capped, or eliminated altogether, in which case park agencies are forced to attempt the nearly impossible task of raising all their operating funds through the revenue they alone generate.[108] A significant number of states have used budget crises to privatize many aspects of park operations, seek out corporate donations, and shift the focus of park systems toward revenue-generating ventures, such as resorts, convention centers, and golf courses.[109] More notes that, at least until now, the full privatization of public land has been a tough sell, but these less-drastic forms of privatization and marketization, such as outsourcing and mandates for 100-percent revenue-generated budgets, are merely steps along the path that weaken the institutional aspects of public land and simultaneously get the public used to the idea of privatization.[110] Indeed, outright divestment, once unthinkable, has begun to occur in several states (see the Preface).

Controversy, contentiousness, and western resentment have all been reliable features of public land politics from the moment the nation turned from a policy of land disposal to retention. This political battle has waxed and waned, flaring into a roaring blaze and dying down to embers numerous times over the past century. The principles at stake are so elemental that it probably can be no other way. In the aftermath of the failed Sagebrush Rebellion, political scientist Phillip Foss writes of privatization attempts:

> The losers in any particular policy dispute are not executed; they live on to fight another day. . . . [T]here are pressures here, both internal and external to federal land management, that may advance the day and insure the privatization proposal a more sympathetic hearing when it arrives.[111]

It is probably safe to assume that that day has arrived, especially given the political domination of a hybrid GOP, consisting of equal parts Trump and Tea Party. Consequently, this fraught moment in American politics represents a huge open window for the cause of privatizing public lands.

FOLLOWING SPREAD: White Sands National Monument, New Mexico. *(Photo by the author.)*

2

Every Man for Himself

The Case for Privatization

> Why should land be an exception to the American consensus
> against government ownership?
>
> —ROBERT NELSON, "The Subsidized Sagebrush: Why the Privatization
> Movement Failed," *Regulation*

Classical Economics and Socialist Bogeymen

AT THE VERY HEART of the arguments for the privatization of public lands lies a fairly conventional libertarian paradigm rooted in classical economics. Indeed, Richard Stroup and John Baden, two of the most prominent privatization theorists, lay out their influences in the preface of one of their books in no uncertain terms: "We have been influenced in our writing by authors too numerous to mention in the neoclassical, property rights, public choice, and Austrian traditions."[1]

It is small wonder, then, that the particular and unique development of America's fairly substantial public lands infrastructure so vexes privatization advocates. To them, it is a strange anomaly that goes against the grain of virtually every other aspect of American culture. Some of the more intemperate observers would go so far as to say that public lands reek of discredited socialism. "It is indeed odd that, in a society that rejects socialism," muse Terry Anderson, Vernon Smith, and Emily Simmons, "such a clearly socialist resource policy survives with such widespread public support."[2] Privatizers see the public domain like some bypassed land that time forgot, as "the last stand of central planning busybodies."[3] Indeed, to the diehards, government ownership, in and of itself, is a form of socialism that leads straight to collectivism and tyranny, whereas, according to Steve Hanke, "the only road to liberty begins with privatization."[4] To B. Delworth Gardner, environmentalists in the post-Soviet era have picked up the fallen baton to become the leading challengers to the classical liberal notions of continual economic growth, technical advancement, and all the social benefits that issue forth from that.[5]

Stroup and Baden, meanwhile, look no further than the U.S. Constitution for evidence that public lands are antithetical to our system of government. It was written above all, they claim, for the protection of private property and contracts and the limitation of the federal government and to "encourage the movement of resources to more highly valued uses."[6] And therein lies the crux of the privatization argument: public land short-circuits the whole process by which a rational market can determine the best use of a given resource and thereby maximize productivity.

The rights to use public land that governments offer to hunters, hikers, ranchers, or loggers are flawed and incomplete, according to the privatizers. This is because they are (1) not directly controlled by the individual (because he or she is not the owner); (2) nontransferable, in that the user cannot sell the land, its resources, or access to it; and (3) insecure, in that the access and user rights are subject to the regulatory whims of government.[7] This scenario, which separates user rights from ownership, creates a system that allows the shifting of costs onto nonusers, which, to the privatizers, is not only inefficient but also grossly unfair.

The market-oriented vision underlying the case for privatization is based on a number of assumptions that are deeply rooted in classical economic theory and could come right out of an introductory economics textbook. As articulated by Stroup and Baden, these assumptions are as follows:

1. Individuals are self-interested.
2. Scarcity increases cost.
3. Individuals are cost-sensitive, so benefits must outweigh costs.
4. The information required to make informed market decisions is scarce and has costs; thus it is like any other scarce good.
5. Individual choices are heavily influenced by incentives.
6. Decision-makers choose options that enhance their own welfare (see item #1).
7. The best system of allocation of scarce resources is one that moves them to their most highly valued uses (and the only way to determine this is through its market price).[8]

From the perspective of these assumptions, it is fairly obvious to privatization advocates that nearly everything about public lands and their management by government agencies violates "best" practices.

Privatization and Environmental Health

In a nation that generally cares about the environmental health of the land, especially the public lands that ordinary citizens have access to, any ideology indifferent to this issue would probably be a nonstarter in the policy-making realm. Not surprisingly, then, the environmental health of the land is often placed at the center of the privatizers' arguments. "Environment and market," according to Terry Anderson and Donald Leal, "are inextricably connected in a positive rather than a negative way."[9] Thus, privatization is seen as creating a "win-win" scenario for the economy and the environment where, as Robert Nelson argues, the best economic decisions are often the best environmental ones, too.[10] And the more efficiently environmental quality is produced by sound economic decision making, the more of it there is to go around.[11]

Much as no one ever washes a rental car, as the old saying goes, privatizers argue that no one takes care of public land because it does not really belong to them. The links of responsibility and accountability that ownership is said to confer are broken in a system of collective ownership, as Holly Fretwell notes:

> Poor land stewardship is first and foremost the fault of politicians in Washington who are controlling the purse strings for our public lands. It is unlikely they would make the same decisions if it were their own private property. . . . Entrusting the care of our federal lands to politicians has resulted in damages that are both widespread and well-documented.[12]

On the other hand, with private land, according to Anderson and Leal, "a discipline is imposed on resource users because the wealth of the owner of the property right is at stake if bad decisions are made."[13] Irresponsible behavior on the part of a landowner reduces his or her wealth by lowering the value of the asset, as Stroup points out:

> If the resource is well-cared for, it will be more valuable and add more to the wealth of its private owner. If the owner allows the resource to deteriorate, he or she personally bears the cost of that negligence in the form of a decline in the value of the resource. The value of a property right to the resource is, in a very real sense, a hostage to the owner's provision of good care of that resource. The same personal financial stake is not present for a government manager.[14]

Conversely, because everyone "owns" public land, no one really owns it, at least not in the way that truly matters, according to the privatizers. Thus, Garrett Hardin's "tragedy of the commons" is often invoked as the operative model. In fact, Hardin himself argued that his thesis could be applied to the national parks every bit as much as the hypothetical sheep pasture.[15] Along these lines, Stroup and Baden observe that the American bison are largely gone because no one owned them nor had any responsibility or incentive to protect them, whereas cows are everywhere because someone owns each and every one of them.[16] "Most environmental problems faced by society," they argue, "result from property being held in common."[17] To privatizers, then, good intentions and moral righteousness rarely deliver the goods; the only factors that can produce good environmental behavior are market incentives.[18] And with a private ownership model, all the right incentives are in place for preserving nature, as Stroup and Baden point out:

> Access to a unique ecological site may be compared with access to a Rembrandt painting. In both cases, the admission fee can make it worthwhile for the owner to share the asset and, indeed, take elaborate precautions against its depreciation.[19]

Anderson and Leal go even further in trying to cement this connection between free markets and environmental quality, as they draw analogies between the workings of ecology to those of the market. Like the free markets, they argue, ecological systems feature "niches" to exploit and thus opportunities to profit:

> As survival rewards species that successfully fill a niche, increased wealth rewards owners who efficiently manage their resources. Profits link self-interest with good resource management by attracting entrepreneurs to open niches.[20]

Central planning by governments, they argue, severs this connection between the steward and his or her reward, as costs get imposed on external actors and market signals get all distorted by the static of politics.[21] As a result of all this interference and indirect decision making, environmental goods tend to be underpriced, and, as a consequence, negative externalities abound. Government management, therefore, "subsidizes destruction of the environment more than it protects it," says Anderson.[22] And if these environmentally virtuous microeconomic features of a free market are not convincing enough, Anderson makes the familiar argument, subject to much debate, that free markets generate the economic growth that they claim is correlated to environmental quality.[23] Matthew Kahn largely echoes this sentiment specifically as it relates to economic growth fueled by urban expansion.[24] This issue of whether private ownership enhances environmental health is explored in great detail in the next chapter.

The Failure of Public Management

To the advocates of privatization, the government's management of public land is the main culprit in the thwarting of rational, efficient, and productive resource policy. The privatizers' case against government is a "kitchen-sink" litany of failures. Government is too distant; does not have enough information or the right kind of information; is too coercive, too malleable, too corrupt, too self-interested, too indifferent, too inefficient, or just plain wrong for the job of allocating natural resources. I review some of these arguments here but examine and test these claims more thoroughly in Chapter 6.

The legacy of the Progressive Era as it regards environmental conservation—and, more specifically, the project of public land retention—was intended to be a model of bureaucratic management guided by scientific expertise, professionalism, and a commitment to the public interest, a model most self-consciously embodied by the U.S. Forest Service (USFS).[25] But to such critics as Nelson, scientific management became less a needed reform than a "moral crusade," while applied science became "a new form of religious faith."[26] Not surprisingly, Nelson sees the century-long attempt at scientific management as a dismal failure, in part, because of real-world limits on obtaining relevant information:

> The failures had occurred because ideas of scientific management would always be utopian. The thinking behind

scientific management, for example, tended to assume
that all necessary . . . information would be readily available to decision makers. In practice, though, important
details would almost always be missing, perhaps because
they were too costly to justify obtaining.[27]

This failure would be especially true, according to Nelson, when
expensive-to-acquire data and analysis are required for low-value
resources (like forage on public rangelands).[28]

Anderson and Leal similarly argue that scientific management is doomed to fail because of its arrogance in assuming that
policy makers have the wherewithal to accumulate and incorporate adequate knowledge about complex ecological systems
within a structure that centrally manages land in a way reminis-
cent to them of Eastern Europe in the Communist era.[29] Consequently, "if scientific management has failed," Nelson points
out, "then this whole system comes into question."[30]

Interestingly, although Nelson soundly rejects the possibility of a policy-making process that attempts to incorporate the
scientific understandings of ecology, biology, soil science, range
science, forestry, and hydrology, to name a few, he wholeheartedly endorses one form of scientific management that he believes would work where the others have failed. He argues that
"if the scientific methods of economics can be introduced, it
will now actually be possible to turn land management over to
the experts (that is, economists)."[31] Thus, Nelson has identified,
in his mind at least, the one and only true science as far as land
management is concerned.

Unable to wall off the intrusion of politics or gain the information it needs, scientific management fails, according to critics,
and begins to dissolve into the crude interest-group free-for-
all best described by Theodore Lowi.[32] Ironically, this situation
was the furthest thing from the minds of the early Progressive
reformers, who abhorred special interests as an obstacle to the
expert implementation of whatever was deemed to be in the
public interest. The interest-group politics that critics argue has
largely supplanted scientific management, was, in their opinion,

helped along tremendously by the multiple-use framework introduced in the Multiple Use Act and solidified in the National Forest Management Act (NFMA) and the Federal Land Policy and Management Act (FLPMA), a concept tailor-made to engender competing claims and allow carve-outs of private privileges on public land. They also suggest that the 1970s expansion of citizen participation and standing to sue further fueled this degeneration of public lands politics into the bazaar of special privileges they claim it is today.[33]

In the flawed structure of today's public land management, according to privatization advocates, the government acts as a broker of sorts as well as the "monopoly supplier," while interests slug it out in a wasteful, illogical, and conflict-ridden process.[34] In the end, the winners secure what Nelson calls "informal private rights" to public resources and, in doing so, enjoy all the benefits of these resources while passing the costs onto the general taxpayer, who does not necessarily share in the benefits.[35] So to the privatizers, the rancher paying below-market cost to graze on the Bureau of Land Management's (BLM's) range or the logger cutting in a steep, marginal, low-productivity area is doing the same exact thing as the "wilderness advocates who successfully pressure the government to set aside their own private playgrounds."[36] Gardner likewise argues that the low or nonexistent fees that recreationists pay to use federal land are an indication of their political power rather than anything special, transcendent, or consensual about the benefits they seek. He therefore sees resource allocation today as nothing more than a process of "public bickering over entitlements and influence peddling," degenerating ultimately into a "rent-seeking frenzy."[37]

At the heart of such attitudes can be seen a profound distaste for "politics" in practically any form. I explore this notion in much greater depth in Chapter 5, but it is important to note at this point that privatizers generally see nothing good coming out of the give-and-take of interest-group competition that David Truman, Robert Dahl, and many others have long presented as legitimate representation and a defining feature of American politics.[38] Instead, conflict is seen as an indication of a dysfunctional method of allocation—a pressure system of carved-out privileges, de facto rights, and externally imposed costs. Conflict is also seen as a monumental waste of resources—a vortex of court battles, appeals, hearings, comment periods, fundraising, and public-relations battles that suck up time, money, and stakeholders' attention.

Privatization advocates even tend to be suspicious of a far-less-cynical version of American democracy based on the ideal of voting as the chief mechanism for identifying society's value preferences. Anderson and Leal argue that voters tend to be "rationally ignorant" and purposefully underinvest in acquiring information on matters of marginal concern to them, yet they still participate.[39] And in the absence of fuller knowledge among voters, interest groups are alleged to have the upper hand in swaying opinion. In the marketplace, by contrast, only those with a clear interest participate, and they also supposedly have a much clearer incentive to become fully armed with relevant information. Thus, people's clearest and most informed vote is, according to privatizers, as consumers in the market, not as voters at the polling station. Furthermore, they argue that because government bureaucrats cannot really rely on vague, unclear mandates that issue from periodic elections and they have no real way to gauge preferences, they either guess or impose their own.[40] The market, then, would supposedly achieve a very welcome depoliticization of land management in which, Stroup suggests, "little acrimony is produced."[41]

The Subjectivity of Value Preferences

To privatization advocates, the central question of resource allocation regards how value preferences are handled. Not surprisingly, the market is, in their view, by far the best, fairest, and most efficient mechanism for determining this response. Joseph Sax explains the privatization argument (with which he disagrees):

In essence, the argument in principle for disposal of the public lands is this: Each person knows what is best for him or her and, therefore, the best system is one that permits the real preferences of individuals to be revealed and implemented. With rare exceptions, the ideal mechanism for implementing these preferences is a private marketplace where each individual expresses his or her desires through bidding. Private ownership advances this goal, and public ownership impedes it.[42]

As theorists generally steeped in classical economics, privatizers understand self-interest as the starting-point assumption, and the idea of an independent public interest that is holistic and something more than an aggregation of individual private interests is seen as ludicrous. Thus, value is not inherent or universally recognized or for or against a so-called public interest—it is simply determined by who values something enough to offer the highest bid. To consider such an expressed preference as somehow wrong, argue Stroup and Baden, represents "intellectual violence directed at individual freedom."[43] Furthermore, references that make any claims beyond self-interest are seen, in their words, as "loaded with emotional baggage."[44] The one and only universal principle in any of this, they go on to argue, are the laws that govern economic markets, which, of course, apply in all settings.[45]

Although not all privatization advocates go so far, Anderson, Smith, and Simmons would not even grant the Grand Canyon special status as a place with universal, transcendent qualities. If it is so special, they argue, then surely it will be protected by selling access, which, because of the scarcity of places like it, will necessarily be worth a lot.[46] Because self-interest is really behind all expressions of value preference, regardless of claims to the contrary, Nelson says that markets are far superior to the political process, as the latter leads to wasteful and destructive outcomes, while the former harnesses self-interest to an effective structure of incentives. And that, despite its immediate focus on self-interest, ultimately serves a greater social purpose—the maximization of scarce resources and the efficient prioritization of clashing preferences:

> Economics seeks to provide an objective measure of the value of each forest resource use. Then, rather than weighing the claims of public forest users by their political power and influence, economic decision-making would weigh these claims by their market prices or estimated social values.[47]

In this scenario, stripped of all subsidies and entitlements, all preferences would compete in the market on equal footing. Scarce environmental goods would need to be priced adequately to reflect their scarcity; once properly priced, argue the privatizers, they should be sufficiently protected, as someone now owns these scarce and valuable resources. And as for those who consume such goods, Anderson, Smith, and Simmons argue that "the social objectives of environmentalist groups would have to be translated into a willingness to pay for preservation."[48] In other words, *put up or shut up.*

Privatization and Productivity

According to Lehmann, the concept of *productivity* lies at the very core of the case for privatization. Summing up the privatization argument, he writes that "free markets direct resources to their most productive uses; hence privatizing public lands would increase their productivity and free for other uses those resources now allocated to managing them."[49]

Thus, allocating resources by bringing buyers and sellers into a market exchange where private rights to a resource compels users to pay all costs would strip away all extraneous and wasteful costs and misallocations. If such a regime governed national forest lands, suggest privatization advocates, logging would immediately cease where the transaction costs and postlogging treatments exceeded revenue, and it would be concentrated only on those lands productive enough to ensure adequate returns. The same would be true for overgrazed BLM rangelands, which the agency, for political reasons, charges a fraction of the market rate to graze. When politics intervenes to distort price signals, claim the privatizers, all sorts of decisions harmful to efficiency and productivity are made.

Besides moving resource allocations to their most efficient uses, the cause of productivity would also be furthered, say the privatizers, by saving all the public money that goes into administering the lands and offering their resources at subsidized prices. Holly Fretwell and Shawn Regan make this point and offer data showing that the federal multiple-use lands (managed by the USFS and the BLM) earned a five-year annual average (2009–2013) of $5.26 billion in revenue while racking up $7.22 billion in expenses, thus earning $0.73 for each dollar spent for a net annual loss of $1.9 billion.[50] The NPS, meanwhile, had an even bigger gap, spending $2.98 billion in 2014 with only about $196 million in 2015 in revenue from user fees.[51] Fretwell and Regan argue that with an appropriate pricing structure and a more productive allocation of resources, federal land should be earning many billions more, not only achieving self-sufficiency but also raising money for the Department of the Treasury.[52]

By contrast, they compare federal multiple-use lands to state-trust lands, which (as discussed in the previous chapter) have a fiduciary duty to maximize revenues in a model much closer to what the privatizers advocate. They find that state-trust lands earn a five-year annual average of $239.9 million with expenses of $16 million. That averages out to $14.50 of revenue for every dollar spent, in contrast with $0.73 on federal land. Per acre, they note that state-trust lands earn more than triple the revenue and incur approximately one-seventh the expense.[53]

The Problem of Bureaucracy

Privatization advocates argue that public managers are unfazed by such seemingly dire balance sheets because they are losing the taxpayers' money and not their own. The public sector, they claim, provides managers and public officials with no incentives to manage resources efficiently or to resist the pressure of special-interest groups. In fact, for those officials who are elected, this orientation can directly translate into tangible political support in the form of votes, mobilization, and campaign donations. And for those who are not elected—the bureaucrats—privatizers point out that their incentives are to increase their agencies' authority, jurisdiction, and budget while furthering their own careers and professional values.[54] But the problem, to privatizers, is that this focus tends to get in the way of productivity, efficiency, and accountability. "Bureaucrats are not evil," Anderson, Smith, and Simmons offer magnanimously, "but they will consciously or unconsciously look out for their own interests."[55]

One particular subset of this "self-interested bureaucrat" model is Randall O'Toole's budget-maximization theory, which suggests that the efficiencies that free-market theorists seek would actually reduce agency budgets, as things are currently structured. So bureaucrats, according to O'Toole, are simply being rational actors when they reject efficiency to enhance their budgets in the face of such perverse incentives.[56] For example, he notes that USFS managers get to keep all their timber receipts but none of their recreation receipts, so which activities would they be expected to focus on? And if the receipts still flowed into their ranger districts, why would they pass up the opportunity to approve a timber sale in a marginal, unproductive area, especially if the costs (of road building or reforestation) were passed to a different account within the agency?[57]

Another problem with the public lands bureaucracy (especially federal) from the perspective of free-market theory has to do with what privatizers see as its coercive, top-down nature. Stressing the larger historical context, Stroup and Baden find the origins of such overbearing government regulation and transfer activity in the Progressive and New Deal eras. They complain that public lands are largely regulated in a heavy-handed, command-and-control fashion.[58] One sign of the failure of such an approach, Nelson argues, is the fact that so many people try to circumvent the law.[59] The Endangered Species Act, a favorite target of free-market theorists, is held up as an especially egregious example of using harsh penalties rather than incentives to influence behavior. Likewise, wilderness designations, roadless-area rules, and other forms of land use restrictions are seen by many critics in a similar light.

In addition to its alleged coercion, federal land policy is also criticized for its top-down centralization of authority over a geographically far-flung system of public lands, a relationship of dependency between the federal government and the states that Sally Fairfax describes as "colonial."[60] Along these same lines, Dale Oesterle suggests that "the claim that Nevada and Alaska" (which are 81.1 percent and 61.8 percent federally owned, respectively) "are sovereign within their boundaries is surely a jest."[61] Nelson, meanwhile, believes that resentment over this imbalanced relationship, which led to the Sagebrush Rebellion in the 1980s, might end up working in both directions:

> Ironically, a different rebellion may spring up in the future, an eastern rebellion against the financial burdens of the western lands. With continuing high budget deficits and pressures to cut many urban programs, easterners at some point could demand that the residents of western states take responsibility for paying for the management of public lands within their own states.[62]

Furthermore, the sheer overwhelming size of the federal domain, according to Oesterle, means that the federal government maintains a commanding market position that allows it to unduly influence markets and prices throughout the economy.[63] And the federal government cannot withdraw resources when it puts land off limits without damaging the economy, he goes on to argue.[64] It should be noted, though, that the public land economist John Loomis refutes this claim, finding that research on this subject has found very little effect of government management on national resource supply.[65]

Anderson and Leal, meanwhile, claim that ecosystems cannot be appropriately managed from afar. Individual property owners, on the other hand, "are in a position and have an incentive to obtain time- and place-specific information about their resource endowments" and thus are "better-suited than centralized bureaucracies to manage resources."[66]

Proposals for Change

The critics of public land all largely accept the basic outlines of the arguments laid out in this chapter, but they part company when it comes to the question of what exactly to do in response. It is here that subtle differences in the critics' backgrounds as libertarians (Stroup and Baden), free-market absolutists (Anderson and Leal), or former federal agency insiders (O'Toole and Nelson) come to the fore.

Full-Fledged Privatization

At the far end of the spectrum would be Anderson and his various collaborators. As a remedy to what they see as the scourge of public management, they advocate the full privatization of all federal lands, and although they never directly address state and local public lands, there is no good reason to assume that their grievances with federal land would not extend, for example, to New York's massive "locked-up" Adirondack Park, Wisconsin's millions of acres of productive county forests, or Upper Michigan's fabled Porcupine Mountains Wilderness State Park, where massive old-growth sugar maple and hemlocks go uncut and fall to the forest floor and decompose when they die. Although Anderson, Smith, and Simmons believe that a simple cash sale of public land in exchange for revenue would meet several important criteria they set forth, it does not allow for broad participation in divesting of what is currently, after all, the public's land.[67] To remedy this concern, they propose an elaborate system centered on issuing public land share certificates (something like no par value stock certificates) to every American citizen. Each citizen would receive about ten fully transferable shares, which could be saved, sold, pooled, and ultimately used to bid on the formerly public land. Resource extractors, private citizens, environmental groups, ranchers, home builders, and recreation companies would be free to purchase or receive through donation or bequest these share certificates.[68]

Also in the full privatization camp are Hanke, who would privatize BLM land by exchanging current long-term grazing leases for land titles,[69] as well as Baden and Stroup, although their proposal is slightly less radical. Recognizing the uniqueness and fragility of wilderness and areas of extraordinary scenic beauty, Baden and Stroup advocate transferring some of these areas directly to qualified environmental groups, such as the Sierra Club or the Audubon Society.[70] In exchange, no more wild land designations would be forthcoming, and careful and compatible resource development under the guidance of these organizations would have to be permitted. Baden and Stroup, however, are pretty sure that these private environmental land managers, being as rational and self-interested as any other property owners, would eventually come around and see the obvious value of such development. This new attitude would develop because, as owners, they would allegedly become more sensitized to the issue of opportunity costs foregone in the name of preservation.[71] Anderson and his colleagues, on the other hand, argue that environmental groups have more than enough money and supporters (presumably armed with their ten land share certificates each) to avoid having to be given any kind of preferential treatment over any other bidder. Still, recognizing that these organizations developed in a fiercely competitive environment, they find environmentalists far preferable to government to hold tracts of wild land.[72] And although they agree that much of the federal estate should be privatized (especially those parcels rich in commodities), still others see a role, albeit much more limited, for the federal government. Oesterle, for instance, imagines that the federal government would still need to manage valuable parks and wilderness areas,[73] while Nelson sees the "crown jewel" national parks and wildlife refuges staying under federal control.[74]

Transfer to State and Local Governments

As illustrated in Chapter 1, western governors, legislatures, and numerous resource-extraction-industry-aligned think tanks and interest groups have been pushing hard for a sequel to the Sagebrush Rebellion that would transfer federal land to the states. Presumably, this land would be more aggressively managed for resource extraction and revenue generation, much more like state-trust lands. However, these transferred lands could just as easily be sold off and privatized by the states. Indeed, some western states, such as Idaho and Alaska, have active disposal programs, which are perfectly allowable methods for generating revenue from their trust lands. For instance, Nevada, which was granted 2.7 million acres at statehood, now retains just 3,000 acres of trust land.[75]

Many westerners are naturally drawn to the idea of hundreds of billions of dollars in assets being transferred to their control, essentially for free, yet not all critics of public land are sold on this solution. Oesterle, for example, wonders how states could possibly absorb the costs of the heavily subsidized, often marginally productive, and expensive to manage federal lands.[76] Anderson, Smith, and Simmons and Stroup and Baden, meanwhile, dislike the notion of transferring land from one level of public bureaucracy to another; given their complaints, this shift would solve nothing.[77] Stroup and Baden note that the most enthusiastic supporters of the first Sagebrush Rebellion tended to be the extractive industries, which simply wanted an even better deal than they were getting from the federal government for heavily subsidized, underpriced resources.[78] O'Toole, meanwhile, finds little evidence that state managers would behave much differently, with the possible exception of trust land managers, who have a legislatively or constitutionally derived fiduciary duty to their beneficiaries (a mandate that transferred federal land would presumably not have).[79]

Of the major privatization theorists, Nelson is probably the strongest advocate for the devolution of land to state and local governments. He worries that outright large-scale privatization would have some very negative unforeseen consequences, as large corporations, not always responsive or easy to regulate, would be in the best position to acquire this mass of newly privatized assets.[80] Instead, he calls for a rather complex, hybrid solution. First, only the most valuable, high-quality recreational lands and wildlife refuges—the "crown jewels," so to speak—would be retained by the federal government. Although he proposes that the USFS, the U.S. Fish and Wildlife Service (USFWS), and the U.S. Department of the Interior all be dismantled, the National Park Service (NPS) would remain intact to manage these limited remnants of the federal domain. Much of the BLM lands, meanwhile, would be transferred to the states, while most national wildlife refuges and many hundreds of less-visited national parks, monuments, and historic sites would be transferred to state or local governments or, in some cases, private nonprofits. Finally, the highly productive, commodity-producing lands (mostly national forests) would be privatized through a slow divestment process, possibly by creating quasi-independent government corporations that would eventually be privatized via the slow sale of government shares to the public (along the lines of the Conrail privatization in the 1970s).[81]

Marketization

Some streams of privatization theory focus more on management than on ownership, and so rather than taking the controversial leap of selling or transferring public land, they prefer instead a *marketization* of its management to bring it in line with how markets would allocate resources. O'Toole offers a good example of this line of thought. The rare libertarian who prefers that federal lands stay public *and* federal, O'Toole calls for a radical shift in budgeting and decision making toward a "pay-as-you-go" model of resource allocation. He would replace the current structure with a system of federal land trusts decentralized down to each individual unit of NPS, USFS, BLM, and USFWS land. All users would be charged fees set at fair-market value, and each unit would keep the fees it generated and be required to cover all costs. However, one-fifth of the fee revenue would be diverted into a Biodiversity Trust Fund to be spent to preserve features of natural ecosystems that are hard to charge user fees for.

Lands that are currently state-owned face, perhaps, less overt pressure to be fully divested than the federal lands, but they have certainly faced much more pressure to move toward greater marketization.[82] Trust lands actually got there long ago, but now increased user fees; budgets cut off from all general funds; revenue "enhancements," such as golf-course or resort development; and outsourced management are all becoming increasingly commonplace at the state level. In this area, then, the forces of privatization have actually made some real, concrete policy gains.

Finally, leasing arrangements and easements are held up by some privatization advocates as possible free-market-friendly alternatives to government ownership and regulation. Leasing can work both ways, in fact, as outright privatizers hold out the possibility of private owners' selling long-term leases or conservation easements to environmentalist bidders to effect preservation, while Nelson broaches the opposite idea of offering exclusive long-term leases on public land to resource users as an alternative to selling the land off.[83] Marion Clawson envisions a system of competitively awarded long-term leasing of federal lands.[84] Thus, on a typical national forest tract, for example, Kampgrounds of America might bid on the campground area, a timber company on the most productive stands of timber, and the Audubon Society on areas like wetlands that are rich in wildlife.[85] The idea, as Anderson, Smith, and Simmons explain, is to get the various competing potential users to bargain with each other and come to some sort of accommodation in the market rather than through lobbyists and the courts.[86]

As a parallel conservation strategy, easements have already become widely used in the United States by nonprofit private land trusts and by governments at all levels that cannot or will not purchase more land outright but still want to achieve conservative objectives. Despite its use of the free market, Anderson, Smith, and Simmons dislike the latter option (government's leasing to users) because, in their minds, it still allows for the interference of bureaucrats over market forces in arranging the terms of the lease.[87] Fretwell, meanwhile, even has doubts about private land trusts, complaining that they serve too often as "real estate agents for the federal government," eventually feeding land back into the public system through the donation or sale of acquired parcels to public agencies for posterity and to lessen the private organizations' management burden.[88] She is also not so keen on perpetual conservation easements, which, in her opinion, operate in a way that "distorts local real estate markets and fetters communities as needs and values evolve over time."[89] One would think, however, that such a strong proponent of free markets as Fretwell would show a bit more respect for the fruit borne by open-market exchanges, even if they produced outcomes (such as an easement for the perpetual protection of a particular tract) that she did not like.

Whether various free-market theorists advocate outright privatization, devolution, land trusts, or other softer forms of marketization, they all share a distrust of the motives and capabilities of public-sector managers as well as the supposed inefficiencies and market distortions that they see as inevitable when land is being held collectively. It is this faith in market exchange as the true realm of rationality, good policy outcomes, and human freedom (as they define it) that informs and propels their seemingly tireless efforts to separate Americans from their public land.

FOLLOWING SPREAD: Coconino National Forest, Arizona. *(Photo by the author.)*

3

Getting Serious about Ecology

The Biological Case for Public Lands

> Every scrap of biological diversity is priceless, to be learned and
> cherished, and never to be surrendered without a struggle.
>
> —E. O. WILSON, quoted in Craig W. Thomas, *Bureaucratic Landscapes*

The False Promise of the Private Eden

AS ILLUSTRATED in the previous chapter, the privatizers' environmental critique of public land is as straight-
forward as it is unsubtle. Simply put, they allege that
federal management is "environmentally destructive"[1] and "has
a poor record of ecological stewardship."[2] According to a representative of a Nevada privatization think tank:

> There is little evidence that government stewardship has
> kept these lands in good condition. We should move these
> lands into private, responsible hands now, rather than
> waiting for them to deteriorate further.[3]

The key, then, to restoring both economic and ecological well-
being to the land is for privatization to proceed. Such bold
declarations, however, fairly beg for some solid and rigorously
obtained empirical grounding to stand on, and whether that
grounding exists is explored in this chapter.

When considering the case that privatization advocates make
on environmental grounds, one might be forgiven if one senses
a certain "have your cake and eat it too" quality, almost as if the

economic theorists who dominate the privatization camp believe they have no choice but to make audacious claims about the environmental benefits of privatization. After all, without a better, healthier environment, what they have left to offer the American public is pretty thin gruel: the bitter medicine of "market discipline," a lot of "No Trespassing" signs, and $300 tickets for Disney's "Yellowstone Experience." Without promising greater environmental health, their policy package would probably be a nonstarter for most people.

At least as a textbook theory, the privatizers' arguments regarding environmental quality just might seem to make some logical sense. But when field-tested, these claims prove to be fundamentally wrong—a collection of anecdotes, cherry-picked case studies, huge assumptions, and blatant omissions and misunderstandings about ecological systems. What is universally and prominently missing from the environmental claims of privatizers is an attempt to offer any sort of comprehensive, systematic body of empirical evidence. Instead, almost as an afterthought, all that is served up are carefully curated horror stories and theoretical conjecture.

Many privatizers are probably quite sincere in their professed environmental sympathies, yet with others, the mask occasionally slips, and their more mercenary motives in making these environmental arguments become clear. For example, in the article "Public Land: How Much Is Enough," a mere thirteen pages after he claims that federal management of public land has been "an ecological disaster," Dale Oesterle questions the whole concept of *ecosystems*, which he derides as "a malleable construct" that is essentially motivated by politics and routinely used to exaggerate the needs of wildlife so that federal managers can expand their domains.[4] One might wonder whether someone who rejects the idea of ecosystems is in the best position to evaluate what is and is not an "ecological disaster." Similarly, Robert Nelson dismisses the conservation of large roadless blocks of wild land as having been accomplished merely "as a symbolic—perhaps even religious—gesture."[5] It apparently never crosses his mind that there might also be at least some biological consideration in conserving such rich, undisturbed tracts.

But even assuming that most privatizers are not just saying what they think the public wants to hear, there are still deep flaws in their arguments. One of the biggest shortcomings with the privatizers' use of the environmental health framework is their shifting and imprecise definitions of the concept. For example, Steve Hanke and Barney Dowdle assert that privatization would "obtain more commercial, recreational, and environmental outputs than with federal ownership."[6] What exactly, then, are these "environmental outputs" they speak of but never elaborate on? Are the resources harvested, trees looked at and admired, oxygen created, carbon sequestered, or wolverine dens established? And how do they know this? They simply assert these ideas in vague market-oriented language without any attempt at greater precision or evaluation. By throwing around the concept of environmental health in such a loose and casual way, they transform it into an amorphous, all-purpose tool. To preserve that advantage, it is never defined through scientifically accepted indicators that any practitioner would ever recognize, let alone validate.

Hanke and Dowdle's language points to one of the great weaknesses in the privatizers' environmental arguments: because they are mostly economists, they conflate concepts of efficiency and productivity with environmental health. Indeed, you may recall from the previous chapter that at the core of their theoretical arguments is this notion that because private owners have a financial stake in the productivity of the particular parcels of land they own, they will do what is necessary to protect that productivity. From the vantage point of this perspective, then, the evidence of environmental health comes to be seen as how many resources some parcel of land is producing. This viewpoint, however, creates a circular logic whereby environmental health on a parcel of land gets measured by the volume of the very activities that cause the most environmental harm to that parcel. More production equals better health; because you are logging so much, it shows that the land must be healthy.[7]

Thus, what ecologists understand as a holistic and dynamic ensemble of interdependent components, processes, symbioses, and interactions is rather crudely reduced by the privatizers to a torturously narrow measure of resource productivity (and of a limited set of resources at that).

Let us, as an example, apply a productivity definition to the environmental health of agricultural land, which might be especially appropriate given that it is the most common category of private land use.[8] Modern, industrial agriculture in the United States is, perhaps, the most productive in the world, and so, according to the privatizers' logic, it ought to follow that U.S. farmland is in tip-top shape ecologically. Yet we know that nothing could be further from the truth, and it is well documented that modern industrial agriculture actually visits enormous ecological degradation on the land, air, and water.[9] Far from being an indicator of health, then, such intense productivity represents an enormous debit from the land's biological account. The short-term productivity (which is usually the only kind being measured) of a single resource—be it corn, hogs, gallons of milk, or timber—is simply not the same as ecological well-being, no matter how emphatically the privatizers claim it is. If we instead employed some alternative and more familiar indicators of environmental health to agricultural production, such as persistence of pesticide residues, soil compaction, erosion, or groundwater pollution or depletion, we would surely draw some different conclusions. Obviously, trade-offs must be made to provide food and fiber for so many (and this book is not necessarily arguing that they should not be made), but the "productivity" this requires should never be mistaken for ecological well-being.

It simply does not hold that because farmers' livelihood is tied up in the land, they will never embark on activities that harm the environment. As one small example, to boost their production of marketable commodities and to take advantage of high grain prices from 2008 to 2012, farmers withdrew millions of acres from the U.S. Department of Agriculture's Conservation Reserve Program and moved toward fence-to-fence plantings, wiping out hedgerows, stream buffers, "back 40" woodlots, and milkweed and wildflower margins so vital to such pollinators as honeybees and migrating butterflies.[10] Furthermore, rather than act to protect resources because they own the land, as privatizers insist, many farmers require subsidies or incentives to do anything ecologically beneficial, such as implementing erosion control or setting aside fallow lands and wildlife habitat. In all these cases, the practices boosting agricultural productivity actually undermine environmental health.[11] That is not to say that farmers are unconcerned about the health of their land, but the pressures and constraints of a ferociously competitive marketplace (with very thin margins) that does not recognize or reward ecological sustainability often overwhelms efforts to do right by the land.

A similarly obsessive focus on productivity measures and unfamiliarity with basic ecological indicators can be seen when Richard Stroup and John Baden call for mining in federal wilderness areas, arguing that, in the context of hundreds of millions of acres of federal land, hard-rock mining's disturbance footprint is miniscule.[12] While that assertion is certainly true, any ecologist would immediately point out that the appropriate indicator of mining's impact on an ecosystem is not usually the terrestrial acreage actually dug up or otherwise disturbed but the geographically wide-ranging pollution to and consumption of surface and groundwater. Such sanguine "win-win" pronouncements, then, should hardly instill confidence in privatizers' environmental assessment skills or their larger message of privatization's advantages.

In fact, the whole privatization theory on environmental stewardship falls apart completely when the wealth comes from nonrenewable resources below the ground (such as coal, gas, oil, and hard-rock minerals) rather than from renewable ones above (such as trees, crops, and animals). Here, the market demands that the highest, best use of the land requires practices that, by definition, harm the underlying biological resource. It is important to be clear: to mine is to strip off the soil and vegetation and to unavoidably poison the watershed to get at the valuable nonrenewable resource. This practice might be necessary if we need those resources, but it is a specious argument to say that doing so does not affect environmental health. Thus, far from being dependent on the health and continued productivity of his or her land, the property owner's wealth—in this case, from mining nonrenewable resources—actually requires damaging said land and, presumably, the productivity of those less-valuable renewable resources.

Another common strategy that privatization advocates use when bemoaning the state of public land is to report with great alarm that our parks are "deteriorating," literally falling apart before our eyes.[13] It is true that drastically reduced budgets at state and federal levels and increased demand have led to maintenance backlogs and serious declines in the condition of park infrastructures, yet notice in this case how ecological health is conflated with the status of lodges, campgrounds, trails, historic buildings, roads, and the like. These amenities are, of course, quite important in their own right, and their deterioration certainly harms the visitors' experience and the public interest, yet they are, once again, scientifically inappropriate indicators of ecological health. After all, how exactly does it harm biodiversity, or habitat availability, or forage quality if an outhouse in Yellowstone has a leaky roof or a park access road in Glacier has bad potholes? Not surprisingly, the answer put forward to address such problems with the health of our parks is, for critics, to stop adding more land to the system and to use existing resources more judiciously to take care of the inventory already in the system (to, presumably, patch up potholes).[14] Sylvia LeRoy disapprovingly quotes a Parks Canada official who confessed, "My feeling is we should grab [new property] even if we do not have money in the budget to maintain it the way we would like."[15] Whereas LeRoy sees environmentally indifferent empire building at work, the quoted official might actually have seen environmentally rich, once-in-a-lifetime acquisition opportunities presenting themselves, and he would be damned if he was going to miss out on them just because his maintenance budget for outhouses and campgrounds was insufficient.

Ecology: Science or Values?

The fatal flaw in the privatizers' argument, and one that no amount of rhetorical jujitsu on their part will resolve, is this: on the one hand, they adamantly proclaim that government land management is ecologically destructive and imply that private lands, by contrast, are in ecologically healthier condition. And yet they dismiss all reasonable, scientifically defensible indicators of healthy land and ecosystems as subjective value preferences or culturally determined desires or tastes rather than objective measures rooted in biological science. Thus, an intact forested wilderness area would be, to a scientist, an objectively rich and biodiverse place with complex and well-functioning ecological systems, whereas, as we have already seen, privatizers would criticize it as little more than a playground suited to the preferences of environmental elites and paid for by nonusers. But if they really are so concerned with ecological health, should they not be a bit more circumspect in their constant casting of wilderness as nothing but a recreational luxury and preference?

Similarly, this failure by privatizers to reconcile their elaborate claims about ecological health with their obtuse refusal to identify any objective standards to measure it by (save, perhaps, productivity) can be very clearly seen when Terry Anderson and Donald Leal argue for allowing the market to decide the highest use for land that hosts endangered species:

> Turning moral values into political issues and arguing that it is a matter of treading more lightly on the Earth, however, becomes another form of rent seeking, wherein people with one set of moral values get what they want at the expense of others.[16]

In other words, the idea that it is a biologically bad outcome to build luxury homes on an endangered butterfly habitat is, in actuality, just a subjective preference being rammed down society's throat at its own expense. But how can anyone espouse that view while still making such ambitious claims about ecological health in a regime of privatization? If ecological health does not prominently include robust biodiversity and fewer extinctions of endangered species, then what could it possibly entail? From the privatizers, we never really know, because they do not ever bother to clearly spell out what they mean with their vague, overly confident, wildly expansive claims about the superior condition of private land.

To the extent that they produce any specific evidence spelling out the ecological failures they allegedly abhor, it tends to be presented in the most ad hoc manner. Selected instances of hapless, purposefully destructive, or ineffective federal management over the past century are meticulously chronicled by the privatizers. They point, often quite persuasively, to such examples as bison and elk overgrazing and starvation in Yellowstone; destructive fire management; poor-quality Bureau of Land Management (BLM) grasslands; U.S. Forest Service (USFS) logging in steep, marginal, erosion-prone areas; or the destructive practice of "drag-chaining" in pinyon pine–juniper habitat to create more open rangeland.[17]

But what all these anecdotes amount to, no matter how accurate they may be, is little more than a scattershot of bad practices from more than a century of managing two-thirds of a billion acres of land. What is desperately needed to bolster the privatizers' claims is a far more systematic review of data to assess the health of similar expanses of public and private land. Most serious observers of public land would readily agree that the "glass" of public management is neither completely full nor empty and that plenty of evidence across four agencies and 635 million acres of widely varied federal land supports either scenario. Pondering this evidence in a more careful, systematic, and comprehensive way instead of delivering a self-serving recitation of selectively chosen failures is what is most needed here to render a fuller judgment on the environmental performance of public land management.[18]

Even if privatization advocates were quite right in their assessment of federal management's being, on balance, more ecologically destructive than not (a question that is explored more fully later in this chapter), they still commit an obvious logical fallacy:

1. Government does an environmentally bad job of managing land.
2. Private management is an alternative scenario.
3. Therefore, private management must do an environmentally better job because it is not government management.

But why can it not do a *worse* job or perhaps a similar job? Again, very little real-world data and systematic comparison are marshaled in support of privatization's claims.[19]

Indicators of Environmental Health

Biodiversity

Any nonsuperficial, nonanecdotal set of indicators of the environmental health of the land must be rooted in biological science. And the biological concept that best captures the essence of what we are trying to measure here is *biodiversity.* Conservation biologists Reed Noss and Allen Cooperrider define biodiversity as

> the variety of life and its processes. It includes the variety of living organisms, the genetic differences among them, the communities and ecosystems in which they occur, and the ecological and evolutionary processes that keep them functioning, yet ever changing and adapting.[20]

That last item is most important, as it is not exactly diversity in and of itself but the state of the systems and processes that support this diversity that most matter in this case. Diversity alone is very unevenly distributed by latitude, climate, soil, and so on. The most abused and degraded Hawaiian forest, for instance, will still have far more biodiversity than a pristine, perfectly functioning

Alaskan wilderness. But the latter, it is probably safe to say, is in better ecological health and is better managed for biodiversity.

If biodiversity, then, is to be the criterion for measuring the ecological condition of public and private land, we need to be exceedingly careful in how such data are applied and compared. For example, it would be unfair to compare national park or national forest tracts to private urban or agricultural lands when measuring biodiversity. In fact, public and private lands are such vast and varied categories that no single data set could possibly allow for the comparison of one to the other as a whole. Thus, despite its conceptual appropriateness, biodiversity as a measure presents a number of problems that make direct comparisons rather difficult. One such problem is that biodiversity is, as just mentioned, regionally clustered by latitude, altitude, and climate. Regardless of ownership, biodiversity tends to increase as one moves south, with the greatest biodiversity found in California, Texas, Hawaii, and the Southeast, especially Florida. Conversely, Alaska, the northern Great Plains, the Upper Midwest, and New England have considerably less biodiversity.[21] Except for California, these high-biodiversity areas, for a number of historical and geographic reasons, happen to have relatively fewer acres of public land than the mean. It would not necessarily follow, therefore, that endangered species prefer the benign management they find on private land because of the high number of privately held wetlands in Florida that have rare species on them.

Another problem is that even specific geographic areas can include vast differences in biodiversity, with wetter and lower elevation habitats, such as marshes, tidal pools, estuaries, and river valleys, naturally having far more, and high-elevation or arid habitats having considerably less.[22] This variation is very significant in the context of settlement patterns and the history of the public domain. At least at the federal level, after homesteaders, speculators, and railroads staked their claims, most of the remaining land amounted to the "leftovers"—areas generally too high, too steep, too arid, and too unproductive to attract any takers. Settlement occurred on the best lands: the broad, fertile river valleys; mesic woodlands; and well-watered plains with deep soils, all of which contained much higher levels of biodiversity; the inaccessible mountain ranges, deserts, and arid grassland, all of which had less biodiversity to begin with, stayed public.[23] As David Wilcove et al. note, right from the start, there has been a poor overlap between biodiversity and public ownership.[24]

Biodiversity and Imperiled Species

When attempting to compare biodiversity on public and private lands, then, it is vitally important to stick, as much as possible, to "apples-to-apples" types of comparisons—whether by ecotype or specific geographic region or, even better, subregion. Given the importance of this question, comprehensive data of this sort are surprisingly hard to find. Perhaps the best and most exhaustive collection of studies on the topic is found in *Precious Heritage: The Status of Biodiversity in the United States.* Bruce Stein et al. report approximately two hundred thousand identified species of flora and fauna in the United States and suggest the possibility of as many as six hundred thousand.[25] Of the known number, about two-thirds are reported to be secure, while the remaining third is split evenly between vulnerable and imperiled statuses.[26] Agricultural activities (threatening 30 percent of imperiled species), urban development (35 percent), water projects (30 percent), and outdoor recreation, especially motorized (27 percent), are identified as the leading threats to these species.[27]

In the most comprehensive study in *Precious Heritage*, Craig Groves et al. use a massive database developed by The Nature Conservancy (TNC) that pinpoints 39,521 discrete population occurrences for species with federal status under the Endangered Species Act.[28] What they find is that, despite all these built-in biodiversity disadvantages on public, especially federal, land, these lands still play a critical and disproportionate role in protecting biodiversity in the United States. Although the authors conclude that the percentages of imperiled species with any presence at all on public and private land are roughly equal,[29] they also offer a much more important and telling measure that compares the individual population occurrences in the TNC database (what the

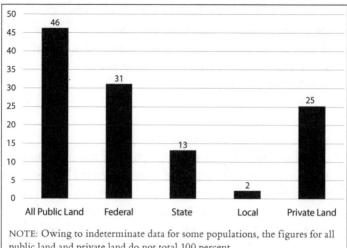

Figure 3.1. Percentage of discrete population occurrences of imperiled species found, by land ownership type. *(Data from Craig Groves et al., "Owning Up to Our Responsibilities: Who Owns the Lands Important for Biodiversity?" in* Precious Heritage: The Status of Biodiversity in the United States, *ed. Bruce Stein, Lynn Kutner, and Jonathan Adams [Oxford: Oxford University Press, 2000], 280–282.)*

authors call "the operative unit for conservation action") by land ownership.[30] They find that 31 percent of discrete populations of imperiled species are found on federal land, 13 percent on state public land, and 2 percent on local public land, for a total of 46 percent on public land versus 25 percent on private land, as is shown in Figure 3.1.[31]

Given the fact that private acres in the United States out-number public acres by an approximately 3:2 ratio, it is even more remarkable that twice the number of imperiled popula-tions occur on public land.[32] The study's authors note that this public-private discrepancy becomes even more pronounced for the federal lands if one removes Alaska from the mix:

Analyzing ownership patterns for population occurrences
. . . one discovers that about one-third of both federally-listed and imperiled species are found on federal lands.
. . . Although this percentage is roughly equivalent to the

percentage of U.S. land under federal ownership (30%),
excluding Alaska—which represents a huge expanse of the
federal estate, yet has relatively few imperiled or federally
listed species—the federal government manages less than
one-fifth of the land area.[33]

They go on to conclude:

The disparity between the population of imperiled and
endangered species populations found on federal lands and
what these lands represent as a percentage of the overall
landscape emphasize the disproportionate importance that
federal lands have for maintaining imperiled and endangered species.[34]

Furthermore, this study finds that 31 percent of imperiled species are found *only* on public land and nowhere else (23 percent
federal, 8 percent state), as compared to 10 percent found only
on private land, as can be seen in Figure 3.2.[35]

Legal scholar Bradley Karkkainen also notes this discrepancy and the inordinate importance of federal land:

Although private landowners own roughly twice as much
land as the federal government, much of the privately
held land is in biodiversity-poor categories such as cropland and pasturage, industrial forest, urbanized areas, or
small-scale rural developments contributing to the fragmentation of habitats and ecosystems.[36]

Biologists Bruce Stein, Cameron Scott, and Nancy Benton largely
come to the same conclusion when projecting into the future.
They find, "Given the current and projected pace of private land
development, we can expect that federal lands will assume greater
importance for the protection of our native species."[37] Yet despite
this critical importance, Karkkainen, like others, notes the pronounced mismatch of federal holdings to biodiversity hotspots
and advocates, therefore, an aggressive program of in-kind land

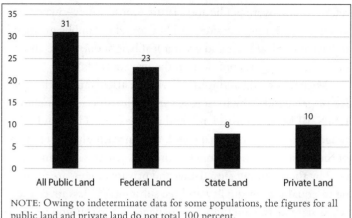

NOTE: Owing to indeterminate data for some populations, the figures for all public land and private land do not total 100 percent.

Figure 3.2. Percentage of imperiled species found *only* in a given jurisdiction. *(Data from Craig Groves et al., "Owning Up to Our Responsibilities: Who Owns the Lands Important for Biodiversity?" in* Precious Heritage: The Status of Biodiversity in the United States, *ed. Bruce Stein, Lynn Kutner, and Jonathan Adams [Oxford: Oxford University Press, 2000], 285.)*

swaps or land sales in one area that would be earmarked to raise funds for purchase in another, richer area.[38]

Other research that compares public to private land has focused on species richness in general rather than on endangered species specifically, and a number of these studies do so in a very direct and useful "apples-to-apples" sort of way. For instance, in one study, biologists studied 31 private and 29 public tallgrass prairie sites in eastern South Dakota using Swink and Wilhelm's Floristic Quality Index (FQI), which measures the presence of conservative, high-quality native species.[39] The researchers found a mean FQI value of 44 on the public sites versus 39 on the private ones.[40] Meanwhile, using the *coefficient of conservatism* (C), another, similar measure that notes the presence of less common species with the most specific needs, the authors found that "statistical analysis showed that privately owned prairies have significantly lower C values than public sites."[41] When the authors applied this same database to grassland bird habitats in a separate study, they came to a similar conclusion, finding "higher wildlife habitat values for public and well-managed reference sites [the reference sites were public and Nature Conservancy–owned] and lower values for private sites."[42] They found the public grasslands to have more leaf litter and greater leaf height due to the absence of grazing that was common on the private lands.[43]

Michael Loring and John Workman also examine the quality of grassland habitats across various jurisdictions, including USFS, BLM, state-trust land, and private land. They find USFS ranges to be in the best shape and, not surprisingly, the recipient of the most investment (much more, it is safe to say, than is covered by their grazing fees). BLM and private ranges, are found to be in equally poor quality and see substantially less investment, while state-trust land (which is managed for maximum revenue) is in the worst shape of all and has the least investment. These findings lead them to conclude that ownership is a less important variable than investment in the resource.[44] But, contrary to privatization theory, the private owners do not seem to have the incentive to invest in the productivity of their own resources, while the USFS does.

Future Projections of Biodiversity

In 2007, scientists conducted research projecting biodiversity levels for the next hundred years in the Oregon Coast Range, an ecosystem of lush temperate rain forests with an ownership profile that is 37 percent public and 63 percent private.[45] What they forecast was a notable increase in biodiversity as habitats for conservative indicator species (such as spotted owls, marbled murrelets, and various lichens) expand substantially. What is significant in their findings is that although public forests make up a little more than a third of the region, the authors find that nearly all the projected increases in biodiversity are clustered on the public land.[46] Currently and in year one hundred, public forests in the region have or are projected to have nearly all large-diameter trees, which harbor the richest biodiversity. When looking at the federal forests, they find that "the potential diversity or resiliency of these landscapes is much higher than that of private forest lands."[47]

Thomas Eichner and Rüdiger Pethig, meanwhile, offer an interesting study that embarks on a similar project of forecasting future ecological outcomes. Their extremely complex and ambitious model explores the relationship between habitat and species status and economic context by predicting outcomes for a theoretical section of land on a continuum that runs from a policy of habitat optimization and conservation to a full-blown laissez-faire market approach. Taken to its end, their model finds that "in the laissez-faire economy, the habitat is consequently squeezed to zero in the long run so that all species are doomed."[48]

Denis White and his collaborators base their twenty-five-year projections on a real rather than theoretical case—that of Monroe County, Pennsylvania, a rural area on the fringes of exurban growth. They attempt to predict landscape changes using development scenarios featuring four different development-to-conservation ratios, ranging from aggressive development to what they call the "park plan," which would preserve all remaining undeveloped land as public.[49] Not surprisingly, after twenty-five years, the park scenario features the least landscape and ecological disruption and the lowest risks of habitat loss and is the only scenario that does not project more species' declining rather than improving. For the private-land-oriented scenarios, the species decline to improvement ratio is 3:1.[50] Although it is certainly true that private property does not necessarily lead to suburban development, the county in this case study was specifically chosen because of the high-pressure situation of rising real-estate demand and value that it was facing, a scenario in which conservation generally occurs only through public or nonprofit ownership.

Landscape Diversity

Ecologists remind us that species diversity depends on and is strongly linked to ecosystem diversity, which, it should be recalled, is an element of Noss and Cooperrider's widely cited definition of biodiversity.[51] To Stein et al., the equation is this simple: *diverse ecotypes = diverse species.*[52] So when comparing the ecological condition of public to private land, the question that naturally arises is "Which one contains a wider array of healthy, functioning ecological communities?" With landscapes, ecologists unfortunately find the state of imperilment to be even more severe than it is for individual species. They find only 25 percent of landscape types secure, while 57 percent are either *vulnerable, imperiled*, or *critically imperiled*, and 1 percent have been eliminated.[53]

Obviously, the same issues exist here as with the broader concept of biodiversity, given the geographic distribution of the public lands by latitude, elevation, climate, and soil moisture. This asymmetrical distribution causes landscapes to be very unevenly represented across the public domain. Studies completed under the auspices of the Department of the Interior's Gap Analysis Program report a relatively consistent result: within a given state or region, approximately 40 percent of community types have less than 10 percent of their land cover in the public domain.[54] Research by David Crumpacker, however, finds better ecotype representation on federal land, with three-quarters of all 135 major ecosystem types relatively well-represented, 24 types underrepresented, and 9 not at all present.[55]

In a fine-scale case study of this uneven distribution of landscape communities from the Southeast, Groves et al. examine two regions: the Southern Blue Ridge and the Atlantic Coastal Plain. In the former, 60 percent of the land is federal, while on the coast, it is less than 10 percent. Not surprisingly, 88 percent of ecological communities are present on abundant federal lands in the Blue Ridge, while on the coast, a still-impressive 60 percent are present on the much smaller parcels of federal land.[56] It is significant to note that although most of these communities are also present on private lands, nearly all the specific sites that are evaluated as the highest quality (A and B grade) are on public lands that are specifically managed for biodiversity.[57]

So, as was found with individual populations of imperiled species, public lands, despite all their geographic deficits, play a crucial and disproportionate role in protecting landscape diversity. As Karkkainen notes, "The federal holdings often include many of the best preserved remaining fragments of critical eco-

systems—the lands with the most potential for serving as biological reserves."[58] He finds this situation to be especially true
in the East, where, according to ecologists, the imperilment of
specific landscapes is actually much worse than it is west of the
Mississippi.[59] Karkkainen argues that although federal ownership may be low overall in the East, it is concentrated in some of
the most important remnants of critical ecosystems:[60]

> The fact that the Federal government owns less than 4% of
> land outside [the West] leads some commentators to con-
> clude we should focus our principal biodiversity conserva-
> tion efforts on private lands. This gross figure may be mis-
> leading, however, if it causes us to overlook the federal gov-
> ernment's substantial land ownership in such disparate and
> critical ecoregions as Hawaii, south Florida, the Upper Great
> Lakes, the New Jersey Pinelands, northern New England,
> the southern Appalachians, and the Ozarks. Gross acreage
> also belies the importance of federal holdings in fragile
> coastal wetlands and barrier islands along the Atlantic and
> Gulf coast, which, although small in acreage, represent
> unique, priceless, and endangered biological assets.[61]

Where public lands seem to compare most favorably to private
lands are with exceedingly rare and endangered ecological communities that present the greatest opportunity costs to preserve.
For example, old-growth forests in the Pacific Northwest contain
exceptionally profitable and desirable straight-grained timber, as
do the redwood forests of coastal California, while midwestern
oak savannas are often in prime home-building or agricultural
areas and have little market value as protected remnants. As the
Savanna Oak Foundation points out, "Since there is no reasonable
way that an oak savanna can be managed for profit, many landowners may be discouraged from savanna restoration."[62]

With such exceedingly rare ecological communities, it is
not unheard of for 90 percent or more of remaining acreage
of a given ecotype to be on public land. For example, various
inventories of old-growth temperate rain forest communities in

the United States range from 90 percent to 99 percent public in a region that is approximately 50 percent publicly owned.[63] The National Commission on Science for Sustainable Forestry reports that "most remaining old growth in the Pacific Northwest is on federal and state lands. There is relatively little older forest on private lands, where a good economic return on investment is a primary management goal."[64] Studies in the Oregon Coast Range (which has 37 percent public ownership) find that 95 percent of true old growth (which constitutes a tiny 1 percent fragment of all forests in the area) is on public land, while for the 17 percent of forests classified as "late-succession mature forest" (biologically rich forests in the slow process of becoming old growth), 77 percent of forests are on public land.[65]

For old-growth forests in the East, the distribution between public and private land is even more skewed. In a landscape of which between 0.3 percent and 0.5 percent remains, half of that is found in just three publicly owned places: Great Smoky Mountains National Park in Tennessee and North Carolina, New York's Adirondack Park, and the Boundary Waters Canoe Area Wilderness in Minnesota.[66] As for the rest, Robert Leverett reports that nearly all of it is also on public land.[67]

For another rare ecosystem, the midwestern oak savanna, Noss, LaRoe, and Scott report a 99.98 percent decline.[68] In the heart of oak savanna range in Wisconsin, between 500 and 1,000 acres of the original 5 million are said to remain,[69] with nearly all notable blocks on state-owned public land, according to a World Wildlife Fund inventory.[70] Freshwater coastal dunes on the Great Lakes are another example of a fragile ecotype with a far greater market value if developed rather than preserved. Not surprisingly, given the demand for lakefront properties, more than two-thirds of remaining state-designated *critical dunes* in Michigan are publicly owned.[71]

Fragmentation on Public and Private Land

At the core of the biodiversity issue for both species and landscape communities is habitat fragmentation, and although the data on public versus private biodiversity can sometimes be a bit murky and difficult to apply, the data on fragmentation are crystal clear. Simply put, private lands, by their very nature, are inevitably far more vulnerable, now and in the future, to fragmentation and parcelization. This fact is crucial to recognize, because this sort of habitat degradation is estimated by scientists to be a contributing factor in 85 percent of cases of species endangerment.[72] It is, according to Karkkainen, nothing less than "the principle cause of biodiversity loss."[73]

Studies have found a net loss from 1992 to 2001 of 29 million acres of rural private lands. For the period between 1997 and 2001, 46 percent of this lost acreage was forest, 20 percent cropland, and 31 percent pasture or rangeland.[74] The USFS, meanwhile, reports 22 million acres of private forest developed from 1982 to 1997 and projects the loss of an additional 1 million acres annually over the next fifty years.[75] This conversion of habitat into urbanized or industrial landscapes is not the only problem for wild ecosystems and their biodiversity. Such conversion also projects ecological changes onto the remaining wild landscapes that lie adjacent, by breaking up large contiguous blocks of habitat and introducing a sprawl of roads, buildings, and infrastructure sprinkled across the landscape.

When considering how to protect biodiversity, Sara Vickerman stresses the importance of *time* (long periods of stability), *space* (adequate amounts of critical habitat for feeding, breeding, and mobility), and *context* (the physical composition of and activities on adjacent land).[76] And all these factors are influenced by the fragmentation introduced by development, be it a new subdivision or fracking sites or a feedlot, and a voluminous scientific literature[77] confirms the ruinous effects that such development has on biodiversity, as Nick Haddad et al. note:

> In summary, across experiments spanning numerous studies and ecosystems, fragmentation consistently degraded ecosystems, reducing species persistence, species richness, nutrient retention, trophic dynamics, and, in more isolated fragments, movement.[78]

These profoundly negative effects, the authors find, are long term and persistent, but they often have a long lag time before finally hitting a point of acceleration into a severe diminishment of populations. The authors term this overall phenomenon an *ecosystem function debt*.[79]

The actual mechanisms by which fragmentation causes this debt to accrue center on habitat reduction, the increased isolation of fragments, and the introduction of *edge* into formerly solid, contiguous blocks of habitat.[80] For example, imagine that a long driveway or access road is built that leads to a newly constructed vacation home deep in a forest. That new road and the boundaries of the property introduce a long series of edges that penetrate what was once interior forest. One might be tempted to downplay the significance of this intrusion, given the relatively small actual acreage of pavement, Kentucky bluegrass, and ornamental shrubbery that has displaced native forest, but this notion would profoundly underestimate how deeply *edge effects* reach into the adjacent land (see Figures 3.3 and 3.4). These effects include changes in sunlight, levels of soil moisture, vulnerability to wind-throw, species composition, and the ability of pests, invasive species, and predators to move in along this new corridor.[81] One of the best-known examples of this phenomenon is the growing threat posed by the brown-headed cowbird, a parasitizing species that lays its eggs in other birds' nests (often those of far-less-common neotropical migrants, such as warblers) and has those birds raise cowbird young at the expense of their own. Increasing fragmentation has allowed the cowbird, which naturally shuns deep interior forest, to access new territory far into the forest adjacent to the new edge. Studies have shown cowbird parasitism and egg predation by raccoons and other edge-dwelling species to be strong contributing factors in the alarming levels of songbird decline in the United States.[82]

Another way that fragmentation harms biodiversity is by stranding species in isolated little islands of habitat, leaving them without the means to migrate through large uninterrupted expanses of wild land or even significant corridors. In an era of accelerating climate change, it is especially important for spe-

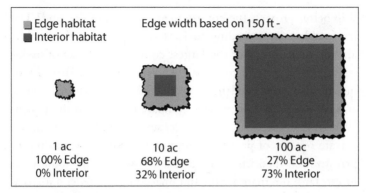

Figure 3.3. Disproportionately greater interior habitat in larger blocks of land—this, in turn, supports greater biodiversity. *(U.S. Department of Agriculture, National Agroforestry Center, "2.2 Patch Primer," Conservation Buffers, available at http://nac.unl.edu/buffers/guidelines/2_biodiversity/2.html.)*

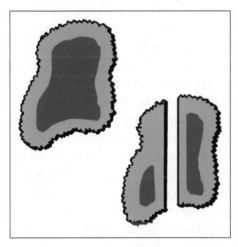

Figure 3.4. Disproportionate effect of road fragmentation on interior habitat—interior habitat is reduced at a rate many times the actual footprint of the developed or otherwise altered land. *(U.S. Department of Agriculture, National Agroforestry Center, "2.2 Patch Primer," Conservation Buffers, available at http://nac.unl .edu/buffers/guidelines/2_ biodiversity/2.html.)*

cies to be able to seek out new habitats if or when their previous habitats can no longer support them because of the changes wrought by increased heat, drought, or flood.[83] This is as true for plant species (which migrate over decades) as it is for wildlife.

Fragmentation, then, is the key mechanism in the unraveling of biodiversity, a fact that privatizers, whether innocently or willfully, seem wholly unaware of. What does this phenomenon mean for the debate over whether public or private ownership better protects the environmental health of the land? The irrefutable fact, according to Karkkainen, is that the "public already owns many of the largest contiguous blocks of undeveloped land" in the country.[84] And of that, more than three-quarters have just one landlord—the federal government, operating through four agencies—compared to 2.06 million farms averaging 469 acres on 968 million acres of land and six million private owners of private nonindustrial forest.[85] According to privatization theorists, those forest-lot owners care about their forests far more than distant and unaccountable federal managers, but that does not seem to stop them from building vacation homes and access roads or subdividing parcels one bit at a time. Indeed, trends in private forest ownership in the past few decades have tended toward increased parcelization among more and more individual owners,[86] especially in areas with rising property values.[87] In fact, according to one study, 61.8 percent of forests in the lower forty-eight states are within 90 meters of an edge, while, conversely, less than 1 percent of the forests are more than 1,230 meters from an edge. Furthermore, almost all significant interior forest is now on public land.[88] Other research also confirms the presence of considerably more fragmentation in private forests than in public ones. For example, in their sampling of high-resolution imagery of eastern forest inventories, Kurt Riitters, John Coulston, and James Wickham find private ownership strongly correlated to fragmentation, with approximately 62 percent of public forest meeting their definition of "intact," compared to 40 percent of private forest.[89]

There is no doubt that many of these private, nonindustrial owners dearly love their little patches of forest and are committed, in principle at least, to biodiversity, but the fact remains that the biggest unfragmented blocks of private forest are owned by industrial forest resource corporations and thus are under the most pressure to be managed for commodity production over biodiversity. The irony is that the private owners most likely to be sympathetic to biodiversity concerns tend to own the smallest, most degraded, and most fragmented parcels of private forests.

Public land is by no means immune to fragmentation (as any visit to heavily fracked BLM lands in Wyoming or a national forest filled with clearcuts and switchbacking logging roads will tell you), but it is still pretty much the only realm where huge expanses of roadless backcountry and long contiguous corridors of habitat still exist. Despite the fact that it was not created for or geared toward biodiversity protection, the federal wilderness system is obviously a critical asset in this regard, as are national forest lands protected under the Roadless Rule and the larger national parks and wildlife refuges. Even the vast, seemingly endless expanses of BLM lands, which such privatizers as Deborah Moeller dismiss as "desolate and nearly valueless,"[90] are, according to Karkkainen, far biologically richer than is commonly assumed,[91] and at least some of this richness is owed to the lands' relatively unfragmented state.

The effects of this clear superiority of public and especially federal land in terms of its contiguity can be seen in data from various conservative species that have large territorial needs and low tolerances for disturbance. For example, research on Wisconsin's wolf population finds that in the study area, 70 percent of wolf packs are situated on public land, even though such land constitutes only 27 percent of the study area. The authors find the greatest predictor of suitable habitat to be road density, which is, obviously, far lower on public land.[92] Similarly, for the wolf packs that have newly moved into northeastern Oregon (which is split fairly evenly between public and private land), researchers find that six of the eight intact packs live overwhelmingly on public land.[93]

Other research, meanwhile, reports similar findings with Pacific fishers (small weasel-like creatures) and pileated woodpeckers on the Oregon Coast Range. In a region that is 37 percent publicly owned, the authors find that

> ownership had a major effect on habitat patterns for most species and vegetative classes across the region. In particular, habitat for species with very large home ranges, e.g., Fishers, occurs largely on federal lands with habitat

on private land being supplemented from adjacent federal lands. Although 55% of private lands occur within 1.1 km of public lands, nearly all Fisher habitat occurring on private lands was within 1.1 km of public lands now (99.9%) and 100 [years] into the future (97%) under current policies.[94]

For the pileated woodpeckers, they find the same result, albeit to a lesser extent. That is, any habitat found on private land is "subsidized" by adjacent public land, which has far superior denning and nesting sites.[95]

In yet another study to find public land to be far better suited for wide-ranging conservative species, Robert Inman examines habitats for perhaps the rarest and most reclusive large mammal in the United States: the wolverine. Overall, he finds very limited amounts of suitable habitat supporting a maximum capacity of perhaps 580 individual wolverines in ten states, and of these habitats, 90 percent are, not surprisingly, on public land.[96] Public land has long played this pivotal role in the welfare of imperiled species. Jodi Stemler reminds us that, at the turn of the twentieth century, public lands acted as crucial reservoirs where wildlife species hunted to near extinction could recover and repopulate back into their former range. She notes that beaver, pronghorn, and bighorn sheep all made their comebacks in the West because of the availability of abundant public land.[97]

Ecosystem Permanence

Along with scale and context, time is the third element of Vickerman's theory on biodiversity. To what extent is an ecosystem vulnerable to or immune from rapid, jarring change? It would seem that the public lands with stable ownership, managed more deliberately outside purely market demands, would have a tremendous advantage in this regard over private land. "Public ownership of forest land," says Bill Cook, "offers promises not possible on privately owned land, especially in terms of the future."[98]

Research in Washington's Olympic Peninsula and the Southern Appalachian Highlands would seem to confirm this statement. The authors find that public lands in both study areas are clustered in larger and more stable contiguous blocks, which also act to somewhat mitigate the ill effects of fragmentation on the adjacent private land.[99] The permanence and relative biological stability of the public landscape is in contrast to the flux and rapid change found in the much more dispersed ownership of the private lands and cause the public lands to act as an *anchor* of sorts. Especially in the Lower Tennessee River Basin case study, when the authors base their change scenarios on recent federal management trends toward ecosystem management, they find an even greater forecasted divergence in rates of landscape change between public and private lands.[100]

Wilderness is especially fragile and ephemeral, and there is a good reason that nearly all that remains is on public land. To the extent that it exists at all, private wilderness tends to simply be wild land on its way to eventually becoming something else. In fact, the legal scholar John Sprankling notes that "all other things being equal, the property law system tends to resolve disputes by preferring wilderness destruction to wilderness preservation."[101] Thus, a distinct antiwilderness bias pervades property law, which favors active users over passive preservers.[102] The notion that vast blocks of ecologically integral wild land, much of which also holds valuable marketable commodities, can retain these wilderness characteristics without purposeful government action is simply fantasy, a point that even some privatizers concede. Without protection, then, from the mercurial whims of the market, private wild lands have a perpetual Sword of Damocles hanging over them.

Forests and Privatization

The Historical Record

One of the best ways to gain insight on privatization is by comparing the effects of public and private ownership of our forests. Such studies are a major focus of the literature, and rightly so.

First, forests are, perhaps, the most crucial and valuable of terrestrial resources, biologically, economically, and symbolically. In fact, as discussed in Chapter 1, it was for their protection that public land policy first moved toward retention with the Forest Reserve Act of 1891. Furthermore, forests cover more than 751 million acres (or 33 percent) of U.S. land. That figure accounts for 40 percent of all public land (about 328 million acres) and 29 percent of all private land (about 423 million acres), which creates a convenient and evenly balanced comparison.[103]

Forestry policy figures prominently in the debate between public lands' critics and defenders. In fact, some of the most commonly cited examples offered by public land critics regard such forest policies as the below-cost USFS timber sales in fragile, unproductive places or overcrowded, poorly managed forests leading to enhanced fire danger. The defenders of the public forests, on the other hand, would say that one needs to look no further than the wholesale pillaging of private forest resources in the nineteenth century to give rest to the myth of the environmentally benevolent private forest owner. As shown in Chapter 1, by the turn of the twentieth century, forests in vast swaths of the East had been essentially liquidated, and those lands unsuited for growing anything but trees had been left abandoned and in shambles.[104] William Shands quotes from a history of Wisconsin's North Woods in the 1920s:

> The whole world of northern Wisconsin was on fire in those years. You could choose a high point in any one of today's ranger districts and see miles of cut-over, burned-over land. Tree stubble and smoldering slash littered the landscape.[105]

This whole notion that landowners will necessarily have a long-term interest in the sustainability of the resources they own and profit from simply does not hold up at all to the historical record. The business model for the nineteenth-century forest industry was simply to cut and run—much as a locust swarm descends on a cornfield, devours it, and moves on to the next. This strategy was inexpensive, profitable, and expeditious. Parcels of virgin timber were dirt cheap; good stewardship was not.[106] Thus, there were no lengthy rotations, no replanting, no sustained yield, and, essentially, no management of any kind. A more appropriate model might have been the mining industry rather than forestry or agriculture.[107]

Privatizers counter this historical narrative with an interesting argument that seems to undermine their claims about the conscientious private owner more than anything else. They acknowledge the wholesale destruction, but they agree with Nelson that it "made much economic and other sense at the time."[108] According to Terry Anderson, in this historical context, aggressive private management was not at all inefficient but rather quite acceptable, because Americans were developing their continent, and, as Stroup and Baden point out, trees were plentiful and had what they claim was a negative value (getting in the way of agriculture and development).[109] Once trees became scarce, they argue, market forces began to kick in, and only then did they become valuable. This approach, however, would seem to foreclose any possibility of good stewardship from the start, as an ethic, so to speak. Instead, stewardship seems to be a goal grudgingly adopted only in the face of scarcity, a standard that practically guarantees environmental degradation. At the very least, then, this explaining away of such wanton, heedless, and mass-scale destruction of a privately owned resource (most definitely not a commons) would seem to undermine or at least limit the applicability of the privatizers' optimistic central theory regarding the environmental benevolence that ownership of a resource supposedly confers.

Privatizers make this contextual argument to explain the great deforestation of the nineteenth century, but the case of the MAXXAM Group's liquidation of its virgin redwood forests in the late 1980s and 1990s offers a modern example of this same disregard by private owners. In 1986, MAXXAM Group, the company run by Texas financier Charles Hurwitz, acquired Pacific Lumber and its holdings in California's redwood country in a highly leveraged buyout financed by junk bonds. To pay off this large debt, the company greatly accelerated timber harvests in its redwood forests at what many considered an unsustainable rate and for the first time began logging in the ancient Headwaters forest, which the previous owners had left intact.[110] Thus, far from sustainably and responsibly managing its valuable (and, in this case, now very *scarce*) resource for the long haul, as privatizers insist owners will do, this private owner, like many others, treated his thousand-year-old redwoods as just another fungible asset in a diversified portfolio, to be cashed out to raise needed capital. In fact, according to mathematician Colin Clark, it is fairly easy to predict the circumstances when the privatizers' notions of careful forest stewardship will break down: "If dollars in banks are growing faster than a timber company's forest, it is more profitable (indeed more economical) to chop down the trees, sell them, and invest the proceeds elsewhere."[111] Indeed, you would be a highly suspect asset manager if you did anything but liquidate your timber stands under those market conditions.

The Question of Old Growth

At the heart of the privatizers' arguments about the government's alleged mismanagement of forest resources is a notion that it logs forests in all the wrong places—concentrating on unprofitable, heavily subsidized, low-productivity logging that damages the environment, while not fully realizing the potential of the richest, oldest, and most-productive mature forests.[112] Nelson echoes most privatizers when he calls for a policy to "harvest old growth to reflect the true capital cost of holding the inventories."[113] This position on logging the biologically richest forests betrays a fundamental contradiction. On the one hand, privatizers make an argument that practically all environmentalists would wholeheartedly agree with when they bemoan all the unnecessary road building, erosion, and fragmentation that accompany the logging of steep, inaccessible, unproductive places, where, to add insult to injury, the taxpayer must pay subsidies to allow the destruction to happen. And yet the environmental concerns they so eloquently give voice to concerning dry, low-productivity sites, seem to evaporate when the focus shifts to the sorts of rich, valuable forests of which relatively few remain. The USFS, for example, estimates that approximately 4.3 million acres of old-growth forest remain in the Pacific Northwest, while Leverett estimates no more than 0.5 million to 1.5 million acres east of the Mississippi.[114]

Privatizers routinely make a binary distinction between, on the one hand, public land that serves a primarily recreational, scenic, or wildlife orientation and, on the other hand, "commercial" land, as if there is no overlap between categories. But, of course, there is much overlap. Commercially valuable mature forests with diverse age structures (especially old-growth, temperate rain forests in the Pacific Northwest) have long been recognized by biologists as the richest and most biodiverse categories of forest ecotypes, not to mention those with the greatest aesthetic and recreational appeal.[115] They also sequester the largest accumulation of carbon per acre of any type of forest on Earth, including tropical rain forest.[116] And because mature forests exist predominantly on public lands, these public forests, overall, store much more carbon per acre than do private forests. Eric White and Ralph Alig report that from 1987 to 1997, national forest lands gained 4.6 percent in their carbon stock, while private industrial forest lands saw a 2.4 percent reduction in carbon storage. In their projections to 2045, they find that private forests will continue their decline, unless carbon comes to be priced, while public forests will continue their increase, regardless of whether carbon is priced.[117]

In fact, old-growth forests are considered so ecologically rich and vital that many biologists urge public managers not only to protect all remaining remnants of old growth but also to manage the more-abundant mature, second-growth forests in such a way that they will eventually take on old-growth characteristics. Yet privatization advocates are having none of this, characterizing old growth as a kind of geriatric care center for old, diseased, dying trees whose rotten timber crashes to the ground and goes to waste, thereby destroying the taxpayers' inventory. Holly Fretwell urges us not to be fooled by "romantic calls to save old-growth forests," because they do not really exist as they once did and are now just sick, over-dense, fire-prone places, like the old-growth areas in Shasta-Trinity National Forest, which she dramatically terms "The Valley of Death."[118] She considers efforts at old-growth preservation to be not at all "ecologically benefi-cial," while she believes that "private timberlands . . . generally exhibit health and vigor."[119] Stroup and Baden, meanwhile, argue that "holding old growth timber off the market while it physically declines is a genuine social loss that does not appear as a cost to agency decision makers."[120] Perhaps not, just as the disappear-ance of old-growth-dependent species, water- and soil-retention capacities, carbon sequestration, and unparalleled aesthetic and cultural qualities never appear as costs on the privatizers' ledgers.

Privatization advocates' biological characterizations of old-growth forest are empirically false and betray a profound misun-derstanding of how ecological systems function. Far from being in decline, these forests actually tend to have an optimally tiered, multiage structure; regenerative capacities; nutrient-cycling ca-pabilities; and overall resilience (they are, after all, the stable equilibrium state of a temperate forest ecosystem). They also have far-above-average fire resistance; when they do burn, the larger trees' thick bark allows much more of the forest to sur-vive than do fires in younger forests.[121] In constructing their case for logging old growth, privatizers seem to conflate old-growth forests with any roadless or unlogged area (most of which are actually not old growth) when making arguments about forest health and vulnerability to fire. It is certainly true that large swaths of national forest land are densely crowded with trees and are fire-prone following a century of official fire-suppression policy. Such policies stopped the smaller, more-frequent cleans-ing fires that most western forests are actually adapted to and re-quire for ecological health, thereby creating conditions for larger cataclysmic fires to eventually explode, especially when drought worsens. Public land managers have attempted to address these concerns and undo a century of mistaken policy by allowing smaller beneficial fires, when and where they can, to burn un-

TABLE 3.1. AVERAGE ANNUAL MORTALITY OF GROWING STOCK ON FORESTS, 1996–2011			
Ownership type	Average annual mortality (thousand cubic feet)	Percentage of total U.S. forest land	Percentage of total mortality
Public	3,457,230	42.0%	43.1%
Private	4,564,635	58.0%	56.9%
SOURCE: Data adapted from Sonja N. Oswalt et al., *Forest Resources of the United States, 2012: A Technical Document Supporting the Forest Service Update of the 2010 RPA Assessment,* U.S. Department of Agriculture, Forest Service, General Technical Report WO-91, October 2014, pp. 6, 153–156.			

impeded, while embarking on thinning operations to improve the condition of overly dense forests and allow them to obtain a more natural and fire-resistant structure.[122] However, given the reality of severe budget constraints and the fact that such a huge portion of the USFS's operating costs go, ironically, to fire-fighting, such projects often end up on the backburner. Because thinning operations are almost always unprofitable, it is doubtful that private owners would have better results in attempting to increase fire resistance. In fact, USFS tree-mortality data show no discernible difference in the rates of mortality on public versus private forests; public forests constitute 42 percent of all forests in the United States and suffered 43 percent of all loss to growing stock from 1996 to 2011.[123] This figure is particularly significant because almost all tree mortality in the United States is due to disease, insects, and fire, all of which are factors that privatizers strenuously argue are out of control on the "diseased, over-crowded, fire-prone" public land, in contrast with the allegedly more-resistant and well-managed private forests.[124]

All forests, public and private, probably do now face greatly enhanced risks of cataclysmic forest fires, as recent western fire seasons seem to suggest. But this risk is much more due to worsening multiyear drought and climate change than management policies. And, as Table 3.1 shows, the vulnerability of western forests to fire has little to nothing to do with the fact that a quarter of public forests are off-limits to timber production.

Public versus Industrial versus Smallholders' Forests

Timber output tends to be lower in federal forests than in private forests for a variety of reasons.[125] First, some sections of public land are taken out of timber production and managed for other purposes (e.g., wilderness, wildlife, water quality). This "reserved" forest amounts to about 22.8 percent of public forests, or about 73.5 million acres.[126] Furthermore, the significant remainder that is still open to logging (the other 77 percent) is subject to far-greater environmental regulation. For example, compared to private forests, herbicides are sprayed much more sparingly and chosen from a much more limited catalog of products. To protect endangered species, a huge amount of coordination, evaluation, and planning must occur for public land, whereas private owners are simply obliged not to "take" an endangered species. Public forests have 60- to 150-year rotations, shelterwood requirements (providing a set number of seed-bearing and nest trees left standing per acre), patch-connectivity requirements, multiple-use guidelines, and sustained-yield limitations, none of which binds or burdens the private forest manager. Regarding riparian habitat for smaller streams, federal standards require buffers of 170 to 340 feet, depending on fish populations, while on private land, no buffers are required. And, most importantly, harvests on public land are regularly monitored by land managers, who are themselves held accountable by an appeals process and, ultimately, lawsuits, which are built into complex systems of public access and participation. Private land, by contrast, is subject only to sporadic state inspections—and usually only after reports of wrongdoing surface.[127] This topic of access, accountability, and participation is explored more fully in Chapter 6.

Another flaw in privatizers' comparison of public and private forest management comes from the fact that when speaking of private forests, they mostly seem to be referring to private *industrial* forest, owned by forest products companies. However, according to USFS data, 62 percent of all private forests in the United States are not industrial but rather owned by individual smallholders,[128] who tend to manage their forests far less intensively than all other types of owners, public or private.[129] Any logging that does occur tends to be without the benefit of professional forestry practices, including any sort of monitoring of forest health or planning for future rotations. In Wisconsin, a state with many acres of smallholdings, only 18 percent of timber sales in private, nonindustrial forests benefited from any kind of professional forestry assistance.[130] Instead, as professional foresters and environmentalists alike bemoan, much of this logging consists of so-called *high-grading*, whereby loggers come in and remove only the highest-quality species. High-grading is very environmentally damaging to forest quality, distorting species and age composition and reproduction, while opening the forest to invasive species.[131]

Restoration versus Preservation

As human activity has come to profoundly influence every last corner of the planet, scientists and environmental thinkers have increasingly stressed the critical need for restoration and stewardship rather than merely habitat preservation. Restoration advocates argue that metalevel changes to the planet wrought by climate change, globalization (invasive species and globe-hopping pests), and the sheer weight of modern humanity's presence have meant that all ecologically valuable systems must be continually monitored and nurtured using good stewardship practices rather than merely held and left alone.[132] For example, if one wished to preserve the globally endangered oak savanna ecotype, it would require far more than just acquiring a surviving remnant. The overwhelming likelihood would be that this parcel had long been denied the periodic, low-intensity fires that, in presettlement days, would have kept the open savanna structure intact. Thus, it would most likely need extensive restoration to reacquire its optimal structural characteristics and species mix. And given that fires no longer sweep what are now the towns, farms, and woodlots of the Upper Midwest, continual stewardship in the form of controlled burns and an active program of invasive species control would be necessary.

This trend toward restoration and stewardship in land management is most clearly seen on state and local public lands, where the reserves tend to be smaller, often more-degraded islands of habitat that cannot fully function as integrated ecosystems.[133] However, the fire-prone tracts of western national forests in need of thinning, overgrazed short-grass prairies on BLM ranges, or second-growth forests that might be managed to encourage future old-growth communities in fifty to seventy years show us that restoration initiatives are every bit as important and relevant (if not more so) on the vast scale of the federal lands. Indeed, in the past two decades, federal land management agencies have begun to make restoration an explicit management priority and a central tenet of their ecosystem management approach.[134] In fact, to meet these goals, the Department of Agriculture has created several programs and budget lines, including *Landscape Scale Restoration*, the *Collaborative Forest Landscape Restoration Program*, and *Integrated Resource Restoration*.[135]

Restoration as a management activity is relevant to this discussion of public versus private management because, rather than simply manage for commodity production, such as timber, it explicitly aims for optimal ecological health and biodiversity. Therefore, in strictly market-oriented terms, restoration, as a time- and labor-intensive effort, tends to be all cost, with little to no market payoff. Of course, the real ecological payoff is hugely important, but, as the next chapter shows, these benefits are almost wholly unrecognized by economic markets as currently constituted. For this reason, restoration efforts on private land (with the notable exception of private conservation organizations, such as TNC) tend to be rather ad hoc, scattershot, and entirely dependent on the owner's own personal values and agenda, in contrast to public-sector efforts, which have increasingly mandated restoration as an explicit policy goal. Thus, although the demand for the restoration of degraded ecosystems vastly outweighs the supply of resources needed to carry it out, the bulk of ambitious, landscape-scale restoration efforts that do occur involve public land, as only the public sector and private nonprofits are routinely willing to "lose money" (i.e., invest in) restoring natural systems. In the public sector, these efforts are justified as the maintenance of valuable ecological assets; in the private sector, because many of these assets have little or no market value, restoration is disincentivized, and any money spent on it is viewed as akin to charity. Furthermore, public land restoration often relies on large, enthusiastic networks of citizen volunteers to heal land for which they feel responsible as collective owners (privatizers' claims that this behavior should never happen notwithstanding).[136] Chapter 5 revisits this role of citizen-led ecological restoration of public land as a form of democratic participation.

Markets and Biological Conservation

Of course, to privatization advocates, markets are the preferred mechanism for the allocation of all resources. The question, then, arises as to exactly how markets can protect ecological assets, such as biodiversity, clean water, healthy soils, and rich forests. It is perhaps quite telling that when privatizers discuss wild land and market preferences, they most often refer to such uses as sightseeing, bird-watching, backpacking, hunting, and other recreational activities, along with aesthetics and perhaps solitude, rather than the nitty-gritty elements of a well-functioning ecosystem, such as the biotic composition of soil, the degree of forest fragmentation, or the presence or absence of invasive species. This focus is because with the former, one can at least try to make a plausible case that markets exist for these things, while for the latter, there really are none. And that, in a nutshell, is the problem for these fundamental elements of true ecological health: they do not readily translate into any sort of realistic marketable commodity, at least not as economic markets are currently constituted (see the next chapter).

The endangered Lange's metalmark butterfly, in Mark Sagoff's well-chosen example, lives in dunes near Los Angeles on land worth hundreds of thousands of dollars per acre to real estate developers.[137] This rather dramatic collision of incompatible demands on a resource perfectly encapsulates the mismatch between market outcomes and ecological realities. In this particular case, Anderson and Leal, for all their "win-win" rhetoric about private markets' being environmentally beneficial, call for the bulldozers to start revving, as market bidding has apparently chosen the highest use. Faced with such tough examples, the best they can come up with is a call for some "entrepreneurial imagination."[138] They argue that figuring out how to charge costs and develop market mechanisms takes tremendous experimentation, creativity, shrewdness, and trial and error. But notice how the onus is on the private owner. What if she just does not care to be bothered to create a "market solution" for the butterfly on her land, just as her neighbor may not care to open a hot dog stand? People are not exactly standing in line to develop and exploit heretofore unmarketable ecological resources. And absent such voluntary "market creativity" to mine some potential untapped value, the fragmentation, degradation, and unraveling of wild ecosystems will continue apace. After all, how exactly does it hurt the value of a private owner's land if the red cockaded woodpecker disappears from his woodlot or a rare salamander no longer inhabits his pond? And because the returns of even the most imaginative marketization of the salamander, if such a thing were possible, would likely be fairly marginal, very few owners would likely go to the trouble. As one private owner who charges a fee for birding access along a river on her Arizona ranch says, "It's very fulfilling. It doesn't pay worth a damn, though."[139]

Anderson and Leal use the ecologically destructive siting of Yellowstone's Grant Village tourist facilities smack in the center of prime grizzly habitat as an example of how unaccountable and politically motivated public management damages the environment. They argue that if, on the other hand, a private owner believed the grizzly habitat was more valuable and could figure out a way to capture that value on the market, he or she would never build that facility in that prime spot.[140] But this very disingenuous argument fails to mention that the market for grizzly bear preservation is practically nonexistent and that theoretical market mechanisms, given the needs and nature of this reclusive and dangerous species, would be, at best, cumbersome and insufficient. So no, a private owner, unless he felt a deep moral or emotional obligation, would most likely not come to the conclusion they predict, especially if the facility's current placement was expedient in some other way.

This stacked deck becomes most apparent, as in the case of Lange's metalmark butterfly, when ecologically valuable resources are found in areas with astronomical real estate values. Does any plausible market scenario or any creative market solution justify the continued existence, in a fully privatized future world, of Cape Cod National Seashore, or Santa Monica Mountains National Recreation Area outside Los Angeles, or Point Reyes or Muir Woods near San Francisco, or the forest preserves that encircle Chicago—or of any city park, for that matter? It does not even need to be in a big city; it must simply have valuable resources, such as old-growth timber or natural gas. Even the pro-privatization theorist Oesterle admits that Yellowstone National Park would have never come to exist if the land had been privately held.[141]

In a brilliant thought experiment, the political scientist Robert Pahre takes privatization on a sort of test drive to see how it might affect the lesser-known, less-visited reserves that make up the bulk of federal land units. For his case study, Pahre specifically chooses Isle Royale National Park, a wilderness island in Lake Superior that has very low visitation (ranking 318th out of 359 units, the lowest for any national park outside Alaska) because of its inaccessibility (it can be reached only by ferry), very short season, and lack of tourist infrastructure.[142] Its most valuable resources are its incredibly wild solitude; its healthy, vigorously functioning forest, wetland, and lakeshore ecosystems; its unique backpacking opportunities; and the renowned scientific research opportunities it has afforded to several generations of biologists who have studied predator-prey relationships and island biogeography there.

Privatizers seem to think that many newly privatized parks could hold their own and protect their special features if they would only properly monetize their attractions on the open market either as private recreation-management companies or, perhaps, as user-organized, nonprofit entities. But when Pahre crunches the numbers, he finds that both scenarios are far easier to vaguely imagine than to actually implement. First, he suggests that given the island's remote isolation, low visitation, and difficult transportation, it is quite likely that a private recreation company would not touch this park with the proverbial ten-foot pole. In its present form and for its present uses, Isle Royale offers no prospect of profit whatsoever, and the costs of investing in the creation of amenities to make it a more enticing and convenient destination would likely never be recouped.[143]

The for-profit scenario's unworkability leaves the nonprofit option for some sort of user cooperative to buy the island. Using the most generously low estimate of the island's market value, Pahre calculates that the fourteen thousand annual backcountry users (assuming all were willing and able to buy into the co-op) would have to fork over between $43,000 and $86,000 each per share. A 2002 operating budget of $3.2 million would add an additional $200 annual operating assessment onto each member's commitment.[144] If, on the other hand, Stroup and Baden's prescription were followed and the park was simply given to an environmental group, it would still, presumably, need to charge $200 per visitor just to cover operating costs, unless the organization had the funds and will to subsidize everyone. Pahre's bottom line is that there is no way for a place like Isle Royale to exist and be preserved in its present wild and ecologically whole state without keeping it public and subsidized. By his estimation, the only workable market alternative (its highest and best use, according to the market) would be for the island to be subdivided into vacation properties for the wealthy.[145] Thus, Pahre concludes:

> Once we move beyond a few parks with commercial resources that could be exploited without changing the character of a park's resources, the case for privatization or creating a conservation trust for many other national parks would not withstand close scrutiny.[146]

Just How Ecologically Minded Is the Public Sector?

This chapter makes an unambiguous case for the proposition that complex ecological systems are in better shape and have better future prospects on public as opposed to private land.[147] However, it would be a grave error if, in the course of making this case, the complicated and decidedly mixed record of public management was sugar-coated and its failures, fiascos, and disastrously bad decisions were overlooked. It is hard to know where to start in cataloguing these failures, but they include

- chronic overgrazing and creeping desertification on BLM lands;
- subsidized clear-cutting in steep, unsuitable areas of national forest land;
- the subsidized building of 380,000 miles of highly erodible logging roads (which is nine times greater than the mileage of the entire U.S. Interstate System);[148]
- a long history of predator-control programs that has extirpated wolves, mountain lions, grizzly bears, and other predators from vast areas of public land on behalf of ranching and big-game-hunting interests;
- the rampant spread of a vast gas-drilling infrastructure of roads, pads, and storage facilities sprawled across large acreages of BLM, state, and even some USFS land;
- massive water projects, which remade nearly every major river system in the West with dam, aqueduct, and reservoir projects during the early and mid-twentieth century (at one point, even the Grand Canyon was slated to be dammed);[149] and
- the aggressive construction of automobile-based tourist infrastructure within fragile parks and scenic areas to bolster what critic Edward Abbey scornfully terms "industrial tourism."[150]

Over the decades, many of these policies have been abandoned or reversed, but others, such as loosely regulated energy development, remain very much intact.

At the state level, these environmentally destructive practices are often even more pronounced. State park systems frequently are more intensively developed than national parks, and although the National Park Service (NPS) has largely moved away from environmentally harmful industrial tourism, it is alive and well at many cash-strapped state park systems cast adrift by state legislatures suspicious of and even outright hostile to public land. The state-trust lands, meanwhile, which account for three-quarters of state land acreage, are probably subject to the most intensive resource extraction of any public land in the United States.

And yet, as previously mentioned, the conclusion that privatizers draw from these failures amounts to a logical fallacy; however destructive government management has been in the past (or even now), this fact, in and of itself, says absolutely nothing about how private management would perform as an alternative. Only data can achieve that, and the comparative data reviewed here are pretty definitive (see Table 3.2); in terms of fragmentation, stability, ecosystem quality, individual populations of imperiled species, forest quality, and wildlife habitat, studies show in fairly clear and convincing terms that public lands, as a whole, outperform private lands.

It is important to note that the conclusions drawn here about the comparative ecological health of public and private land, apply strictly to the American context. In many parts of the world, public-sector control has meant something else altogether. State-owned land, especially in the developing world, where so much of Earth's biodiversity lies, is often more akin to the situation in the United States before the late 1800s, when a policy of disposal reigned; in other words, the purpose of public land is to be distributed for development. Even where it is formally retained as protected land, the public domain in such places as Brazil, Indonesia, Malaysia, Gabon, or the Congo suffer from a host of dysfunctions, be they irregular or non-

TABLE 3.2. COMPARISON OF PUBLIC AND PRIVATE LAND BASED ON SELECTED ECOLOGICAL MEASURES

	Public land	Private land
Less forest and habitat fragmentation	X	
Greater number of imperiled species found on specific land ownership type		X
Greater number of imperiled species found on one land ownership type	X	
Greater number of discrete populations of imperiled species	X	
Greater proportion of suitable habitat for conservative species	X	
Greater ecosystem stability and permanence	X	
Greater acreage of imperiled landscape communities	X	
Greater proportion of forest as mature or old growth	X	
Greater proportion of land undergoing ecological restoration	X	

existent enforcement, corruption, collusion, or impunity, that make them every bit as vulnerable as private land. In many parts of the world, then, governments that are aggressively oriented to short-term development can often be the worst enemies of ecological systems rather than their defenders. Elinor Ostrom argues persuasively that, in this context, the best stewardship is neither centralized government control nor strictly exclusive private property but rather a system of common pool resource management collectively self-governed by the resource users in the community.[151] Chapter 6 revisits this issue of local versus national control.

In sum, the weakness of privatization advocates' theories about public land, and especially what arrangements would best serve their ecological health, stem largely from their unfamiliarity with, and perhaps some indifference to, the basic notions of ecological science. So when Stroup and Baden, for example, decry wilderness as an unfairly privileged consumer preference with some pretty but unpriced scenery and good backpacking, they are really missing the proverbial forest for the trees. Where in this description is the well-functioning ensemble of biologically integrated systems of water, wildlife, soil, vegetation, and carbon cycling that helps hold the web of life on our planet intact? Brands of shampoo are consumer preferences—functioning ecological systems are not.

FACING PAGE: Spring Creek Canyon Wilderness Study Area, Bureau of Land Management, Utah. *(Photo by the author.)*

FOLLOWING SPREAD: Oak savanna, Owen Conservation Park, Madison Park District, Wisconsin. *(Photo by the author.)*

4

The Valuation of the Invaluable

The Economic Case for Public Lands

Some proponents contend that wilderness is "priceless" and cannot be subject to economic valuation. Nevertheless, such contentions must be taken as largely rhetorical; society obviously has a limit on the sacrifices it will make to create more wilderness.—ROBERT NELSON, *Public Land and Private Rights*

The American People wanted to save these places, not because they brought money. We knew they would cost money. We saved them because they were worth money. They are precious. That is why we preserve them.

— ROGER KENNEDY, former NPS director, quoted in Bill Wade, "A New Tragedy for the Commons," *George Wright Forum*

Ideally economic analysis for resource management should consider all relevant values, not merely those that are easy to quantify. Utilizing nonmarket values provides a more complete picture of the consequences of a proposed activity than market data alone would allow.

—U.S. DEPARTMENT OF THE INTERIOR, 2013 Bureau of Land Management Memorandum

Public Goods and Public Bads: Markets and Market Failure

TO MANY OBSERVERS, the debate over public lands ultimately boils down to a matter of economics. As discussed in Chapter 2, privatizers argue that free markets are generally the most rational and efficient means by which to allocate resources and that the private ownership of these natural resources provides all the right mechanisms and incentives to keep landscapes productive and to maximize benefits to society.

To critics, however, this notion is willfully blind to some hard and undeniable realities. They point out two real-world scenarios in which a purely free-market framework can be counted on to fail: (1) when the good in question is a public good or common pool resource and (2) when private market transactions external-ize the costs of producing a good onto the broader public.

The first scenario arises when the good in question is either an intangible thing, such as wilderness, solitude, aesthetic beauty, or a well-functioning ecosystem, or is a common-pool resource, such as an aquifer, clean air, or a river that, by its very nature, cannot be divvied up among private owners as a stand of timber or lode of ore can. Because neither type of resource can be exclusively enjoyed or controlled by any one owner, economic theory tells us that markets tend to underproduce such *public goods*.[1] According to public lands advocates, such as John Loomis, only government intervention in the market can make up for this discrepancy and provide more public goods by using taxes to pay for agreed-on benefits. In this way, the free-rider problem is also minimized; otherwise, no market actor would have an incentive to buy a public good, because it can theoretically be enjoyed without payment, as its benefits are not exclusive. This logic, incidentally, is precisely the same that underlies public education, public roads and bridges, national defense,[2] and perhaps the economists' favorite, if arcane, example, the now-defunct United States Lighthouse Service.[3]

The second scenario for market failure is the externalization of costs, or what Loomis calls "public bads," and it comes into play when a privately held commodity is produced and its benefits are exclusively enjoyed, but its costs are externalized onto the wider public.[4] For example, if a coal seam is strip-mined, the coal produced belongs solely to the mining company, but the egregious costs of water pollution, deforestation, constant blasting, and heavy trucks grinding up local roads are passed almost entirely onto the public. Public-sector environmental regulations and, according to Loomis, government ownership of public land allow for the internalizing of externalities[5] and the conscious balancing of costs and benefits to find the sort of optimum that eludes purely free-market mechanisms. Thus, the government's job, in Loomis's view, is to find the optimal amount of a public good to supply and then weigh that against competing opportunity costs (for commodity production) that must be paid to provide the good.[6]

As Chapter 2 showed, privatizers resolutely believe that this mission is a fool's errand that politicians seeking favor and government bureaucrats using their misguided "scientific management" principles are destined to botch. Rather than government intervention, they essentially advocate a doubling-down on the market framework. In other words, if the problem for the market is the underproduction of unpriced or underpriced public goods, then the answer is to reform the infrastructure of the market and our attitudes toward it to allow for a fuller exchange of valued items whereby the idea of public goods are reconceived and transferability and, where possible, exclusivity are somehow introduced. This reformation, privatizers argue, will take a great deal of creativity, entrepreneurship, and trial-and-error. As far as externalities are concerned, free-market dogma, ever suspicious of government, insists that creative and well-designed market mechanisms can more fully capture the costs that are currently pushed onto others. And should that prove inadequate, the judicial arena can always sort out costs that are unfairly imposed on others and cause them damage.[7] In the privatizers' world, then, people are not free to use their government to stop pollution but merely to get compensated for the damages they sustain.[8]

Critics of privatization suggest that such arguments fall somewhere between naïve and disingenuous. As Loomis plainly puts it, "The conditions for operation of a private for-profit competitive market simply do not exist for most . . . natural resources,"[9] and no amount of creativity or ingenuity will likely change this fact. Who would or could create this massive and far-reaching new infrastructure of markets that trade in every last species, endangered landscape or plant community, geologic feature, place of solitude, aesthetic wonder, or cultural/historical artifact? Is the onus on those who wish for its protection? Is it on those who wish to own the exclusive and transferable rights to these resources? And will the demand for each of these resources and amenities be sufficient to command prices that (1) realistically compete with alternative consumptive uses and (2) are greater than the *transaction costs* (which are the direct costs of the logistical efforts necessary to identify often-dispersed customers and to devise a way to collect payment from them)?

The unlikelihood of an affirmative answer to either criterion should make one dubious that free-market theory in this particular context can stand up to the rigors of real-life situations and human behavior. Suppose we tried to create a market for the preservation of the endangered Kirtland's warbler. Most Americans would likely hold its protection as a collective value, but how would we determine this value in a way that would allow for exchange on a market? Economists might suggest that the bird's value be determined through a survey research tool known as *willingness to pay* (WTP), which sets a threshold for how much money something is actually worth to someone. What are the chances that the average WTP figure for this little bird would exceed the transaction costs, let alone the alternate commodity-oriented uses, for its habitat? And if the numbers did not work, should we pull the plug on this rare bird?

The issue of transaction costs equally applies to the use of law and the courts to account for externalities, as legal representation and other court costs are expensive. Furthermore, the bearers of externalized costs are often dispersed and unorganized, while the burdens of proof and liability are quite often difficult to establish (especially when the externalizers have armies of well-paid staff attorneys). Americans already can sue for damages from environmental externalities, yet their relatively low success rate in securing redress[10] and the fact that externalities continue to be imposed unabated should raise some serious doubts about this strategy as the sole means of dealing with externalities.

Costs and Benefits: Who Defines?

At the root of their arguments is privatizers' belief that the very nature of public ownership prevents natural resources from being allocated productively and efficiently, and this flaw, in turn, means that they are not, in essence, earning their keep—that is, their benefits are not justified by their supposedly substantial costs in terms of public expenditures and of foregone development opportunities. To the defenders of public land, on the other hand, this stance betrays the privatizers' torturously pinched definition of what constitutes a benefit. Public land supporters invariably speak to a much wider constellation of benefits that issue from our public lands, and, in contrast to the strictly market-derived, individually focused values of free-market theory, these might often be intangible, collectively held, and not necessarily found on any market.

Thus, it is crucial to recognize that the spectacularly narrow bandwidth from which privatizers conceive of and identify economic costs and benefits does not negate the existence or veracity of alternative calculations. For example, when judging efficiency and cost-benefit ratios, privatizers often point admiringly to private or state trust-owned forests, which are much more aggressively logged than nearby federal forests.[11] In this construction, only two considerations come into play: (1) revenue from the timber harvest and (2) the larger administrative and capital costs to manage the land in question. Conspicuously missing on either side of the cost-benefit ledger is anything else linked to this complex resource deeply embedded within a context of larger cultural, social, economic, and ecological systems. Where on the balance sheet are water quality, erosion, habitat loss, tourist and recreation activity, quality-of-life concerns, or carbon storage, just to name a few relevant factors? Depending on how wide the net is cast, such a fuller accounting becomes a much more complicated, not to mention imperfect, endeavor— but, nevertheless, one crying out to be done.

In addition to strictly market-derived costs and benefits, privatizers also widely use the criterion of productivity (with a similarly cramped definition) to judge the proper allocation of resources. To them, as Scott Lehmann notes, productivity is always measured in terms of a marketable commodity and never anything else. So, for example, given its astronomical property value, Cape Cod National Seashore would be most productive as land open for real estate development, even though it sits astride a region of millions of people and is, therefore, actually extremely productive when it comes to providing other things that privatizers happen to neither hold an interest in nor recognize. Similarly, Alaskan national parks could have spectacularly productive copper mines *or* be equally productive at creating grizzly bear cubs; it is just that one option is recognized by privatizers as legitimate on the market and the other is not. But even if we accept the questionable proposition that copper is somehow objectively worth more than grizzlies, Lehmann asserts that this is still a losing argument. In crude market terms, he concedes that privatizers often win the argument that some use x produces more than use y, but if the productivity criterion for x is whether it produces more of *everything* of value (not only copper but also grizzlies, salmon, clean water, wilderness experiences, solitude, and so forth), then privatization is nearly certain to fail this productivity test.[12]

This chapter's purpose is not to create an indisputable and perfectly all-encompassing account of costs and benefits and productivity, as such a task is quite impossible. Rather, the goal is simply to explore just how much the privatizers' incomplete accounting misses. When this fuller economic picture emerges, so does the realization that holding on to our public lands makes abundant economic sense.

Casting a Wider Net: Economic Benefits beyond Commodity Production

The classical free-market economists' view that wild land derives its value only in terms of its marketable commodities could not go unchallenged for long. In his seminal 1967 essay "Conservation Reconsidered," the economist Joseph Krutilla lays out a strong case for why nonmarket resources have real and legitimate economic value.[13] Whereas free marketers would consider preservation of wild places as a sort of expensive indulgence or a form of subsidization, Krutilla offers an alternate view of conservation as a policy choice that earns its keep and provides plenty of previously unrecognized and often quite tangible economic benefits:

> When the existence of a grand scenic wonder or a unique fragile ecosystem is involved, its preservation and continued availability are a significant part of the real income of many individuals.[14]

In the ensuing decades, numerous other scholars have provided similar economic analysis building a very solid case for the existence of real and substantial nonmarket value.[15] This exercise has not all just been theoretical. Valuation models have long been used by public land managers in constructing long-term plans as required by federal law (the National Forest Management Act [NFMA] and the Federal Land Policy and Management Act [FLMPA]). Pete Morton describes how the old U.S. Forest Service (USFS) FORPLAN valuation tool was a disaster for most noncommodity uses of national forest land when conducting cost-benefit analyses. According to Morton, FORPLAN was a superconstrained model that structurally undervalued all noncommodity uses.[16] This weakness resulted in forest plans overly biased toward commodity production as well as lots of questionable valuation data used by critics of public lands in their calls for privatization. Not until new economic models of valuation became more widely adopted in the 1990s did the USFS experience a paradigm shift toward an ecosystem management approach.[17]

It is important to note that this growing body of work focuses not just on the value of the natural resources that are nonmarketable but also on their much wider effect on values that are very much market-derived, such as income, property values, and spin-off consumer spending. Such a multifaceted approach to resource economics necessitates that one distinguish between the two elements these studies routinely measure: (1) economic *value* (what some particular item is worth to someone) and (2) economic *impact* (how that item spurs related economic activity throughout the rest of the local or regional economy). Resource economists also distinguish between different levels of value: (1)

direct-use value stems from the production of goods or services that result from the use of a particular resource, and (2) *passive-use* value refers to value that is drawn merely from knowing that some resource exists and is protected. So although most Americans will never visit Denali National Park in Alaska, they very well may be glad that it is protected (existence value) and will be there for future generations (bequest value). Because passive-use values are fairly intangible, quantifying them can prove challenging. Among the tools that economists tend to use (but that are not without their critics)[18] are "willingness-to-pay" surveys (discussed earlier in this chapter), which attempt to determine an actual dollar value for a passive use. Between the continuum of direct and passive use, Morton adds several additional dimensions, including community benefits (and all wider spin-off effects), scientific benefits (research, education, health), and ecological benefits.[19]

It should be clear, then, that the past few decades of thinking broadly about true costs and benefits and attempting to conduct a more comprehensive and accurate economic valuation have really let the genie out of the market bottle, so to speak, and have thus moved the conversation into all sorts of interesting and diverse realms that end up revealing just how economically precious our public lands are. This torrent of research by resource economists has managed to create a huge, complex, and multifaceted body of literature,[20] which comes at this question from a number of angles. Ultimately, it shows that public lands, especially those that are most protected, are far more valuable and have a far greater economic impact than has been traditionally estimated.

Multiplier Effects

As we have seen, privatizers' claims about productivity depend on the narrowest definitions and scopes of economic activity. And perhaps nothing tends to be more consistently neglected in their calculations than the wider multiplier effects that public lands, especially those with abundant intangible values, have on their local and regional economies.

Perhaps the place to start is with the federal land management agencies' own fairly conventional analyses of their wider economic impact. Recent USFS data from its system-wide Land Management Planning efforts show total economic output (sales) from the national forests and grasslands to be $71.9 billion, which, by the agency's calculations, adds $34.5 billion to the U.S. gross domestic product (GDP) and creates 430,238 jobs and $20.4 billion in labor income.[21] It is significant to note that, for the USFS, recreation-oriented resources generate economic benefit roughly equivalent to that generated by commodity-oriented ones.[22] By comparison, National Park Service (NPS) contributions to the economy add an estimated 295,339 jobs and $32.04 billion in economic impact, all of which are generated by recreation-oriented resources.[23] (It should be noted that subsequent valuation research of the NPS lands using broader methods covered later in this chapter produced a figure nearly three times higher; see Table 4.5). As a smaller agency with fewer recreational amenities and little to no commodity production, the U.S. Fish and Wildlife Service (USFWS) has a comparatively smaller economic footprint, contributing 35,684 jobs and $4.72 billion in economic impact.[24] Finally, the energy- and mineral-rich Bureau of Land Management (BLM) lands add an estimated 374,419 jobs and $88.02 billion in impact; only in this case is the impact much more heavily tilted toward commodity production, with recreation constituting only 11.7 percent of jobs and 6.7 percent of economic impact.[25] The Trust for Public Land (TPL), meanwhile, estimates that state parks in the United States contribute a further $20 billion to their respective local and state economies,[26] while numerous studies peg individual park visitors' spending at between $40 and $98 per day.[27] Table 4.1 summarizes this impact.

John Bergstrom and his colleagues peer deeper into this economic contribution at the state level, examining the direct, indirect, and induced effects of recreational visits to state parks in four southern states (North Carolina, South Carolina, Georgia, and Tennessee). What they confirm is a ripple effect on the regional economy, with a mean employment *multiplier* of 1.58.[28] In

TABLE 4.1. ECONOMIC AND EMPLOYMENT IMPACT OF PUBLIC LAND SYSTEMS, BY JURISDICTION

Jurisdiction	Economic impact (in billions of $)	Jobs added (in 1,000s)	Proportion of impact from recreation
USFS	34.5	430.2	45.0%
NPS	32.0	295.3	100.0%
USFWS	4.7	35.7	100.0%
BLM	88.0	374.4	6.7%
State parks	20.0	NA	100.0%

DATA SOURCES: U.S. Department of Agriculture, Forest Service, "Contribution of National Forest and Grassland Resource Management to the U.S. Economy," Appendix M in *National Forest System Land Management Planning Final Programmatic Environment Impact Statement*, January 2012, p. M-3; U.S. Department of the Interior, Office of Policy Analysis, *U.S. Department of the Interior Economic Report FY 2015*, June 17, 2016, pp. 22–23; Trust for Public Land, *Return on Investment from the Land and Water Conservation Fund*, November 2010, p. 14.

other words, for every one job directly created by state park recreation, another 0.58 jobs are created in the regional economy by these ripple effects—for example, the person hired at the counter of an ice cream shop to serve the people brought to the area by the park. The total income multiplier they calculate is even more pronounced, at 2.39, while the gross output multiplier (for all other aspects of economic activity) is 2.08. They note that this result is roughly on par with other leading industries in Georgia (one of the four states in the case study), such as wood products (2.42), agriculture (2.66), other recreation (1.85), and miscellaneous others (ranging from 1.92 to 2.70).[29] Their conclusion is that state parks that produce no commodities could still hold their own and directly contribute to the regional economies on par with most other industries. Jeffrey Prey, David Marcouiller, and Danya Kim come to similar conclusions in their exhaustive, fine-grain study of the economic impacts of the Wisconsin state park system. Finding the parks to be "linchpin regional assets to economic vitality,"[30] they report a multiplier effect of 1.65 for total economic output and 1.70 for income.[31]

Although they are significant wherever public lands exist, the direct and indirect effects of public lands on employment and economic activity stand out in especially stark relief in poorer, more-isolated rural areas. Take, for example, Harney and Grant Counties in eastern Oregon, which were at the epicenter of the Bundy militia occupation of the Malheur National Wildlife Refuge in January 2016 (see Chapter 1). Eventually, the standoff became a major source of economic disruption in tiny Harney County because so much of its workforce was sidelined. Compared to a state-wide average in Oregon of 1.7 percent, a far greater percentage of the workforce of Harney and Grant Counties (11.7 percent and 11.2 percent, respectively) is employed by the federal government (mostly by the BLM, the USFS, and the USFWS, in this case).[32] In Harney County, the federal government accounted for 240 jobs, in contrast with 100 jobs in ranching and 65 in growing hay.[33] And while approximately one in nine jobs is federal, an even more concentrated 1 in 5 dollars of total income earned in the county is also federal in origin, as these are among the best-paying jobs in the area.[34] Public-sector jobs are, perhaps, not considered fully real or legitimate to a libertarian or a Tea Party militiaman, but in these two counties at least, they provide the economic backbone and pay the bills. And if the Bundy militants had gotten their wish and somehow convinced the authorities to transfer these lands to the adjacent ranching communities, enormous economic pain would have been visited on these counties' tax revenues, budgets, household discretionary incomes, and all the spin-off business these federal incomes generate.

As more bills get introduced in Congress to sell federal lands, open up wilderness areas, or strip the president's authority to create national monuments, perhaps one way to track the real economic ripple effects of public land is to observe how certain public land–dependent towns, regions, and industries have responded to this growing threat. Increasingly, they have commissioned research, mobilized lobbying efforts, and engaged in vigorous public-relations outreach to protect their perceived economic interests. Perhaps no private industry's economic research and outreach have made a bigger impression than those of the outdoor recreation industry, which is acutely aware of its dependence on abundant public land. According to a comprehensive and oft-cited 2012 analysis done on behalf of the Outdoor Industry Association, this industry has a market of 140 million Americans and accounts for 6.1 million jobs (which exceeds those in real estate, oil and gas, information, education, transportation, construction, and finance—for some of those categories, by a factor of two or three).[35] In addition to providing $80 billion in state, local, and federal tax revenues, the study finds $646 billion in direct consumer spending, with economic ripple effects on the U.S. economy totaling an astonishing $1.6 trillion.[36] Even one rather obscure subcategory of recreation, trout angling, in just one specific region in the Upper Midwest is shown to punch far above its weight economically. A 2008 Trout Unlimited study finds a $1.1-billion economic impact ($647 million direct and $465 indirect/induced) in the Driftless Area (where Wisconsin, Minnesota, Iowa, and Illinois border the Mississippi River), which is, incidentally, a sum greater than the $728-million impact of Chicago-area professional sports.[37] So outdoor recreation seems to have become something of an unheralded giant in the American economy.

Property Values

Another important element in the wider economic spin-off effects that environmental economists have identified is enhanced property values. Simply put, public land is desirable to live near, and thus it bestows an average premium of 20 percent onto adjacent properties.[38] Niall Garrahan cites research by the city of Boise, Idaho, showing an even more pronounced increase in property values for homes adjacent to newly acquired preserves versus similar homes in the same area but not directly adjacent.[39] And this premium is not just exclusive to urban or suburban areas, as research finds that wilderness designation on remote federal tracts enhances nearby private property values as well.[40] The proximity to public land not only seems to create extra value for property owners; it also, in turn, increases property-tax revenues for local governments—an especially important consideration, given the common complaint that public land starves the tax rolls.[41] Furthermore, public land in suburban and exurban communities often saves those communities money for infrastructure and utilities, which, in many cases, cost more than the new tax revenues that development brings.[42]

Return on Investment

These data on the economic ripple effects of public lands show that, far from being the costly indulgence that privatizers argue is foisted on an unsuspecting public, they are generally a prudent expenditure (in terms of not only acquisition but also operation), featuring a healthy return on investment (ROI). In fact, the Trust for Public Land, which has produced a raft of meticulously calculated ROI studies, dependably finds ROI figures of 400 percent to 1,100 percent for every state land acquisition program it examines (that is, for every $1 invested in buying land, a return of $4 to $11).[43] The TPL has also conducted an analysis for a sample of tracts of federal land obtained through the Land and Water Conservation Fund and discovered an average ROI of 400 percent.[44]

What is most significant about these studies is that they compare the costs of land acquisition to the economic benefits that have flowed only for the period during which those costs were incurred. And yet once a tract is fully acquired, those costs inevitably end (except, perhaps, for lost property-tax revenue), while the benefits generally keep accruing indefinitely. As time goes on, then, the ROI for land acquisition could be expected to grow increasingly lopsided in favor of the acquisition.

Privatizers, however, complain about not only the costs of governments' buying land but also the ongoing operating expenses, which, unless the parcel in question is returning a surplus of direct revenues, is described as "losing money." If economic gains are more widely conceived of than just commodity sales or entrance fees, though, we see that ROI for ongoing operation expenses is every bit as robust as it is for acquisition, if not more so. For example, USFWS economists painstakingly accounted for the economic impact of national wildlife refuges by using a fairly large eighty-refuge sample. As has already been pointed out, the refuge system has the *least* economic impact of all federal land jurisdictions, and yet the mean return on investment for $1 of operating budget is still $7.27 (or an ROI of 727 percent).[45] The ROI figure for NPS operational budgets, meanwhile, is an even greater, at 1,000 percent, while North Carolina state parks annually return 925 percent.[46] The fact that the results of these disparate ROI analyses of operational expenses (done by different researchers) hover so close to one another would seem to corroborate their validity. Table 4.2 summarizes the findings of these ROI analyses.

TABLE 4.2. RETURN ON INVESTMENT FOR LAND ACQUISITION AND PARK OPERATIONS		
Jurisdiction	Type of expenditure	Return on investment
PA	Acquisition	700%
MA	Acquisition	400%
NH	Acquisition	1,100%
OH	Acquisition	400%
ME	Acquisition	1,100%
NY	Acquisition	700%
WY	Acquisition	400%
NC	Acquisition	400%
NC (state parks)	Operations	925%
CO	Acquisition★	600%
Federal (LWCF)	Acquisition	400%
Federal (USFWS)	Operations	727%
Federal (NPS)	Operations	1,000%

SOURCES: Trust for Public Land, *Return on Investment from the Land and Water Conservation Fund*, TPL Report, November 2010; Erin Carver and James Caudill, *Banking on Nature: The Economic Benefits to Local Communities of National Wildlife Refuge Visitation*, Division of Economics, U.S. Fish and Wildlife Service, Washington, DC, October 2013 (for more on calculations, see Chapter 4, note 45); U.S. Department of the Interior, National Park Service, *Fiscal Year 2016 Budget Justifications*, 2015, Overview 1; Trust for Public Land, *North Carolina's Return on the Investment in Land Conservation*, TPL Report, February 2011, p. 15.
★Acquisition of conservation easements rather than land itself.

Public Lands as a Spur to Growth

In November 2011, more than one hundred economists and other natural resource scholars wrote an open letter to President Barack Obama:

> As economists and academics in related fields, we believe that federal protected public lands are essential to the West's economic future. These public lands . . . are an essential component of the region's competitive advantage. . . . The rivers, lakes, canyons, and mountains found on public lands serve as a unique and compelling backdrop that has helped to transform the western economy from a dependence on resource extractive industries to growth from in-migration, tourism, and modern economy sectors such as finance, engineering, software development, insurance, and health care. . . . Businesses are recruiting talented employees by promoting access to beautiful, nearby public lands. This is happening in western cities and rural areas alike. . . . Together with investment in education and access to markets, studies have repeatedly shown that protected public lands are significant contributors to economic growth. . . . We urge you to create jobs and support businesses by investing in our public lands infrastructure and establishing new protected areas such as parks, wilderness, and monuments.[47]

The argument these academics are trying to make is that, given all the demonstrable economic impacts of public lands as well as demographic, cultural, and structural changes to society and the economy, the real value of public land lies in its status as a supercharged lifestyle amenity and a central element in quality-of-life considerations. And this perception, in turn, has enormous and tangible economic benefit.

The larger context of this argument concerns the structural changes in the economy over the past few decades, especially in the public-land-rich West, which has seen a dramatic shift away from manufacturing and resource extraction toward a service and information economy. In fact, by 2010, 72 percent of the economy in the West was in the service sectors and another 14 percent was in the public/government sector, leaving only 14 percent in traditional extractive and manufacturing sectors.[48] In this new economy, attracting human capital has become every bit as important, if not more so, as attracting physical capital, and this area is where public lands' magnetic attraction exerts its gravitational pull on creative and highly educated individuals and thus serves as an engine of growth. Gundars Rudzitis and Rebecca Johnson call this fresh approach the *Amenities/Quality-of-Life* model of economic development, noting that "traditional economic models of wildland development don't consider the context of people's lives and how they interact with, shape, and are affected by the social and spatial environments."[49] Wilderness and wild land, they argue, exude a "sense of place" that many people desperately seek and deeply value.[50]

A voluminous literature bears this opinion out.[51] Headwaters Economics, an environmental think tank, for instance, cites data it has collected that show a strong correlation between the amount of federal land protected as parks, wilderness, monuments, or wildlife refuges in a given western county and that county's employment growth rates from 1970 to 2010. Counties whose land was more than 30 percent protected saw a 345 percent increase in jobs versus an 83 percent increase for counties with no protected federal land, as can be seen in Table 4.3.[52]

The same dynamic seems to be at work regarding per-capita income, which increased $436 (in 2010 dollars) for every additional 10,000-acre increment of federally protected land within a western county's borders. So for a county with 150,000 acres protected, that would translate to an increase of $6,540 over the average rural western per-capita income (in 2010) of $34,870.[53] To economists, at least, population growth is another key indicator of the economic health of a region; here, too, the data show that the increased presence of public land is associated with in-

TABLE 4.3. EMPLOYMENT GROWTH RATE BY PERCENTAGE OF FEDERALLY PROTECTED LAND IN COUNTY, 1970–2010

Percentage of county land that is federally protected	30%	20%	10%	0%
Employment growth rate, 1970–2010	345%	297%	108%	83%

SOURCE: Headwaters Economics, *West Is Best: How Public Lands in the West Create a Competitive Economic Advantage*, November 2012, p. 19.

TABLE 4.4. PERCENTAGE OF CHANGE IN POPULATION, EMPLOYMENT, AND INCOME FOR NONMETRO WESTERN COUNTIES WITH THE MOST AND LEAST FEDERAL LAND, 1970–2014

Nonmetro western counties	Population growth	Employment	Personal income (inflation adjusted)	Per-capita income (inflation adjusted)
Top 25% for federal land	124%	242%	333%	81%
Bottom 25% for federal land	26%	73%	122%	71%

SOURCE: Megan Lawson, *Federal Lands in the West: Liability or Asset?* Headwaters Economics Report, February 2016, p. 1.

creased population growth.[54] Megan Lawson, meanwhile, finds these positive effects on population growth, employment, personal income, and per-capita income for counties with higher percentages of *all* federal land[55] (including multiple-use lands) and not just specially protected lands, showing perhaps that their appeal and economic value extend beyond just the most "glamorous" lands. This correlation of federal land to other economic indicators can be seen in Table 4.4.

All told, the presence of abundant recreation and scenery provided by public lands, Richard Reeder and Dennis Brown point out, "results in generally improved socioeconomic well-being," with lower poverty rates and improved health and education,[56] and correlates with, according to Rasker, some of the fastest-growing communities in the West.[57]

Ecosystem Services:
Casting the Net Wider Still

The idea of ecosystem services (ES) has been incubating since the 1970s but was not fully articulated and popularized until the 1990s, by such theorists as Gretchen Daily, Robert Costanza, and Paul Hawken.[58] Until that point, economists focused mostly on ecosystem *products*—that is, the usually marketable tangibles, such as timber, whitetail deer, bushels of corn, or drinking water, that come out of natural systems. The ES framework, however, shifts the focus to the services that provide these products; thus, no services means no products, as Robert Smail and David Lewis point out when they argue that "the conversion of forest land to development reduces both the product coming off the assembly line, and the assembly line itself."[59] Simply put, then, ecosystem services refer to the myriad processes and systems by which the natural world produces the things that help to sustain all life on Earth. Rudolf de Groot, Matthew Wilson, and Roelof Boumans try to catalogue some of the more important ones, including (1) regulation of atmospheric gases (CO_2 and O_2), (2) climate regulation, (3) disturbance moderation, (4) water quality and quantity, (5) soil retention and formation, (6) nutrient cycling, (7) waste treatment, (8) pollination, (9) biological control of pests and diseases, (10) habitat and biodiversity, (11) photosynthesis, and (12) biomass production.[60]

These vital, fundamental processes churn along day-in and day-out and are generally taken for granted. In fact, they are treated by traditional economics largely as a given, with no attempt made at valuation.[61] And yet when these services are impaired or distorted by human activity, society pays quite dearly. For example, erosion or desertification destroys valuable crop-production or grazing capacities, while a water supply ruined by pollution or overdraft might require multi-billion-dollar treatment facilities or desalinization plants. In fact, the oft-cited case study of New York City's watershed in the Catskills Mountains might be considered the poster child of ecosystem services in action. Rather than spend $6 billion to $8 billion to build water-filtration facilities and another quarter billion dollars annually to operate them, New York City invested $1.5 billion to acquire forest land and conservation easements to protect and improve the watershed, thereby relying on basic ecosystem services.[62]

Thus, when the public lands critic Robert Nelson complains about tens of millions of acres of federal wilderness as being "locked up and out of service,"[63] he displays an utter disregard for the real, tangible services that intact ecosystems provide—a disregard that is quite commonplace in mainstream economics. As it turns out, the value of the services provided by a well-functioning, intact ecological system is nothing short of monumental. Costanza et al. put forward the oft-cited estimate of *$33 trillion* (in 1994 dollars) annually, or $5,000 per capita for all the world's ecosystem services.[64] David Holzman updates this figure to an annual $44 trillion in 2012 dollars, or twice the global gross national product (GNP).[65]

Valuation Using Ecosystem Services

As the ES framework has gained currency, it has unleashed a torrent of fairly detailed valuation studies done at much closer range than Costanza et al.'s global estimate. Some measure specific parks, a given state's forest resources, a particular watershed, or a policy initiative to protect a given species, but what all these studies have in common is that they attempt to put an actual dollar value on the services that nature provides and that have gone, heretofore, completely unrecognized. And these values are anything but insignificant, as shown in Table 4.5, which presents the results of selected ES valuation studies.

For the sake of context, in the last study in Table 4.5, Rebecca Moore et al. remind us that the forest products industry contributed $27 billion to Georgia's economy in the same year that nontimber ecosystem services contributed $37.6 billion.[66] In the Skykomish Watershed study, meanwhile, the authors go a step further, calculating the value if the watershed were treated like an asset with a hundred-year lifespan and a standard

TABLE 4.5. SELECTED ECOSYSTEM SERVICE VALUATION STUDIES

Author	Year	Focus/location	Annual benefit (in millions of $)
Loomis	2005	Sea otter recovery projects in coastal California	172.0
Kroeger	2005	Protected public land in four northern Florida counties	3,200.0
Defenders of Wildlife Report	2004	Lynx conservation projects nationwide	2.5–19.2
Ingraham and Foster	2008	National wildlife refuges in lower 48 states	26,900.0
Buckley et al.	2011	Services provided by beavers in Escalante Watershed, Utah	833.7
Trust for Public Land (USFS)	2010	Water flowing off U.S. national forests	3,700.0
Garrahan	2012	73,387 acres of newly acquired conservation land in Boise, Idaho	9.0–152.7
Simpson et al.	2013	Public and private forests in Texas	92,900.0
Schmidt, Batker, and Harrison-Cox	2011	536,000-acre Skykomish Watershed, Washington	245.0–3,300.0
Kovacs et al.	2013	123,966 acres of acquired conservation land in Minnesota	117.8–985.5*
Moore et al.	2011	Private forests in Georgia for non-timber-related ecosystem services	37,600.0
Haefele, Loomis, and Bilmes	2016	NPS land and programs	92,000.0

DATA SOURCES: John Loomis, *Economic Benefits of Expanding California's Southern Sea Otter Population*, Defenders of Wildlife Report, December 2005; Timm Kroeger, *The Economic Value of Ecosystem Services in Four Counties in Northeastern Florida*, Conservation Economics Working Paper #2, Defenders of Wildlife, Washington DC, 2005; Defenders of Wildlife, *Economic Impact Assessment of Designating Critical Habitat for the Lynx (Lynx canadensis)*, Defenders of Wildlife Report, Washington DC, 2004; Molly Ingraham and Shona Foster, "The Value of Ecosystem Services Provided by the U.S. National Wildlife Refuge System in the Contiguous U.S.," *Ecological Economics* 67, no. 4 (November 1, 2008): 608–618; Mark Buckley et al., *The Economic Value of Beaver Ecosystem Services: Escalante River Basin, Utah*, EcoNorthwest Report, Eugene, OR, October 2011; Trust for Public Land, *Return on Investment from the Land and Water Conservation Fund*, November 2010, p. 11; Niall Garrahan, *Open Land Utility: A Study of Conservation, Ecosystem Services, and Recreation in Boise, Idaho*, James Monroe Scholar Program, College of William and Mary, Summer 2012; Hughes Simpson et al., *Texas Statewide Assessment of Forest Ecosystem Services*, Texas A&M Forest Service Report, College Station, October 2013; Rowan Schmidt, David Batker, and Jennifer Harrison-Cox, *Nature's Value in the Skykomish Watershed: A Rapid Ecosystem Service Valuation*, Earth Economics Report, Tacoma, WA, December 2011; Kent Kovacs et al., "Evaluating the Return in Ecosystem Services from Investment in Public Land Acquisitions," *PLoS ONE* 8, no. 6 (June 11, 2013); Rebecca Moore et al., *Quantifying the Value of Non-timber Ecosystem Services from Georgia's Private Forests*, Georgia Forestry Foundation Report, June 2011; Michelle Haefele, John Loomis, and Linda J. Bilmes, *Total Economic Valuation of the National Park Service Lands and Programs: Results of a Survey of the American Public*, Harvard Kennedy School of Government Faculty Research Working Paper Series, RWP16-024, June 2016, p. 26.
*This particular valuation does not include flood reduction, pollination, or air quality.

4.125 percent discount rate at between \$5.8 billion and \$79.5 billion (or about 24 times the annual benefits). However, with a more realistic 0 percent discount rate (recognizing the ecosystem's renewability and permanence), one finds a \$24-billion to \$334-billion asset.[67] Compare this figure for a single modest half-million-acre watershed to the Office of Management and Budget's non-ES estimate of a \$463-billion asset value for the entire 635-million-acre federal land system,[68] and you start to get a sense of the yawning gap in value when precious resources and services are essentially treated as free goods versus when they are not.

Ecosystem Services and Markets

The ES framework gives us a better sense of the intense concentration of value embedded within natural ecosystems, yet what is far less clear is what should practically be done with such information. Some advocates seek to use an ES paradigm in an ambitious project to dramatically reenvision and remake market exchanges, but others are content to employ it much more modestly to widen the debate and to serve as a source of leverage to rebalance land management priorities and reaffirm the value of wild land, whether inside or outside markets. If the former aim could be successfully achieved and markets could somehow be created for ecosystem services, benefits that are now received for free would require payment, thereby turning recipients into buyers and, in the process, theoretically internalizing externalities.[69]

In the real world, however, creating ES markets has proven to be a daunting task for many of the same reasons pointed out earlier in this chapter—namely, that easily marketable items need to be exclusively enjoyed and transferable and need to have reasonable transaction costs for bringing them into a market. Like most environmental amenities, however, ecosystem services have some real problems in meeting these conditions, as they are, of course, classic public goods. Other reasons beyond their status as a public good also make creating markets for them challenging.

Robert Salzman points to the sheer ignorance in the wider world of what ecosystem services are, how they function, and how to provide them as being the most serious obstacles to creating markets.[70] After all, without proper knowledge, information, and price signals, markets cannot function. Brown, Bergstrom, and Loomis similarly point to the enormous difficulty in properly administering ES markets, which are much more complex than most other markets and would require huge inputs of measurement, assessment, and monitoring to function.[71] Kent Redford and William Adams point out that climate change and its wild unpredictability would make this task of assembling predictable, reliable market information harder still.[72]

Given these difficulties, Brown, Bergstrom, and Loomis have attempted to systematically assess the likelihood of markets' being established for nine distinct ecosystem services measured along six criteria of suitability for market exchange (clear measurement, excludability, low transaction costs, lack of negative externalities, rivalness, and sufficient buyers and sellers). For the fifty-four total intersections of particular services and criteria, they find that forty combinations (or 74 percent) rate as poor, five as fair, and nine as good. All nine of the "good" scores involve only one criterion—lack of negative externalities—which, of course, is hardly surprising.[73] The main conclusion to draw, then, seems to be that ecosystem services have some fairly lousy market prospects.

Not surprisingly, then, the creation of ES markets has gotten off to a very slow and uncertain start. Most schemes exist as isolated programs scattered around the world. Perhaps the most-established examples of ES market exchanges in the United States are the buying and selling of conservation easements, wetland mitigation banks (required by federal law for filling in wetlands so there is no net loss), and the U.S. Department of Agriculture's Conservation Reserve Program for farmers to voluntarily set aside some agricultural land for cash payments.[74] Such limited and underdeveloped markets with not enough participants could easily devolve into a monopsony with only one dominant buyer (the government, in the case of the three examples above), which, according to Salzman, then becomes more of a payment scheme than a true market.[75]

Environmental Services and Public Land

Just because ecosystem services are so poorly marketable does not mean that these services are not real and desperately valuable, and this distinction is where public lands prove so crucial. Public agencies are uniquely positioned to absorb the costs of land management to "pay" for valuable ES that benefit all of society as public goods. And until that unlikely day arrives when truly functioning markets develop for all these services, only public ownership can resist market failure and recognize and even work to maximize the otherwise unrecognized economic value of Earth's basic ecological functions.

Theoretically, the government could begin to identify and directly charge for the ES it provides. For example, it might charge municipalities for the clean water that flows off a national forest watershed, although city residents may resent paying again for an amenity their federal tax dollars already paid to protect. Perhaps a bigger question, though, is who will pay the wolverine's bill for the services it enjoys in its undisturbed wilderness habitat? It might, then, be a far better use of the ES model to allow public managers to rightly justify those difficult management decisions they sometimes make that seem to fly in the face of market demands. If a mining permit is declined in the context of an ES approach, reams of valuation data would show that such a denial was a prudent decision not only ecologically but economically. Likewise, restoration projects (for forest quality, prairie maintenance, habitat improvement, stream rehabilitation, and the like) are often relatively expensive and certainly not lucrative in market terms, but they can be readily justified as investments to improve the productivity of many valuable ecosystem services. In other words, ecosystem services provide a very legitimate form of cover and public support for environmentally sensitive decisions and allow managers to shift from the strictly market-oriented rubrics of the past (such as board feet of timber or animal unit months of forage) to much more "sophisticated objectives."[76] According to Jeffrey Kline et al., "The Forest Service hopes that the ecosystem services concept will allow forest managers to tell a richer story to Congress and the public about the benefits and tradeoffs associated with managing national forest lands."[77]

Perhaps it is not surprising that the four major federal land management agencies have all come to enthusiastically embrace the ES framework. For instance, the USFS formally adopted ES as a management guideline in a 2012 Planning Rule, which removes all reference to net benefits and efficiency and speaks instead of providing benefits and contributing to social and economic sustainability.[78] Adopting a new stance and new language is one thing, but successfully integrating this concept into day-to-day planning and decision making is quite another. Given the tremendous information inputs and analysis this mind-set requires, some doubt whether agencies under such severe budgetary constraints and political opposition can really pull it off.[79] And what exactly would it mean to "pull it off"? Is it merely to account for ES values in all future planning and decisions, or is it to support, cooperate with, or even help create formal ES markets?[80] Whatever the answer, it is clear that precisely valuing nonmarket benefits and services is a fiendishly difficult task. However, even if public managers cannot quite assign perfect values to competing nonmarket claims, at least they are no longer marked as "zero" on the ledger sheet.

Environmental Critiques of Ecosystem Services

> For the master's tools will never dismantle the master's house.
>
> —AUDRE LORDE, "The Master's Tools Will Never Dismantle the Master's House," in Cherrie Moraga and Gloria Anzaldúa, eds., *This Bridge Called My Back*

The ES model goes far to reclaim clear value long denied, yet it is not without its strong detractors in the environmentalist camp. In fact, a very lively debate rages as to how, where, and even whether the concept should be employed. One particular indictment of the ES model revolves around its very strong anthropocentrism and utilitarianism. That is, it focuses almost exclusively on how humans derive benefit from nature, and as such, it might be seen as simply the latest version of the century-long debate between Gifford Pinchot's utilitarianism and John Muir's preservationism. Arguing against the instrumentalism of ecosystem services, biologist Douglas McCauley points out that nature is full of things that do not directly benefit us, and some—such as tropical forests harboring the Ebola virus, trees sucking water from an arid watershed, or coyotes eating an occasional lamb—can even be seen as "ecological disservices."[81] Where is their place in this ES paradigm? Or conversely, asks McCauley, what about things like the invasive but commercially desirable Nile perch, which has dramatically increased the market value of Africa's Lake Victoria fishery, but at the expense of nearly destroying local biodiversity and traditional cultures?[82]

In fact, biodiversity as a value is often swirling at the center of much of this ES debate, as it is not uniformly categorized by all ES theorists as an ecosystem service in and of itself, for some of the reasons cited above.[83] This division gives rise to all sorts of potential conflicts between, say, the obvious ecosystem service of carbon sequestration and the carbon-releasing tree clearance and controlled burns necessary to maintain rare prairie ecosystems—or, for another example, planting invasive, nonnative eucalyptus trees as erosion control.[84] Which ecological processes and outputs are more important? Do we squelch some aspects of nature to enhance the ones we identify as having more utility and market value? Do we more vigorously protect the watershed near human populations and ignore the clear wilderness stream that flows untapped into Lake Superior? McCauley goes further and asks what happens when technology or market demands (which are always in flux) shift? Using the famous Catskills Watershed example, he asks whether an ES justification could still be made to spend considerable resources to preserve an intact, pristine forest if new water-filtration technologies come online in the future to dramatically reduce the costs of a treatment plant.[85] Don't we want, he seems to imply, a more durable basis on which to protect natural ecosystems?

Other critics, meanwhile, worry that ecosystem services are the proverbial camel's nose under the tent that will eventually lead to a complete marketization of nature, which, if successful, would bestow a newfound megavalue onto natural resources, which would, in turn, lead to privatized corporate control and consolidation.[86] In light of this possibility, Mark Sagoff complains that environmentalists have become intimidated by economists and too often surrender to their instrumentalist frames of reference and adopt their same individualist views of preferences and markets.[87] According to these critics, conservation must be framed in moral terms because nature is priceless and has intrinsic value far in excess of any instrumental value. "The scientistic and self-referential controversies in which ecological economists engage," claims Sagoff, "drain away the moral power that once sustained environmentalism."[88]

Indeed, by adopting this framework, Sagoff argues that ES advocates have abandoned the principles that infused so much of the landmark environmental legislation of the 1970s—namely, that because environmental degradation represents market failure, which harms people and nature as a form of "invasion and trespass," binding standards have to be set.[89] The Endangered Species Act even explicitly rules out consideration of economic costs. Saving species, like saving wilderness, is simply considered a moral imperative. "Why do they prefer to tell stories about the possible economic benefits of the furbish lousewort," asks Sagoff of ES proponents, "rather than offer moral reasons for supporting the Endangered Species Act?"[90] He sums up his position as follows:

> The things we are unwilling to pay for are not worthless to us. Love is not worthless. We would make all kinds of sacrifices for it. Yet a market in love—or in anything we consider "sacred"—is totally inappropriate. These things have *dignity* rather than a *price*.[91]

For this reason, McCauley argues that "we will make more progress in the long run, appealing to people's hearts rather than their wallets."[92]

In the face of such critiques, supporters of the ES framework certainly push back. Lynn Maguire and James Justus, for example, claim that intrinsic value arguments are actually the weaker ones because they tend to be vague and not very useful in the sort of competitive and comparative decision-making processes that routinely occur in this policy-making realm.[93] To have to make choices and weigh policy tradeoffs is, by definition, to determine the value of things, and finally the ecosystem just might get its due. For these very reasons, then, they argue that intrinsic value arguments have amassed a very poor track record of convincing policy makers.[94] Framing natural resources in terms of their profound instrumental value is, it would seem, the only language that many policy makers comprehend, and so, perhaps, it tends to sink in and convince where moral arguments fail, especially among those with very different moral codes.

Many other supporters of ecosystem services, including the leading theorist Robert Costanza, stress that despite being framed as polar opposites, intrinsic and instrumental values toward nature are not necessarily in conflict at all. He argues that ecosystems matter for all sorts of reasons and in all sorts of ways, "hearts, minds, and wallets included."[95] Walter Reid similarly suggests that it is not an either/or proposition. Is it not more effective, he asks, to advocate for the protection of coastal wetlands in Louisiana on intrinsic *and* utilitarian grounds rather than just the former?[96] Does one really negate and cancel out the other? Can these wetlands be places of sublime beauty and inherent, indescribable worth *and* prevent destructive and expensive storm-surge damage while adding value to nearby fisheries?

In a similar vein, nothing is more intrinsically valuable than a human life, and we rightly recoil at attempts to quantify its value—yet we do just that in court when we calculate compensation in cases of liability for death or injury. In the name of inherent human worth, should we give the widower nothing because life is priceless? And in giving this compensation, are we really successfully negating the pricelessness of human life? Another apt parallel might be found in the realm of public education. We support the education system because most of us agree that education is an intrinsic and imperative moral good, but who would deny that it also has a profound economic impact on income, socioeconomic status, GDP, and so forth? Are not both, side by side, excellent reasons to invest in education?

And valuation need not lead to marketization, according to Costanza, especially because most ecosystem services are public goods with poor market prospects. It is, rather, merely an attempt to show fuller value to policy makers in places where it has previously been ignored so that they may make more ecologically prudent choices going forward.[97] This enhanced valuation, then, seems to be what ecosystem services do best. Rather than as a way to commodify or monetize natural resources and struggle to create artificial and poorly functioning markets for them, it is best employed as evidence and testimony to the treasure-trove of value stored for the American people on their public lands and as an impetus to protect the services that churn out all this value.

Perhaps all these powerful critiques have made some ES advocates a bit more circumspect and even defensive, leading them to this middle-ground approach as illustrated in the preface to Francis Choi and Tim Marlowe's groundbreaking valuation formula used in their analysis of Joshua Tree National Park:

> There are those who believe that the value of the National Parks is infinite, and who therefore may consider this research to be unseemly. While we acknowledge that the true value of some of these resources may rest in the realm of the unknowable, we believe that the necessity for re-allocation of resources to and within the Park Service merits a duly diligent attempt at valuation. And yet we have undertaken this research in the spirit of advocacy for those for whom the worth of the parks is unimaginable, and in the pursuit of increased and stabilized funding for an American institution whose value runs deep.[98]

Some Caveats on Valuation

Given the tremendously high values that environmental economists find on public land, it should come as no surprise that
privatizers would cast a skeptical eye on this whole enterprise.
To them, it is a project that is woefully imprecise at best and,
more likely, arbitrary to the point of being wholly made up. But,
as previously pointed out in this chapter, huge margins of error,
imprecision, and the necessity to operate on certain assumptions
that may or may not come to pass are all freely acknowledged by
most scholars doing ES valuations or even more-conventional
ROI or economic impact studies. This uncertainty, in fact, is
one of the reasons that value estimates are often given as a fairly
wide range or the midpoint of said range. To some extent, this
estimation is unavoidable and due to the unique characteristics
of the values being measured. This fact does not negate their
value; it simply means it is harder to pin down.

Regardless, critics argue that this imprecision and these
questionable assumptions cripple ES valuations beyond the point
of usefulness.[99] In Choi and Marlowe's analysis of Joshua Tree,
for example, their upper estimate of the value of climate regulation ($313 million) is based on the assumption that without the
national park, that particular spot would sequester no carbon,
which is a somewhat dubious proposition.[100] Similarly, not all
analysts build into their models so-called *counterfactuals*—that
is, the value of the timber harvesting, mining, motorized recreation, or real estate development that may have occurred if the
site being analyzed were not protected (though the best studies
do). The opportunity costs, of course, vary among jurisdictions,
in that most would be lower on multiple-use land and higher on
wilderness areas or national parks.

Another potential weakness in these valuation studies concerns how certain values are calculated in the first place, especially for the very common situation where there is no market for
the service. In the absence of an established market price, economists generally look for the *replacement cost* to achieve roughly the
same service in a different way (e.g., forested watersheds versus

water-treatment plants). However, this situation begs the question of how to value something for which there is no technological replacement (such as photosynthesis, perhaps). If replacement costs cannot be ascertained, then an even more controversial method is, as previously mentioned, to survey people's *willingness to pay* to see what a certain preference is worth to someone by directly asking. While this is a widely accepted technique in economics, it strikes skeptics as an especially squishy and arbitrary measure, with respondents potentially grabbing values out of thin air.[101]

But even imprecise valuations with huge margins of error still tell us some very crucial things; most importantly, we know now that the value is not zero, which was precisely the assumption that most valuations and decision-making matrices worked from before the advent of ecosystem services. To go back to the example of compensation claims for death or injury, does anyone really believe that the figure for lost earnings, companionship, and so forth that requires such calculations comes anywhere close to accuracy and precision, as if such a thing is even possible? Again, is the answer to this imprecision to throw in the towel and to just say the life is worth zero dollars? So even if we are not able to exactly pin down the value of natural systems as a market does, it does not follow that all such value is therefore negated.

Budgets and Revenue

At the core of the privatizers' indictment of public land is that they are said to mostly "lose money" in that their operational budgets exceed their revenues, "producing a balance sheet," according to Fretwell, "that in the private sector would have sent shareholders fleeing."[102] As a result, taxpayers are alleged to be getting a bad deal while subsidizing all sorts of policy preferences, such as wilderness preservation and recreation, that they may not share. The revenue and appropriation data for Fiscal Year (FY) 2013 in Table 4.6 make this "deficit" abundantly clear.

Most galling to privatizers is the ratio for the multiple-use-oriented USFS, whose receipts since the limitations imposed by

TABLE 4.6. FY 2013 APPROPRIATIONS AND REVENUE FOR
FEDERAL LAND MANAGEMENT AGENCIES

Agency	Appropriation (in millions of $)	Revenue (in millions of $)	Ratio
BLM	2,048.0	525.0	3.9:1
USFS	5,710.0	223.6	25.5:1
USFWS	2,592.0	18.9	137.1:1
NPS	3,306.0	333.4	9.9:1

DATA SOURCE: Carol Hardy Vincent et al., *Federal Land Management Agencies: Appropriations and Revenues,* Congressional Research Service, Washington, DC, December 10, 2014, pp. 6, 15.

the Northwest Forest Plan in 1994 and the agency's adoption of an ecosystem management approach have declined by a factor of ten, from an inflation-adjusted figure of approximately $2.7 billion in 1989 to $254 million in 2015.[103]

This mind-set, however, depends on several questionable assumptions. The first is that the operating budget exists solely for the facilitation of revenue-producing commodity extraction or recreation. So if the revenue lags the budget, then this enterprise would automatically be understood as unacceptably bloated and inefficient. Therefore, the default mode for an agency's operation, in this privatization mind-set, should be that it generates the revenue necessary to meet (and, ideally, exceed) its operational costs.[104] By this standard, however, the Department of Defense, public libraries, schools, prisons, police and fire departments, and, really, any public service all fail the test as well. So, this standard seems to be unusually stringent and not applicable to most other public agencies and programs. It is also, perhaps, the acid test of how one views the role and purpose of the public lands: are they a critical bundle of public goods, services, and intangibles linked to our collective well-being, or are they a business that is currently being run poorly?

The second related assumption (already discussed in this chapter) is that commodities that can be produced for revenue are the only valuable items worth spending money for on public land. But if one accepts the premise behind ecosystem services, then it begs a crucial question: are such systems that churn out so many critical services and relay so much tangible and intangible value to taxpayers not worth an annual investment to keep the services as productive and healthy as possible through restoration, replanting, infrastructural improvements, and so on? Lehmann notes that although privatizers uniformly believe that public management absorbs far too many resources, they never show that this spending is, in fact, wasted. He argues that they "are still some distance from establishing what they take to be obvious . . . that federal land management is relatively inefficient."[105] But what if it is relatively efficient, just not in the way that privatizers want (i.e., commodity production)? What if, instead, it is efficient in juggling diverse and difficult ecological, economic, cultural, and aesthetic goals?

Unfortunately, federal budgetary trends have become increasingly restrictive, while some states, such as Wisconsin under Governor Scott Walker, have entirely zeroed out their state park budget lines, forcing them to rely on revenue alone.[106] Restrictive budgets have led to state park closures across the country,[107] and, at the federal level, an estimated $9.12 billion to $13.42 billion in deferred maintenance for U.S. Department of the Interior agencies and $5.56 billion on national forest lands.[108] Meanwhile, state park systems, desperate for cash, often turn to questionable revenue-generating commercial ventures and private partnerships to build such amenities as resorts, golf courses, restaurants, and ski facilities, which often conflict with their mission and damage the parks' natural features.[109]

But is public land management really such a profligate expenditure? A little context might go a long way toward putting into perspective this idea of public lands' being a budgetary extravagance that does not pay its own way. In 1977, the category *Natural Resources and the Environment* accounted for 2.75 percent of the federal budget; as of 2013, it is less than 1 percent.[110] Meanwhile, the budgetary subfunction *Conservation and Land Management* (within the category above), which specifically consists of the budgets for the four main federal land management agencies, has dropped from 0.12 percent of GDP in 1977 to 0.06 percent in 2015.[111] That is *six-hundredths of 1 percent* of our GDP to manage 28 percent of the American landmass and protect and nurture its invaluable natural capital.

How do these costs for the management of nearly one-third of the country's land—containing, perhaps, trillions of dollars of ecosystem services (not to mention timber, oil, minerals, and so on)—compare to other commitments and expenditures in the federal budget? Table 4.7 shows some selected outlays for context.

What engenders such fierce indignation among the critics of public lands that they fixate on one of the comparatively more modest federal outlays (especially given the enormity of the task), instead of, say, NASA or military or commerce programs? One might charitably speculate that they are focusing on that portion of the expenditure that goes toward such items as under-cost grazing, unpriced recreation, or low-value timber harvests and seeing objectionable subsidization. Indeed, Dale Oesterle complains that "the request for a private subsidy from recreationists who do not want to pay for their personal enjoyment of federal lands is raw interest group politics, not a public goods argument";[112] thus, if it is not a public good, the agency would presumably have no business spending money to provide it as a subsidy. But none other than the USFS critic Randall O'Toole points out that these subsidies have nothing on those that flow to the private sector. He compares $15 billion to $20 billion in direct subsidies (thus, not including irrigation and tariffs) in 1995 going to 20 million acres of private farmland to $6 billion going to users of 640 million acres of federal land, a figure that amounts to 100 times less per acre for public land.[113]

The budget grounds alone hardly seem adequate for these complaints; one would think that privatizers and deficit hawks in Congress who rail against public lands under the banner of deficit reduction would want to go after bigger fish. And there is no big-ticket item bigger than Iraq and Afghan War appropriations, the ultimate costs of which are projected to be in the range of $4 trillion to $6 trillion.[114] At its peak, one *month* of that very expensive and possibly futile war cost a billion dollars more than a year's worth of all federal land management, and the annual cost for *just air-conditioning* on military bases in Iraq is almost double

TABLE 4.7. SELECTED FEDERAL BUDGET OUTLAYS	
Budget category	Annual outlay* (in billions of $)
National defense	677.9
Food assistance	106.9
Ground transportation	61.0
Veterans' benefits	55.9
Elementary, secondary, and vocational education	47.5
Advancement of commerce	39.4
Air transportation	21.7
Air-conditioning expenses for military bases in Iraq	20.0
Space flight and research	16.6
Conduct of foreign affairs	13.5
Farm income stabilization	13.1
Higher education	12.1
Cost of one month of Iraq War operations	12.0
Disaster relief	11.9
Conservation and land management	**11.1**
Veterans' education and rehabilitation	10.4

SOURCES: All figures except Iraq War–related figures: Office of Management and Budget, *Fiscal Year 2016 Historical Tables: Budget of the U.S. Government*, February 2, 2015. Iraq War–related figures: Michael Kelley and Geoffrey Ingersoll, "The Staggering Cost of the Last Decade's US War in Iraq—in Numbers," *Business Insider*, June 20, 2014.
* With the exception of Iraq War operations, which are *monthly* outlays.

the federal land management bill.[115] So, is privatization of our public lands, a rather meager budget category, really the panacea to deliver us from an ocean of red ink? Or is it something else about collective ownership that disturbs privatizers more and tantalizes those who covet control of its resources?

Privatization is often held up as a net gain, as the government could sell the land and raise much-needed funds, stop having to pay for its management and built-in subsidies, and get the land back on the tax rolls. But the tremendous stored value of ES provision on the collectively owned public lands and water, not to mention the immense mineral and energy value below ground, as well as all the clearly demonstrable economic spin-off effects suggest something else altogether: that privatization would actually amount to nothing less than the most massive boondoggle of the century, rivaled perhaps by only the railroad and mining giveaways in the nineteenth century. The modest sum that we annually invest in the health and productivity of a massive base of natural capital that we all own and that provides us with invaluable public goods is actually one of the greatest bargains we will ever enjoy.

FACING PAGE: Okanogan-Wenatchee National Forest, Washington. *(Photo by the author.)*

FOLLOWING SPREAD: Tahquamenon Falls State Park, Michigan. *(Photo by the author.)*

5

The Fundamental Democracy
of the Commons

The Political Case for Public Lands, Part 1

> National Parks are the best idea we ever had. Absolutely
> American, absolutely democratic, they reflect us at our best
> rather than our worst.
>
> —WALLACE STEGNER, "The Best Idea We Ever Had," in Page Stegner, ed.,
> *Marking the Sparrow's Fall*

> There is the serious question of whether it is at all appropriate
> for people to use the power of a democratic constitutional
> government to impose their values on society through the
> allocation of natural resources.
>
> —WILLIAM DENNIS and RANDY SIMMONS, "From Illusion to
> Responsibility," in Sheldon Kamieniecki, Robert O'Brien, and
> Michael Clarke, eds., *Controversies in Environmental Policy*

> The Economic Man and the Citizen are, for all intents and
> purposes, two different individuals.
>
> —STEVEN MARGLIN, "The Social Rate of Discount and the Optimal
> Rate of Investment," *Quarterly Journal of Economics*

> Commonly known as public lands, the federal estate is more
> appropriately thought of as "political lands."
>
> —TERRY ANDERSON, "Back to the Future," in *Challenging Federal
> Ownership and Management*

Homo Economicus versus *Homo Politicus*

WHEN THE PRIVATIZATION ADVOCATE Terry
Anderson describes public lands with the phrase
political lands, he intends it to serve as a harsh rebuke

of the public domain and its management, and yet even public lands' greatest sympathizers would not necessarily disagree with this label. And herein we find the crux of the issue: to privatizers, politics are a dirty, chaotic, illegitimate business that ruins all it touches, while to those not inclined toward such an unfettered free-market perspective, politics are simply the unavoidable and, indeed, desirable give-and-take of democratic deliberation in action, as institutions, groups, and individuals try to advance and reconcile disparate visions and values. This debate is the focus of this chapter.

As previous chapters have shown, privatizers are adamant that bureaucratic control of our common land thwarts accountability, fiscal discipline, and the possibility of a rational, efficient, and fair allocation of resources. It allegedly substitutes flawed notions of science, imperious bureaucratic whim, and interest-group pressure for the "truth" of the best and highest uses, as can be revealed only by the wisdom of the market. Deeply embedded in this worldview is a profound skepticism toward democracy typical of the more strident versions of neoclassical and libertarian economic thought. This tradition puts forth a vision of *Homo economicus* for whom economic exchange is natural, in contrast with politics, which is invariably seen as an artificial and, at best, necessary evil, and even then only for the purpose of protecting markets, property, and the economic rules of the game. The only truly legitimate form of "democracy" in this paradigm is the democracy of the market, where all are free to come and exchange without coercion and where outcomes are thought to reflect free and open pursuit of individual preferences.

To privatizers, the easily vilified public-sector bureaucrats are not the only element of governance not to be trusted; even voting itself is suspect, at least when it comes to determining citizens' preferences. Rather than bestowing guidance or legitimacy, voting is seen as being compromised by low information and its vulnerability to special-interest influence so that it ultimately becomes little more than a conduit for these same special interests, as Terry Anderson and Donald Leal argue:

In the marketplace, prices lower information costs by converting subjective values into objective measures. In a democratic political process, the main counterpoint to prices for signaling values is voting. Voting is a signal that, at best, communicates the subjective values of the median voter and, especially given that voter turnout is often low and representative of organized interest groups, communicates the subjective values of special interest groups.[1]

Privatizers seem to reserve their greatest revulsion for the back-and-forth competition between organized interests (which is discussed in greater depth later in Chapter 6). It might seem odd that adherents of an ideology that lauds competition in the private market finds the same competition so distasteful in the political realm. Speaking of future policy fights over the public lands, Dale Oesterle paints a portrait of interest-group politics typical for a privatization advocate:

> These new disputes will be just as ugly as the old ones, with each group marshaling raw political power, throwing out a smoke screen of arguments based on collective values while staking claim to a subsidy for their activity.[2]

And the simple answer to end this ongoing travesty? According to Terry Anderson, Vernon Smith, and Emily Simmons, it is that "land use should be depoliticized."[3] And if, as Richard Stroup and John Baden contend, "public ownership of many natural resources lies at the root of resource control conflicts,"[4] then it would follow that no public ownership means no politics and thus no unpleasant conflict. Comparing this situation to one in which "toys are taken away from children who can't stop fighting over them," the journalist Hal Herring muses that privatizers would "solve the conflict over the public lands by simply getting rid of them."[5] Therefore, "what happens on federal land," Scott Lehmann points out, "would no longer be everyone's business."[6]

Public land advocates, on the other hand, are far more sanguine about the political conflict they see as inherent to the democratic process and question the extravagant and self-serving price that privatizers are so gladly willing to pay to end such conflict. As Jodi Stemler observes:

> Yes public land management can be messy and controversial, but no wise person gives away a mansion because of disputes over the bathroom fixtures or where or how to build a new staircase.[7]

Public land advocates, then, would respond to the privatizers' *Homo economicus* with a vision of *Homo politicus*, for whom politics and deliberation represent a positive and natural seeking out of the public good and the balance between individual needs and social obligations. And despite the privatizers' constant invoking of constitutional principles of property and limited government, supporters would argue that *Homo politicus* is much more in keeping with the Framers' vision of civic republicanism, whether of the Jeffersonian or Hamiltonian variety, whereby fierce and inevitable competition and self-interest are tempered by a shared commitment to the public interest. Without a vigilant public-spiritedness and sense of civic obligation among the elites and masses, the Framers knew that democracy and liberty would be swept aside by a tide of avarice.

But while this ideal of public spiritedness is one face of the American subspecies of *Homo politicus*, the ferocious competition for power and influence is certainly the other, and public land advocates most definitely realize this. "The United States," argues the legal scholar George Cameron Coggins, "is a democratic republic in which politics are inherent, indispensable, and unavoidable—'raw politics' is how we operate as a society."[8] With this sentiment, Lehmann would certainly concur:

> Federal ownership has, from the beginning, been a compromise between competing interests. . . . [L]and-management decisions are generally not the product of central planning or bureaucratic whim. To a large extent, they

reflect the outcome of competition between these interests in open political processes.[9]

To public land supporters, then, the "open processes" of politics, whether of the "high" or "low" variety (both of which privatizers seem to hold in great disdain), are actually nothing to
apologize for.[10]

Individual Preferences versus Collective Values

In the privatizers' universe, there are only individual desires and
preferences held by individual consumers "behaving atomisti-
cally," as Joseph Sax puts it.[11] And to the extent that anything
resembles a social good, it is simply the decisions that most efficiently maximize the distribution of goods to satisfy these preferences. What the social good most definitely is not, to privatizers,
is any sort of holistic concept, whereby the good is indivisible
and greater than the sum of its parts. Also, privatizers see no fair
or legitimate mechanism to adjudicate between clashing private
interests other than the market.

Public land advocates, on the other hand, see a much sub-
tler and more nuanced picture of this age-old push-and-pull between individual and social claims. Political life, according to
Sax, is "a complex interplay, a mixture and a tension between
atomistic behavior and collective behavior, and . . . both kinds
of behavior are reflected in routine preference-expressing activity."[12] The key point that privatization's critics make, then, is that
in addition to individual preferences, there are also collectively
held preferences every bit as, if not more, legitimate, which are
sometimes held simultaneously by the same person. And to ignore them should void any claims to a serious consideration of
preferences. Mark Sagoff's very influential work on this question
posits that ordinary people have a dualistic identity regarding
their preferences: as consumers with certain personal, market-
oriented interests but also as citizens and members of a community pondering what they think would best for the larger group.[13]
The citizen has a much broader and, some would say, loftier set

of concerns and preferences that include moral, ethical, cultural, and aesthetic interests. As a result, Sagoff notes:

> When citizens and their representatives deliberate in moral and aesthetic terms about the fate of the environment, they often reach conclusions utterly at odds with those they would reach if they considered only the economic aspects . . . of things.[14]

He further claims:

> We may be concerned as citizens, or as members of a moral and political community, with all sorts of values— sentimental, historical, ideological, cultural, aesthetic, and ethical—that conflict with the interests we reveal as consumers, buying shoes or choosing tomatoes. . . . The individual as a self-interested consumer opposes himself as a moral agent and concerned citizen.[15]

Sagoff uses his own students to illustrate this phenomenon in action. Many of them, he reports, are quite avid skiers. However, when presented with the real-world proposal to build an elaborate and enticing Disney ski resort in Mineral King, a wild valley in California's Sequoia National Forest,[16] they almost uniformly reject that option and prefer ecological preservation. Thus, their preferences as citizens, it would seem, clash with but outweigh their preferences as consumers in terms of their own moral constructs. As Sagoff puts it, "The political result, then, depends on what people agree after deliberation is best for the community, not what is efficient in satisfying their pre-existing consumer demands."[17] "Democracy at its best," he goes on to say, "invites people to take the point of view of the community" and to "ponder what best expresses its values."[18] And in doing so, Lehmann argues, one may discover that *what I'm interested in* can differ from *what's in my interest.*[19]

These collective preferences, however, are not always obvious or shared by all; rather, they are forged into something that approaches a working consensus only through the hard work of politics, as Sagoff points out:

> We do not become a functioning political community simply by sharing public goals. . . . To function as a community we must also reach the compromises necessary to move beyond incantation to political and economic achievement.[20]

And in this regard, collective decision making might have an advantage. Turning the free marketers' theories of scarce information on their head, Sax argues that collectivities can much more readily obtain and access the costly information to act prudently (by "crowdsourcing," if you will) than can autonomous individuals acting alone in the marketplace.[21] Similarly, Lehmann wonders whether democratic institutions might actually be better than markets in assembling and acting on certain types of information, such as the effect of externalities, that markets are routinely blind to.[22]

Thus, to give up on politics, as privatizers urge, is to permanently privilege individually held preferences while essentially ignoring collective ones. The problem is that some values, by their very nature, can be realized only collectively. For instance, only an entire political community can decide to act to save the grizzly or to set aside the Grand Canyon; no private citizen acting on individual preferences in a free market can, under any circumstances, achieve this goal. According to Sax, not only do groups have collective preferences; many individuals' own personal preferences are also precisely in line with the collective preferences—for example, to achieve some goal together with others and to have a say in collectively managing it.[23] This sort of individual preference, by definition, cannot be privately satisfied in the marketplace either.

While public land advocates tend to strongly equate the collective values that are invoked to justify conservation with the broad public interest, privatizers are unmoved, insisting that all preferences are subjective and rank in importance only relative to what people are willing to pay to realize them. To them, all this talk of collective values, moral imperatives, and intangible public goods smacks of elitism masquerading as populism. Oesterle, for one, finds the notion that "hiking, unlike bowling, somehow elevates people" to be a "self-righteous" argument that leads to "ugly overtones of elitism."[24] Similarly, Stroup and Baden complain of the "intellectual violence" embedded in the notion that some desires are wrong.[25] So, to privatizers, all preferences—from preserving rare species to building ski resorts to driving ATVs across fragile dunes—are simply subjective matters of taste that only the market can sort out and prioritize and that force people to put their money where their mouths are. Any claims to any sort of self-evident, a priori objective good— such as, say, biodiversity, ecological health, or scenic wonder—is often dismissed as emotionalism or even "quasi-religiousness."

However, the free-market orthodoxy trips itself on this question of the objectivity versus subjectivity of preferences. It treats the central criteria for free-market allocation—productivity and efficiency—as precisely the sort of objective, a priori truth that it denies to all other values and preferences. Lehmann points out that privatizers use these loaded concepts as neutral, technical terms, with "no normative force," when nothing could be further from the truth.[26] Lehmann goes on to note that to privatizers, "increased productivity is not, in their view, something we can just take or leave. They value increased productivity and think *the rest of us should too.*"[27] Well, maybe we should and maybe we shouldn't, but how did their preferences come to be a scientific imperative, whereas concerns for biodiversity or a stable climate remain as mere desires, fads, or even pseudo-religious mumbo-jumbo? "That a policy could be good or bad in any other sense, for example, morally, aesthetically, culturally, legally, or politically, would be a surprise to them," says Sagoff of privatizers.[28] According to Sagoff, they believe "that the principal function of politics is to satisfy the pre-existing preferences of individuals, however arbitrary or ill-considered."[29] Moreover, the supposedly "neutral" arbitration of the market in determining our preferences is often anything but, as relentless advertising, fickle whim, and a deep, culturally embedded consumerist ideology all work to shape, channel, and even generate consumer demands, which, in market ideology, must never be constrained or have their motives questioned.[30]

According to Sagoff, this all means that privatization theory engages in "a specious tautology" that upholds allocative efficiency by defining *social welfare* in terms of it and then turns around and uses social welfare as a stand-in for allocative efficiency.[31] Furthermore, he claims that privatizers seem utterly disinterested as to whether social welfare as they define it has "anything to do with human well-being as ordinarily understood."[32] What exactly is better about increased productivity and efficiency to make it a universal good and a given? We are never really told. Instead, according to Lehmann, "critical normative assumptions" such as these are "never defended; they are apt to go unnoticed or to be mistaken for empirical claims."[33] In reality, collective values are no harder or easier to judge, weigh, and consider than individual preferences; the same thicket of relativity and universalism applies to either.

But the apparatus of the democratic state, however flawed or dysfunctional, is the only means by which to figure out and then achieve collective values and civic goals. Sax suggests that if a collective decision-making body, such as the federal government, decides, for example, to restrain itself from logging a wilderness tract that market-efficiency criteria would otherwise claim to be the "best use," this choice is not *wrong* in any way if it reflects the political community's goals and values.[34] And because the land is already collectively owned, this preference does not need to be "paid for" any more than a farmer has to pay for her decision not to allow fracking on her own land. Yes, there are opportunity costs, of course, but there are alternative benefits as well, which landowners, be they individuals or collectives, can in either case freely choose to prioritize. Thus, according to Sagoff, "the protection of what is beautiful, authentic, charming, historic, and inspiring is right and good *whether or not* it is economically efficient."[35] According to Lehmann, property rights provide for individual freedom, but they do not guarantee its wise use.[36]

The Collective Values Embedded in Public Lands

Like a radio that cannot tune in on a certain frequency, collective values as they pertain to the public lands do not seem to register with privatization advocates—they appear to be an indecipherable concept. But these values have long registered with ordinary citizens, which is why a political consensus has developed over the past century, as have many ferociously protective citizen-led movements. Privatizers might blithely dismiss them as "elite special interests," but the history of these movements and the evolution of public opinion tell us otherwise.[37]

So what exactly are these collective values that have so animated the American people and their public officials to create such an extensive public domain? Chapter 3 discussed the values of biodiversity and ecological integrity, and Chapter 4 discussed the immense collective value of the goods, services, and economic well-being that issue from public land, but there are also profound cultural values to be found. First and foremost, our public lands have, over the centuries, come to be a central element of our identity as a nation and a people. As the writer Terry Tempest Williams reminds us, "the American character has been shaped by the landscapes that we live in."[38] The unity, pride, cultural resonance, aesthetic power, and well-being that radiate from our public lands are precisely the sort of intangible benefits that rarely make it onto the privatizers' spreadsheets, but, nonetheless, they allow "us to be the best of who we are as human beings,"[39] according to Williams. The historian William Cronon strikes a similar note:

> The work of land conservation is not just about protecting material nature—plants, animals, and ecosystems—but also about protecting human values and cultural land-

scapes. Put simply: we protect nature because we love the land. We protect preserves and natural areas and open space because they stand for some of our dearly held values. . . . History and the land are the core of our patriotism as a nation, and sustain our vision of what the United States is and should be as a nation: our best dream of what we aspire to become.[40]

Indeed, for at least a century and a half, poets, writers, historians, and naturalists have waxed poetic about the glories of the American landscape as embodied by our public lands, and, as such, these narratives have become embroidered into our cultural DNA and national identity, telling of something utterly unique, precious, and quintessentially American. To contemplate Yellowstone, the Grand Canyon, the Okefenokee Swamp, Yosemite, Mount Desert Island, the Boundary Waters, or the Olympic Forest is to glimpse some of the very architecture upholding our national story.

Because they play such a role, argues the historian Michael Frome, public lands contribute to our growth as better citizens in that they "are like art galleries, museums, and libraries, meant to enrich society by enlightening and elevating individuals who come to them."[41] To continue with this metaphor, would privatizers find that users of the neighborhood public library are free-riders imposing their elitist preferences onto society by getting everyone else to pay for their reading hobby—just as their fellow citizens who use public lands are accused of doing? Or is the storing of accumulated wisdom and knowledge (like biodiversity and aesthetic wonder) in an accessible commons a self-evidently transcendent and ennobling goal that makes society a better place? Why is the market and its criteria an objectively superior forum in which to make these choices than our democratic processes? Privatizers, of course, would label these collective ideals as paternalism, to which Sagoff replies, maybe so, but it is the paternalism of wanting to leave to people in the future something *worthy of happiness.*"[42]

Restoration as the Embodiment
of Collective Values

The pride, affection, and responsible citizenship that can get forged by this shared proprietorship of the commons are benefits that should not be underestimated. A perfect illustration of the civic virtue engendered by this common ownership can be seen in the explosive growth in the last several decades of volunteerism on our public lands. Individuals have long served indispensable voluntary roles as caretakers, naturalists, tour leaders, educators, trail maintainers, and campground hosts, but their role in ecological restoration and monitoring is perhaps the most compelling. Although definitive nationwide data measuring all volunteer citizen restoration activity on public land are quite elusive, it can be safely estimated that, at a minimum, hundreds of thousands of citizens working through thousands of stewardship groups annually volunteer tens of millions of hours on many thousands of sites.[43] What is most remarkable about many of these efforts is how sophisticated, long-lasting, and productive they have been. In his book profiling Chicago's North Branch Prairie Project, one of the nation's pioneering restoration groups, the science journalist William Stevens describes a close-knit community of citizen-scientists coming from all walks of life who have together developed a deep pool of knowledge and expertise on the ecological workings of the place they inhabit.[44] This considerable effort comes out of a profound love for, commitment to, and passionate fascination with the precious ecological remnants found in their local public lands, which they have meticulously attempted to nurse back to health.

As discussed in Chapter 3, none of this ought to happen if the world worked in the way that privatizers describe. In that world, which is governed only by laws of ownership and contract, because no one owns the land, no one cares or takes responsibility for it (i.e., *nobody washes the rent-a-car*). The general public would be expected only to use it, either as free-riders or fee-paying customers. In this rather bleak scenario, there are no real citizens bound together in collective purpose, and it is rather unfathomable to speak of love, commitment, responsibility, or a stewardship paid back in something other than economic productivity. But in the real world that these restoration volunteers inhabit, land gets healed, knowledge gets applied, responsibilities are fulfilled, and hearts and minds bind tighter to a particular piece of land that belongs to everybody.

To have such a stake in a commons as magnificent and valuable as the one Americans enjoy has become, for some, a powerful rallying cry for its defense, as shown by the writer and activist David Bollier:

> A reckoning of what belongs to the American people is a first step to recovering control of common assets and protecting them for public purposes. When we argue for the American commons, we assert the right to public control over public resources. . . . The idea that human beings share a moral and civic inheritance that cannot be alienated, commodified, or sold is part of an American tradition that has its roots in the Declaration of Independence.[45]

Access and Egalitarianism

Another important element of the collective values embodied by public lands has to do with the fundamentally democratic egalitarianism they represent. It is nothing short of remarkable to consider that nearly one-third of this country is a common inheritance that all can, for the most part, share and access equally, whether a dishwasher or a CEO. As one Wyoming outdoorsman puts it:

> I live in western Wyoming because a large portion of the land belongs to me. It is not mine exclusively and I would not want to be the sole owner. . . . I cannot put a price on public land, but I know it is one of my most valued possessions.[46]

Because this egalitarianism of public lands puts them in the reach of all, Americans are free, according to Stemler, "to wander in a way that is utterly unique in the modern world."[47] In an America that lacks guaranteed access to traverse private lands, as is common in Europe, this abundance of public land is no small thing. As Thomas More points out, one cannot be excluded on public land.[48] Likewise, for millions of hunters without access to expensive hunting clubs or other private lands, public land is the one place where their access is guaranteed. Not surprisingly, then, nearly seven in ten western hunters rely on public land.[49] Therefore, it should be clear, as the economist Arthur Okun notes, that you can treat people equally or efficiently, but you cannot do both.[50] Privatizers, on the other hand, find wide access to public land to be a bad place to address distribution and equity concerns. In fact, the poor, according to Sylvia LeRoy, might resent their tax dollars going to something they tend not to use.[51]

Public Lands and the Idea of Freedom

Large swaths of public wilderness, the writer Edward Abbey suggests, also represent nothing less than the ultimate realm of human freedom and the crucial yin to civilization's yang. In fact, to him, it is the forge on which civilization was hammered out:

> Wilderness is not a luxury but a necessity of the human spirit, and as vital to our lives as water and good bread. A civilization which destroys what little remains of the wild, the spare, the original, is cutting itself off from its origins and betraying the principle of civilization itself.[52]

Abbey, the anarchist, unintentionally channels the economic principle of existence value (discussed in Chapter 4) when he observes that one need not even sojourn into the wilderness for it to nurture a sense of freedom:

> A man could be a lover and defender of the wilderness without ever in his lifetime leaving the boundaries of

asphalt, powerlines, and right-angled surfaces. We need wilderness whether or not we ever set foot in it. We need a refuge even though we may never need to set foot in it. We need the possibility of escape as surely as we need hope; without it the life of the cities would drive all men into crime or drugs or psychoanalysis.[53]

Democracy, Choice, and Public Opinion

The debate over the political status of public lands comes down to the fundamentally unbridgeable ideological and paradigmatic chasm separating *Homo economicus* and *Homo politicus*. Privatizers express revulsion at the coercion exercised by governments upholding restrictive land management policies. And public land advocates consider these same policies to be democratically legitimate and reflective of deeply held collective values. But privatizers, as we have seen, not only reject the notion of collective values as thoroughly subjective but, going further, also characterize public land advocates and users as a rather small and elitist cabal seeking to impose its will and get society to pay for its preferences.

At this point, a look at what we know from the data on public preferences regarding this issue might be quite instructive. One finds that the privatizers' characterization is not borne out at all. The available survey research on public attitudes nationwide and in the western states would seem to suggest a scenario far closer to the public land advocates' shared collective values model than the privatizers' "elite cabal" model. Indeed, far from confirming a picture of indifferent, put-upon masses, as privatizers portray, polling data show lopsided and bipartisan majorities in favor of protecting public lands as well as keeping federal lands in federal hands. They also show a public that heavily uses and values its public lands, with an incredible 95 percent of westerners reporting a visit to federal lands in the prior year, 58 percent reporting more than six annual visits, and 24 percent reporting more than twenty.[54]

TABLE 5.1. NATIONAL SURVEY DATA ON PUBLIC ATTITUDES TOWARD CONSERVATION GOALS

Conservation goal (N = 7,069)	Agree/disagree (strongly agree = 5; strongly disagree = 1)
Conserve and protect watersheds	4.73
Preserve natural resources through such policies as no timber, no mining	4.22
Protect ecosystems and wildlife habitat	4.58
Preserve "wilderness" experience	4.15
Natural resources must be preserved, even if some people must do without.	4.14
Future generations should be as important as current in public land decisions.	4.52
I am glad there are national forests, even if I never see them.	4.66
People can think public lands are valuable even if they don't go there.	4.46
Forests have a right to exist for their own sake.	4.11
Wildlife, plants, and humans have equal rights.	4.28
The decision to develop resources should be made mostly on economic grounds.	2.92
The primary use of forests should be for products useful for humans.	2.95
The government has better places to spend money than on strong conservation programs.	2.33

SOURCE: Deborah Shields et al., *Survey Results of the American Public's Values, Objectives, Beliefs, and Attitudes regarding Forests and Grasslands,* U.S. Department of Agriculture, Forest Service, Rocky Mountain Research Station, Fort Collins, CO, Gen. Tech. Rep. RMRS-GTR-95, 2002, pp. 22, 28.

At the broadest level, U.S. Forest Service (USFS) data from a very large national survey in 2000 portray deep levels of support for conservation and preservation goals in public land management, as Table 5.1 shows.

Meanwhile, more-current national data on more-specific policy proposals show a similarly strong stance on behalf of public land conservation, as is evident in Table 5.2.

TABLE 5.2. NATIONAL SURVEY DATA ON PUBLIC ATTITUDES TOWARD PUBLIC LAND POLICY PROPOSALS AND NATIONAL PARKS, 2015

Proposal (N = 1,101; M.O.E. ± 3.1%)	Total percentage opposed	Percentage strongly opposed	Percentage supporting or undecided
Sell public lands to help balance budget	73	58	27
Allow oil/gas drilling in recreational areas of national parks and forests	71	52	29
Stop creating new national parks, monuments, and wilderness areas	69	48	31
Loosen protections on endangered wildlife	67	49	33
	Total percentage supporting	Percentage strongly supporting	Percentage opposed or undecided
Presidential initiatives to permanently protect some public lands as monuments, parks, and wilderness areas	90	70	10
Proposal (N = 708; M.O.E. ± 4.0%)		Total percentage agreeing	Percentage neutral or disagreeing
United States should sell off some national parks.		6	94
I do not benefit directly from national parks.		15	85
It is important that trails, parks, and open spaces are protected for current and future generations, whether I use them or not.		94	6
It is important that national parks are preserved for current and future generations, whether I visit them or not.		95	5
National parks are important to me because I enjoy visiting them.		81	19
Private businesses could probably do a better job than the federal government protecting historic sites and buildings.		22	78

SOURCES: Hart and Associates Poll, December 5–9, 2014, available at https://cdn.americanprogress .org/wp-content/uploads/2015/01/Public-Opinion-on-US-Energy-and-Environmental-Policy_ Interested-Parties-Memo.pdf; Michelle Haefele, John Loomis, and Linda J. Bilmes, *Total Economic Valuation of the National Park Service Lands and Programs: Results of a Survey of the American Public*, Harvard Kennedy School of Government Faculty Research Working Paper Series, RWP16-024, June 2016, p. 15.

Perhaps the most detailed data on public land attitudes come from Colorado College's State of the West poll, which specifically measures respondents from seven Rocky Mountain states who are, for better or worse, most affected by the federal government's massive land holdings in the region. The regional polling data find, again, a notably strong level of support for federal public lands, as Tables 5.3 and 5.4 show.

It is significant to note that the Rocky Mountain survey data are from a region of the country arguably more conservative than the nation as a whole, and yet the data still clearly show a strong preference for policies that conserve and protect public, and specifically federal, land.[55]

In fact, this strongly bipartisan support for public land found in the Colorado College survey was considered noteworthy enough in this superpolarized political environment to catch wider media attention.[56] Thus, the privatizers' characterization of public land as being foisted on an unaware and uncommitted general public seems to strongly conflict with the empirical evidence, which instead portrays a public fully cognizant of public lands' biological value, value to their regional economies, and value to their quality of life. Consequently, the survey research data would seem to lend considerable weight to the *environmental values as collective values* model articulated by Sax, Sagoff, and Lehmann.

These attitudes got a real-world test in October 2013, when the federal government partially shut down after House Republicans engineered a budget showdown by demanding the repeal of the Affordable Care Act. Included in the shutdown were all national parks and many other federal lands that the Obama administration made a dramatic show of closing, with blocked roads and abundant signage intended to drive home the dual points of GOP intransigence and the extent to which government services matter to the public. Charles Goodsell calls these sixteen days a "natural experiment" that revealed the deeper meaning of the situation.[57] In many ways, the closed-off national park system became a highly symbolic and sympathetic mascot

TABLE 5.3. ROCKY MOUNTAIN REGION SURVEY DATA ON PUBLIC ATTITUDES TOWARD PUBLIC LAND POLICY PROPOSALS, 2015–2016

Policy positions (N = 2,100; M.O.E. ± 2.74)	Total percentage opposed	Percentage strongly opposed	Total percentage supporting
Transfer federal lands to the states.	59	39	33
Sell significant holdings of federal land to reduce the debt.	60	46	26
	Total percentage supporting	Percentage strongly supporting	Total percentage opposed
Reduce coal mining on public land.	48	30	31
President continuing to have power to protect land as national monuments	80	59	11
Endangered Species Act	54	34	19
	Percentage viewing as helping economy	Percentage viewing as hurting economy	Percentage viewing as having little impact
Federal lands' effect on state economy	72	6	19
	Percentage viewing as a serious problem	Percentage viewing as not a serious problem	
Lack of resources to take care of federal public lands	67	27	
Impact of mining on land and water	60	27	
Loss of fish and wildlife habitat	67	33	
	Percentage wanting to continue protecting natural areas	Percentage viewing as having too many restrictions	
Which comes closer to your view?	63	28	

	Total percentage viewing as an important priority	Percentage viewing as a very important priority	Percentage viewing as not an important priority
Protecting natural areas for future generations	96	82	4
Conserving wildlife habitat	95	75	5
	Percentage viewing federal lands as belonging to all Americans	Percentage viewing federal lands as belonging to people in the state	
How do you characterize federal land in your state?	68	24	

SOURCES: Questions 1–8: Colorado College, *2016 Western States Survey*, available at https://www.coloradocollege.edu/dotAsset/1ae5d935-6a3d-4139-a128-e62d2441ec1f.pdf. Questions 9–13: Colorado College, *2015 Western States Survey*, available at https://www.coloradocollege.edu/dotAsset/f8b242ee-17a7-426d-8c5f-a970bde80f74.pdf.

of the larger shutdown, and the Obama administration gladly pushed this view because the parks represented such a universally beloved and noncontroversial government service. The closure also elicited howls of pain from tour operators, concessionaires, and tourist-dependent gateway communities, many of which were in deep-red Republican districts. So economically painfully were the closures that many state governments pleaded with the federal government to allow them to pay for and reopen the shuttered national parks.[58] Republican legislators tied themselves into knots trying to defend the larger federal shutdown while simultaneously criticizing the park closures as a stunt that was hurting innocent people. But to make this latter argument, these same legislators, many of whom had long expressed unremitting hostility toward public lands, were now forced to implicitly concede that the American people deeply love their parks and that those parks are also economically vital to their own communities.

TABLE 5.4. NEVADA AND COLORADO STATE SURVEY DATA ON PUBLIC ATTITUDES TOWARD PUBLIC LAND POLICY PROPOSALS, 2015

Public land policy proposals (*N* = 5 00; M.O.E. ± 4.38)	Total percentage opposed	Percentage strongly opposed	Total percentage supporting
Transfer federal lands to the states.	62	40	32
	Percentage viewing as helping economy	Percentage viewing as hurting economy	Percentage viewing as having little impact
Federal lands' effect on state economy	73	4	22
	Total percentage agreeing	Percentage strongly agreeing	Total percentage disagreeing
Public land recreation and tourism are essential part of state's economy.	82	52	17
Public land recreation and tourism are essential part of state's quality of life.	94	70	6
Public lands are so essential, we must preserve them for future generations.	97	76	3
	Total percentage viewing as an important priority	Percentage viewing as a very important priority	Percentage viewing as not an important priority
Protecting and conserving public lands for future generations	98	82	2
Ensuring access for recreational activities	94	66	6

	Percentage viewing federal lands as belonging to all Americans	Percentage viewing federal lands as belonging to people in the state	
How do you characterize federal land in your state?	76	18	
SOURCE: Public Opinion Strategies, *OIA Swing State Surveys*, October 6–10, 2015, available at https://outdoorindustry.org/wp-content/uploads/2015/10/15455-15454-OIA-CO-NV-Statewides-Combined-Final-IS.pdf. NOTE: Figures were calculated by averaging the Colorado and Nevada survey results and rounding up.			

FOLLOWING SPREAD: Apostle Islands National Lakeshore, Wisconsin. *(Photo by the author.)*

6

A Closer Look at Government

The Political Case for Public Lands, Part 2

> The BLM does not worry about bankruptcy. In fact, it has converse incentives: higher administrative costs mean a larger agency budget, which is the ultimate goal of many bureaucrats. When a bureaucrat can dress up an increased budget request in the mantle of the public interest, so much the better.
>
> —DALE OESTERLE, "Public Land," *Ecological Law Quarterly*

> The ranks of the Forest Service, the Park Service, the Bureau of Land Management . . . and the Fish and Wildlife Service are filled with men and women of high moral caliber, some of the world's most outstanding physical and biological scientists, and some of its best engineers and designers. . . . [I]f we needed to, we could not quickly create another body of professional land managers such as these without a hundred years of trying.
>
> —ELIZABETH ESTILL, "The Benefits of Professional Public Land Management," in *Challenging Federal Ownership and Management*

Bureaucratic Management of Public Lands: Tyranny or Democracy?

ALTHOUGH PUBLIC OPINION and democratic theory bolster the legitimacy of collective preferences as well as our elected representatives' role in securing them through legislation, the real action lies in the day-to-day management of public land by state, federal, and local bureaucratic agencies. And this realm is where privatizers focus their most intense scorn. As illustrated in Chapter 2, free-market theorists accuse government land managers of a host of grave abuses, including corruption, inefficiency, budget-maximizing self-interest, incompetence, unaccountability, and a misguided fealty to what they see as the false god of scientific management—that last item representing something more akin to Soviet central planning than anything else.

When these alleged shortcomings are combined with public agencies' decidedly mixed record on protecting the environmental health of the land, privatizers remain thoroughly confounded as to why environmentalists have not joined their crusade, as Dale Oesterle ponders:

> The conservationists' marginal record of success on federal lands, coupled with their severe criticism of current management practices, makes it difficult to understand their indefatigable optimism in government ownership.[1]

Perhaps, though, the stubborn environmentalists in question see through what Mark Sagoff calls "the fallacy of disparate comparison" (whereby the actual flaws of real-world public management are held up against a pristine theoretical market).[2] Furthermore, as indicated in Chapter 3, if one establishes that X is not carrying out a task as well as hoped, it does not necessarily follow that the alternate Y (privatization, in this case) must necessarily do a better job. So environmentalists may not trust federal managers all that much, according to Scott Lehmann, but they trust the private sector even less.[3] And the reasons for this attitude should be abundantly obvious: in one scenario, no matter how much policy makers might let them down, they have guaranteed access and recourse, mechanisms for ensuring accountability, and a large stake as members of the American public, while in the other system, what they are most likely to face is a proverbial shut door with a "Do Not Enter" sign hanging on it.

Models of Bureaucratic Governance

Public administration theorists tend to place bureaucratic agencies along an axis that roughly corresponds to how open and permeable or closed off and technocratic an agency is. On the one hand, the open agency sees its role as a facilitator or an "honest broker" in a complex, pluralistic political environment in which competing interests must be heard and accommodated to some extent; from this perspective, responsiveness, accessibility, and flexibility are held up as important qualities. At the other end of the spectrum, the closed agency is one where technical mastery, professionalism, and expertise along with a certain resistance to change reign supreme. This latter model is deeply rooted in the Progressive Era's conception of an efficient, scientific, and public interest–focused management that was seen as necessary to replace the corrupt and self-serving raw patronage of Gilded Age politics.

Specifically regarding public land management agencies, a fairly large literature has taken turns placing the main land management agencies at various points along this continuum. For example, the U.S. Forest Service (USFS), perhaps the most studied agency in the federal government, has been alternately cast as open and flexible[4] or as closed, rigid, and locked into its professional values.[5] Although this debate is often presented as an either/or proposition, the changing sociopolitical context in which the agencies operate has made it much more of a both/and situation. Thus, the two imperatives of responsiveness and professionalism can be seen to exist side by side, often clumsily and with great conflict, as a tightrope walk between two truly authentic impulses that are both taken very seriously by the agencies in question.

State and local land management agencies, meanwhile, feature their own unique bureaucratic political dynamics, each with their own place on this professionalism-responsiveness continuum.[6] Ironically, it might be at the state and county levels, insulated as they are from lawsuits, participation requirements, biocentric laws, and progressive hiring policies, where a rigid resource management–based professionalism can actually flourish in a more pristine form, as noted in this study of public managers in the Upper Midwest's abundant county forests:

> This near-total immunity from legal challenge creates a vastly different political environment in which county

foresters operate and one which gives them a much freer hand to do as they please within the bounds of the mandate they operate under. The great irony, then, is that Gifford Pinchot's Progressive Era creation, the U.S. Forest Service, with its considerable lore and proud agency culture of bureaucratic professionalism and scientific expertise, is actually the forest agency that must act most often as referee, conciliator, honest broker, and juggler of diverse public needs, goals, and preferences, while tiny little county forest departments operate as they see fit according to the tenets of professional forestry. In other words, it can be argued that county forest managers are much more the practitioners of the form of "expert" scientific forestry that Pinchot so clearly envisioned for his federal agency.[7]

As bureaucratic organizations with diverse clientele (from wilderness users to recreationists to resource extraction companies) and substantial legally mandated citizen-participation requirements, the federal agencies have really had no choice but to adopt a more facilitative role than they typically employed throughout the first half of the twentieth century. Elizabeth Estill notes how trained land managers have found themselves thrust into the role of peacemakers, doing as much conflict resolution as scientific management in local communities embroiled in bitter and polarized land-use disputes.[8] These disputes have grown more contentious and complicated, as economic and demographic changes have placed a more diverse and sometimes seemingly irreconcilable set of demands on public land.

Especially at the USFS, the "professional expert" role has been further muddied by an incredible diversification of employees since the 1980s, which inevitably raises the question "Which expertise are we talking about?" The 1950s agency that Herbert Kaufman notably profiled as almost military in its structure and esprit de corps and made up almost exclusively by white male foresters from perhaps a half dozen schools of forestry[9] has given way to a much more diverse organization in terms of race, gender, and, even more so, specialization. Between 1986 and 1994, the USFS saw a 7 percent and 15 percent decline, respectively, in foresters and engineers, while increasing the numbers of hydrologists (+36 percent), fishery biologists (+189 percent), botanists (+318 percent), wildlife biologists (+84 percent), and ecologists (+293 percent).[10] Jeanne Clarke and Daniel McCool report a similar diversification in the ranks of the U.S. Fish and Wildlife Service (USFWS) and other land management agencies.[11] So, in place of a dedication to a singular agencywide professionalism, there is now dedication to many professions, and some, like engineering and aquatic biology, might often be at odds with one another. It is interesting to note that Kaufman considers loyalty and dedication to the agency as indistinguishable from dedication to the professional values of forestry, which made perfect sense at a time when the agency was a homogenous mass of foresters. But because it and the other federal agencies feature such a complex tangle of forms of expertise, Craig Thomas argues that there are now actually three poles of influence on a land manager: (1) the public and outside groups; (2) his or her own professional values as a hydrologist, ecologist, forester, or the like; and (3) his or her dedication and loyalty to the agency and its mission and mandate.[12]

The Progressive Era's model of professionalism and scientific management has certainly been altered and adapted to the times, yet it still persists as a notion that has been doggedly maintained by land management agencies for the better part of a century. For most of this period, scientific management strictly meant range science, game management, and silviculture, but the move toward ecosystem management in the 1990s—even if adopted somewhat reluctantly—gave this notion powerful new relevance. Scientific management now means using expertise collaboratively to protect biodiversity, sustainable resource use, and the uninterrupted flow of productive ecosystem services.

Privatizers, for their part, have rarely bothered to differentiate between any of these complex and varied aspects of land management agencies. They see scientific management as hopelessly wrong and flawed, while pluralist facilitation is a corrupt morass of influence peddling. Thus, they have all the bases covered; public officials are alleged to be, all at once, naïve and cunning, hapless and ruthless, unpredictable and overplanned. But privatizers see their greatest crime, when all is said and done, as using the coercive power of the state to restrain markets on behalf of the public.

The Motivations of the Bureaucrat

As we have already seen, true to their neoclassical economic theories, privatizers believe that what motivates public land managers is simply a matter of self-interest, or what is termed in the literature *principal agency*.[13] Much as their ideological cousins in the climate-denial camp think that atmospheric scientists push theories of climate change to advance their careers, gain tenure, and secure research funding, privatizers tend to see the successful maintenance of his or her career as the prime factor in explaining a land manager's decision making. A corollary to this personal success, of course, would be to expand the larger agency's jurisdiction, budget, and decision-making authority. A CATO Institute publication speaks of land management bureaucracies that "skillfully manipulate public opinion and members of Congress to increase their budgets," thus becoming the biggest beneficiaries of this supposedly rigged game.[14] This so-called budget-maximization theory, as articulated by William Niskanen generally and by Randall O'Toole as well as Richard Stroup and John Baden regarding public land agencies, holds that budgetary incentives perversely punish efficiency with lower budgets, and because managers lose tax dollars rather than their own money, they are not overly concerned.[15]

Despite how ubiquitous and widely held these theories are, critics find the evidence for them to be rather thin and inconclusive.[16] What is perfectly clear from the literature, moreover, is that individual bureaucrats *themselves* are not personally benefiting when agency budgets are increased—a point that seems to suggest that the motives are something else, such as agency mission or professional values, rather than naked self-interest.[17] In fact, for the vast majority of managers outside the top echelons, budgets are a "rather distant concept" over which they have little to no direct control.[18] Similarly, critics argue that theories of turf expansion are overplayed as well, especially for the rank-and-file.[19] New turf certainly brings more authority, but it also brings more administrative headaches, more conflict, and sometimes an actual dilution of the core mission, thereby representing more of a liability than an asset on the balance sheet of agency power. Perhaps more important than the gaining of new ground, according to Thomas, is the strong aversion to losing existing turf.[20]

So if naked self-interest in the form of budget maximization or turf expansion is an unsatisfactory explanation, what motivates the public land manager? Regarding federal land managers, Estill argues that they simply need to be understood, first and foremost, as *public servants*. To her, this identification implies that they entered into a "calling" more than a job, often at considerable personal expense (in terms of educational attainment and sacrificed wages), to carry out a mission they are deeply committed to.[21] In their rather cynical view, privatizers, conversely, assume the worst about bureaucrats' motives. But why, Lehmann wonders, should professional ethics, self-respect, or dedication not serve as a constraint on self-interest?[22] Indeed, one needs to look no further than the many highly educated but relatively low-paid social workers, environmental lawyers, or school teachers to see evidence of alternative motives trumping narrow self-interest. In fact, the literature in public administration strongly suggests a clear link between public-sector employment and individual levels of altruism.[23]

Similarly, in his renowned defense of the bureaucratic sector, Goodsell reviews a number of studies that find more empirical support for models rooted in professionalism and dedication than in individual self-interest (principal agency theory).[24] In making this point, he quotes the findings of John Brehm and Scott Gates:

> Ultimately, our data . . . turn the phraseology, if not meaning, of principal agency theories around: Bureaucracy

works in the United States because of "principled agents." We found that [public employees] were highly professional and strongly influenced by principles that cohere with the mission of their organization. . . . Scholars, as well as the public and politicians, need to credit bureaucrats for being public servants, for working as hard as they do, and for being as responsive as democratic government demands.[25]

Goodsell also reviews a quarter century of literature that compares public-sector to private-sector motivation and finds a consensus that public-sector employees are equally motivated and report higher levels of work satisfaction, a greater commitment to benefiting society, and stronger values of self-sacrifice and integrity.[26]

Finally, Thomas's research finds *autonomy*, not self-interest, to be the main motivator of bureaucratic behavior.[27] Given that autonomy protects professional values and prerogatives, his findings are not necessarily at odds with Estill's or Goodsell's more-idealistic takes on the matter.

Assessing Bureaucratic Performance

Perhaps even more important than what motivates a public land manager is how well he or she performs the job. Given the complex, multifaceted, and often contradictory nature of this position, making such an assessment is no easy task. However, the only version of bureaucracy that privatization theorists seem willing to evaluate is the ideological straw man they themselves have constructed. Consequently, they seem to show far less interest in assessing the real-world version by any sort of criteria less predetermined than the ones they routinely employ. Such criteria would have to take into account an agency's legislative mandate, organizational mission, and willingness to achieve these goals with enough responsiveness to satisfy the requirements and expectations of democratic governance. The problem with the privatizers' arguments is that they usually begin with their a priori rejection of public ownership, management, and collective values, and then they work backward from there, coming to an inevitably negative appraisal of the actual performance of land managers. In other words, there is no separation between the land managers' supposedly illegitimate public goals and whatever it is they do to carry out those goals. To privatizers, doing a good job realizing what they see as bad goals or a bad job realizing bad goals is ultimately the same.

But if one largely accepts these public goals and missions, as Estill does, the view might turn out to be quite a bit different. "The United States," she boldly declares, "is perhaps unknowingly blessed with a hundred years of selection for the finest, most competent body of professional land managers existing in the world today."[28] In the face of such divergent views, a look at what the data say might be instructive. Goodsell devotes much of his book to dispelling via data what he considers to be the popular myths and false narratives surrounding the broader bureaucracy. These include data gleaned from the research on public-sector/private-sector productivity as well as customer service surveys, each measuring an important aspect of performance. Regarding public-sector productivity, Goodsell cites data measuring 34.3 percent growth in the nearly three decades between 1967 and 1994, which is nearly identical to the productivity growth rate found in the private sector during the same period.[29] Meanwhile, in terms of customer satisfaction, he finds that evaluations of employees of federal, state, and local agencies are consistently high across numerous measures over numerous years and types of agencies.[30] More importantly, they are, once more, commensurate with those in the private sector.[31]

As far as natural resource agencies are concerned, the customer satisfaction data are even more positive. The U.S. Department of the Interior, which includes the Bureau of Land Management (BLM), the National Park Service (NPS), and the USFWS, ranked the highest among the cabinet departments on the University of Michigan's 2015 American Customer Satisfaction Index, with a score of 75 out of 100.[32] As for the USFS, only one of its divisions, Research and Development, was measured

TABLE 6.1. USFS AND NPS CUSTOMER SATISFACTION
(0–5 SCALE)

	USFS	NPS
Developed facilities	4.6	4.6
Condition of environment	4.6	4.6
Employee service	4.7	4.8
Safety	4.7	NA
Value	4.2	4.7
Overall	4.7	4.7

SOURCES: U.S. Department of Agriculture, Forest Service, *National Visitor Use Monitoring Results: National Summary Report*, May 22, 2012, pp. 16–22, available at http://www.fs.fed.us/recreation/programs/nvum/nvum_national_summary_fy2011.pdf; U.S. Department of the Interior, National Park Service, *National Park System 2009 Visitor Survey Card Data Report*, Report #NAPA09, 2009, available at https://www.nature.nps.gov/socialscience/docs/napa_09.pdf.

with this same tool in 2015, scoring 76 out of 100.[33] Meanwhile, the agency's own customer-service data show visitors overwhelmingly satisfied by their experience, with 78 percent very satisfied, 16 percent somewhat satisfied, and only 3 percent reporting to be somewhat or very dissatisfied.[34] NPS visitor-satisfaction data, meanwhile, are nearly identical.[35] Table 6.1 shows the levels of satisfaction with specific aspects of national forest and national park visits.

Evaluating Scientific Management

There are, of course, many other facets to an agency's performance beside customer satisfaction. Because most land management agencies operate along this previously discussed continuum between professional expertise and flexible responsiveness, perhaps we need to consider them separately. On one end, privatizers scoff at the professional expertise that defines and motivates public land managers, viewing it as a pseudo-science or, as Robert Nelson puts it, an "emotional crusade" that willfully ignores the one truly relevant science of classical economics.[36] For this reason, all attempts by public agencies to engage in planning are seen as doomed to failure, as "efficient public planning," according to Stroup and Baden, "is a logical impossibility."[37]

This assertion certainly might be true, to some extent, for commodities, but John Loomis counters that it is wholly untrue regarding the provision of public goods.[38] Indeed, the *only* way that public goods can be optimally managed and protected is through continual monitoring, planning, and evaluation. Perhaps, then, what privatizers are ultimately suggesting is that planning and scientific management are bad and do not work because they do not necessarily produce the outcomes that privatizers themselves are ideologically committed to—namely, maximum commodity production.

Let us be clear that the meaning of scientific expertise in today's land management agencies differs quite a bit from the days before the great diversification of professions, when it pretty much meant silviculture, range management, and engineering. Indeed, in times past, this so-called scientific expertise has been nothing short of an environmental disaster, as measured in steep clearcuts at unsustainable rates, destructive dams, exterminated predators, overgrazed range, and polluted streams. And consequently, as Hanna Cortner observes, citizens came to be rightly suspicious and skeptical of such so-called agency expertise.[39] But over time, because they are public and thus ultimately accountable entities, these same agencies were slowly, and not without great difficulty, pulled in the direction of openness and responsiveness through legal mandates, public input, and changing collective values. As a result, they ultimately embraced a broader and more ecologically informed range of scientific insights and practices.

Another barrier to ecologically enlightened scientific management has been largely structural: complex, dynamic, and interdependent ecological systems existing within a heavily fragmented political framework. And this political world's boundaries (jurisdictional and geographic) rarely, if ever, coincide with those of the natural systems they are intended to manage. Where coordinated, comprehensive action to effectively manage complex ecological systems is needed, all this fragmented political system can seem to muster is piecemeal and ad hoc. It was, after all, designed by the Founders to prevent the abuse of power, not to cohesively manage biodiversity. Thomas notes that alongside this external fragmentation also exists internal fragmentation, as most land management agencies (federal and state) have some degree of a divided mission and conflicting legislative mandates.[40] By the 1990s, however, the pressure to move toward an ecosystem management approach led agencies to slowly, and perhaps a bit grudgingly, move beyond their usually competitive stance toward a more institutionalized form of interagency coordination, at least among the multiple-use agencies.[41]

External Factors

Another factor hindering agencies' performance involves external matters over which they have little control, such as appropriations, legislative micromanagement, and other circumstances related to the larger political climate. This issue is especially prevalent during political cycles of austerity, whether induced by fiscal conditions or ideological hostility. Simply put, when faced with inadequate resources to properly implement an overload of mandated responsibilities, performance is guaranteed to suffer, which then becomes a self-fulfilling prophesy to those critics looking for excuses to give privatized solutions a chance. This downward spiral is especially evident in those state park systems cut off from general state tax revenues. They, in turn, respond with higher fees and reduced services and maintenance or else are forced to rely on external private-sector support, such as corporate donations, friends groups, and volunteers, just to cover basic operations. And the fact that private sources do often step into the breach only further emboldens the budget cutters and privatizers.

According to Bill Wade, such outsourcing, especially of basic park functions, is rarely successful and may actually increase costs and decrease productivity. This result develops because park staff are often jacks-of-all-trades who shift roles as seasons and circumstances demand in the parks they know and love and are so deeply committed to.[42] How does one efficiently outsource that?

Agency Performance and the Courts

A last and sometimes underestimated influence on agency performance, at least at the federal level, has been the courts. Since the 1970s, environmental groups have embarked on a strategy of relentless litigation in the federal court system to uphold various aspects of federal land management legislation, such as the National Forest Management Act (NFMA), the National Environmental Policy Act (NEPA), and the Endangered Species Act. And the resulting effect on federal agencies has been nothing short of dramatic. In fact, Elise Jones and Cameron Taylor find that administrative appeals, lawsuits, and even just the threat of lawsuits have been "significant factors" in driving institutional change at the USFS as well as concrete change in the agency's management practices.[43] Thomas finds much the same, as he identifies court enforcement of environmental legislation as the most important motivator in jump-starting efforts at interagency cooperation.[44] If this impact could be encapsulated into a single case, it would have to be Judge William Dwyer's 1991 spotted-owl ruling, whose remedy was the complete shutdown of all logging on federal forests in California, Oregon, and Washington until a suitable recovery plan for the owl could be devised (which did not happen until 1994). This decision ultimately led to a drastic reduction in national forest harvest volumes as well as new policies on old-growth forests and biodiversity. More indirectly, according to a number of scholars, this case and others have pushed the USFS toward a wholesale embrace of the ecosystem management framework[45] and lasting organizational change.[46]

One of these changes has been a newfound willingness to engage in interagency collaboration on behalf of biodiversity. According to Thomas, national forest managers post-Dwyer switched to a proactive approach and jumped onto the biodiversity bandwagon, so to speak, to protect their autonomy and exercise it on their own terms.[47] Conversely, Thomas reports that because the NPS, which is sued far less frequently and was not affected by Dwyer's injunction, lacks the court-induced incentive, it has been much slower to join efforts at interagency coordination.[48]

One indicator of how profoundly the federal courts have shaped land management can be seen by comparing federal to state and local forest management. For example, in comparing the USFS to selected state forest agencies, Tomas Koontz finds the former to achieve far more environmental protection and citizen participation, while the latter delivers proportionally greater volumes of timber and higher revenue.[49] Other research has found county forests to be managed even more aggressively for timber and revenue production.[50] The one important common denominator that distinguishes state and county forests from their federal counterparts is that land-use statutes at the subnational level are written in a way that denies environmentalists much of a legal foothold from which to sue forest management agencies. As a result, lawsuits at this level are a negligible factor. This circumstance, in turn, creates a very different set of facts on the ground, which, to some observers, makes state and county forest management agencies far less democratically responsive.

Interest Groups: Bane or Boon to Democracy?

At the opposite pole from a public land manager's job description as a scientific expert is the role of facilitator and honest broker between warring interest groups and sectors of the public. Not surprisingly, privatizers are every bit as critical of this role as the other, finding it to be an unseemly "hodge-podge of . . . special interest favors," which allow for unchecked rent-seeking and special privileges for the few, paid by the many.[51] But, as shown in Chapter 5, this alleged political bazaar can also be viewed as an unavoidable and intentional aspect of American politics, whereby diverse factions of the public who believe they have a clear stake in the public lands democratically mobilize to influence policy in an open system.

Regardless of the scenario, it is clear that this facilitator role did not come easily to most land management agencies.

Although certain powerful local interests (stockmen, logging companies, mill owners, and so forth) have always had a certain degree of guaranteed access and input due to their economic and political importance, it is, nevertheless, safe to say that most land managers understood their preferred and central role to be that of professional expert. Some agencies, such as the USFS, were able to keep business interests at arm's length, but this position was possible, according to some observers, only because there was so much overlap in the agency's professional values of forestry and commodity users' commercial goals.[52] On the other hand, the BLM (in the past, jokingly called the "Bureau of Livestock and Mining"), became so intertwined with commodity-using groups that many critics accused them of being captured outright, as professional values were no match for the political power of commercial clients.[53]

Not until what Jeffrey Berry terms the "Advocacy Explosion" in the 1960s and 1970s did countervailing public interests, including many environmental organizations, begin to mobilize in large numbers. This was as a result of not only the sociopolitical ferment of the times, but also the proactive attempt of a reformist government to encourage public participation.[54] As previously noted, this leveling of the playing field was achieved, in part, through the mandates that were built into the major pieces of environmental legislation from the time (such as the NEPA, the NFMA, and the FLPMA), requiring extensive notification, comment periods, and other forms of citizen input and participation in the Environmental Impact Statement (EIS) process. Concurrently, the role of environmental groups was also secured and expanded by favorable court rulings, which expanded environmental groups' standing to sue. Freed from having to show direct personal injury, environmental lawyers were now able to represent the public interest more broadly and in a wider variety of situations.

Faced with these mandates and the aggressively changing political environment, federal land management agencies began, over time, to adapt to and to accommodate the participatory demands placed on them and the new roles this change brought on. There has been much debate in the literature over whether this responsiveness has really been just a begrudging, pro forma "going through the motions" or an authentic and earnest embrace of new roles.[55] However, after nearly five decades of working with outside interests, the agencies in question certainly seem to have internalized this facilitative aspect of their job. Wendy Espeland, for example, finds the Bureau of Reclamation in the Department of the Interior to have become truly more democratic and responsive in its procedures and organizational culture as a result of the NEPA requirements thrust upon it in 1969.[56]

Once again, studies of state and county public forest management show that they generally feature a tiny fraction of the formalized public input procedures that exist for federal forests.[57] And where such procedures do not or barely exist, only powerful, local, commodity-using interests seem to have a voice, albeit one that is often more hidden. As for private forest management, which is the ultimate goal of privatization advocates, the public or interest groups, for the most part, do not have even the slightest input, consultation, or influence, as this role would be anathema to all notions of private property.

There is no doubt that today's interest-group competition over public land policy, raging as it has for almost a half century, has hardened into deeply conflictual and dysfunctional patterns that have become, subsequently, very easy to criticize for their seeming disregard of the public interest. But our nation, with its weak party system, divided government, and easily penetrated and highly fragmented political institutions, was set up in such a way as to develop into the "Interest Group Society," as Berry calls it.[58] Is any other major policy area (health care, abortion, civil rights, financial regulation?) not similarly dominated and defined by interest-group competition?

The privatizers' disgust with all this unseemly conflict and bickering and competition might, at first glance, seem principled, yet it is important to remember that environmental politics in America did not become this ferociously contested trench war until members of the public concerned about the environment mobilized into a profoundly democratic mass movement that was helped along by guaranteed citizen access and input in the 1970s. Without this grassroots mobilization, the role of interest groups might have remained a version of what it was in the 1940s or 1950s—that is, an elite "good old boys" network of commodity users, whereby the president of the local Stockmen's Association and the BLM district manager sit together at a Rotary Club function or play an occasional game of golf together while informally discussing "business." Would this situation leave privatizers as disgusted and indignant at the currying of special favors as the current situation of spirited competition seems to? Indeed, the procedural reform and advocacy explosion that brought environmental groups to the table and into the fray have made this policy realm infinitely more open, democratic, and representative of the views of ordinary people than it would have been otherwise. As the Canadian political scientist Robert Paehlke points out, democracy is good for environmentalism, and environmentalism is good for democracy.[59]

On the other hand, the privatizers' solution to the problem of interest-group competition is one of decidedly *less* democracy. They would "solve" matters by moving the entire decision-making process out of the public realm and placing it behind the closed doors of whichever commodity user bid the most. What was once an infuriatingly slow, conflictual, and messy democratic process would, overnight, become almost antiseptically clean, but wholly unilateral and private.

Centralization, Decentralization, and Democracy

Critics of the federal domain question its democratic bona fides by invoking its centralized nature, controlled as it is by distant departments and agencies in Washington, D.C. For western states whose landmasses are 50 percent to 80 percent federally owned, this arrangement is likened to some kind of colonialism. In fact, privatizers have gotten far greater political traction in calling for local devolution than for outright privatization, as is evidenced by at least two cycles of the Sagebrush Rebellion.[60] Instead of being perceived as embedded within a collective set of national values, federal lands are seen (against the evidence of western state survey data reviewed in Chapter 5) as representing an imperial imposition of Washington, D.C., on the distant states. Oesterle notes how unfair it is that eastern representatives and senators, often lobbied by environmentalists, outvote western legislators on public land issues.[61] Baden, meanwhile, complains that government's top-down imposition of environmental restrictions has "robbed rural communities of their traditional user-rights over forests, waters, fisheries, and wildlife without offering appropriate remuneration."[62]

On the other hand, Estill reminds us that the lessons of the biodiversity and ecosystem services frameworks recommend the moving of decisions upscale to a coordinated federal level despite the political trends that are pushing in the exact opposite direction. "It's hard," she suggests, "to hold biological integrity in the face of politically centripetal forces."[63] Other observers, such as George Cameron Coggins, push back even harder, calling what he sees as the undue influence that local actors *already* have on federal management an "immoral, unlawful," and "undemocratic . . . abdication."[64] In his view, the worst problems on the federal lands are the result not of misguided federal authority but of the ceding of said authority to local interests, such as farmers, water districts, ranchers, ATV clubs, sawmills, or chambers of commerce.[65]

Even if one disagrees with Coggins and believes, instead, that it is perfectly legitimate for managers to be responsive to local stakeholders, his broadside points to the fact that federal-local interactions are far more complicated and nuanced than the privatizers' simple story of colonial domination. In reality, federal land managers are already quite decentralized, scattered as they are across thousands of management units dispersed across every far-flung corner of the country, many quite distant and remote from Washington, D.C.[66] Furthermore, federal managers down to the most decentralized level (such as the USFS Ranger District or the BLM Grazing District) are empowered by broad discretion in interpreting and implementing fairly ambiguous multiple-use mandates.

When this discretion is combined with the fairly open access afforded by required participation mandates and generous access to the courts, the result is anything but a top-down model. Rather, it is a complicated political ecosystem that requires a monumental and continual balancing act on the part of federal managers. If they move too far toward the direction of local interests, they risk being co-opted and taken down a path that will soon violate their mandates and the national public interest. Koontz reminds us that federal lands have a national constituency, which creates a much more varied and environmentally supportive set of demands that would get lost if only a local constituency focused exclusively on economic demands gets heard.[67] On the other hand, if managers remain aloof and closed to local interests, as Coggins seems to advocate for, they risk alienating themselves from the communities they are part of and inextricably bound to.

According to Estill, this tension requires good land managers to take a hybrid approach, whereby the federal manager serves as the *agent* to apply science and to facilitate collaboration to "provide the connective tissue across local jurisdictions[,] which ensures protection of the commons of larger scales."[68] Such a policy toward local collaboration on federal land tends to manifest itself through such vehicles as citizen advisory boards, workshops, and, increasingly, what are called grassroots *consensus groups*.

In this last category, the best-known of these attempts at what Randall Wilson calls "collaborative conservation"[69] has been the Quincy Library Group (named for its meeting place) in the northern reaches of California's Sierra Nevada. Although this initiative has had many detractors, its supporters have hailed it as a model and persuaded Congress in 1998 to fund and institutionalize the group's role in the national forests in the immediate area. Around the same time, many other attempts at collaborative conservation sprang up across the country in all sorts of natural resource management settings, each with a focus on intensely local, place-based consensual problem solving.[70] During the 1990s and 2000s, the participation of such groups increasingly came to be institutionalized in state and federal legislation, regulations, and planning rules.[71]

Even where they have not become quite as formalized as the Quincy Library Group, examples of collaborative local-federal partnerships are not hard to find. They have spread from their origins in highly contested national forests to the BLM's Resource Advisory Councils, and even to the USFWS. In fact, many ranchers near the Malheur Refuge thought it ironic that Bundy militia chose that particular place for its armed occupation when such great strides had been made in the past decade in building cooperation and partnership between local ranchers and refuge managers, culminating in a landmark 2013 management plan that had wide support in the community.[72] "To me," said one rancher near the refuge, "what is important is that the refuge has really listened and taken a more collaborative approach. Automatically that helps build better relations with the community."[73]

Collaborative community-based partnerships have also become a vehicle for involving long-ignored constituencies, such as Native Americans. For example, in December 2016, President Obama used the Antiquities Act to designate Bears Ears National Monument in southern Utah on BLM land sacred to a number of area tribes, and a commission of tribal representatives was established to help manage the land.[74] Another good example of inclusive community-based management is the Kickapoo Valley Reserve in southwestern Wisconsin. In the late 1960s, the federal government condemned 140 farms on about 8,600 acres to build a large dam. The environmentally destructive dam was bitterly opposed and ultimately never built, but the Army Corps of Engineers did not get around to divesting the land until the 1990s. The land was ultimately transferred to the state of Wisconsin and the Ho Chunk Tribe, which together created a unique reserve run by a state-appointed board of local people and tribal members with a preservation and recreation mission.[75] This very local governance model helped address the grievances of Native

Americans whose ancestors had been dispossessed a century and half before from that very spot as well as of the families of the farmers forced off their land for the dam.

Collaborative conservation, however, is not without its detractors. Some USFS personnel believed the Quincy Library Group, for example, undermined their mandated responsibilities, and some environmentalists saw the effort as subverting the hard-won advances toward ecosystem management and biodiversity protection they had already achieved.[76] More broadly, skeptics believe that consensus groups grant an undue amount of power to hyperlocal interests, thereby diluting and damaging the national interest.[77] Furthermore, these ad hoc local interests may not be wholly representative of the community. Such groups are also seen as short-circuiting the legitimate role of litigation, advocacy, and values conflict in forcing policy changes. Instead, the search for consensus, it is argued, usually leads to the lowest common denominator, policy-wise.[78]

Supporters of consensus groups, on the other hand, see them as a potential breakthrough in moving away from the intense conflict, lobbying, and legal paralysis of the traditional interest-group model and toward a more consensual and effective search for policy compromises. Mary Chapman stresses the place-based rootedness this approach can bring to decision making, while Sarah Parks and John Gowdy speak of the power of "collective consciousness" and deliberative valuation as being crucial to efforts to determine the value of natural systems.[79] They find that it dovetails quite well with Ostrom's groundbreaking work on communal resource governance.[80]

Regardless of how much faith one places in the collaborative approach, it is clear that criticisms of a monolithic federal juggernaut's besieging of local communities is just not accurate. The reality is a far more mundane, more nuanced, and much less tidy incremental slog. It involves federal managers' simultaneously acting on behalf of centralized goals and decentralized needs while juggling a plethora of constituencies, interest groups, mandates, policy demands, legal requirements, lawsuits, and values. Like the famous saying comparing the making of laws to the making of sausage, it may not be pleasant to look at, but it beats by a long measure any alternative put forward by privatizers. Despite its flaws, shortcomings, and abundant failures, our imperfect system still manages to keep faith with the public interest in that it is essentially open, responsive, and accountable, unlike the alternate model of private ownership.

FOLLOWING SPREAD: Three Rivers Petroglyph Site, Bureau of Land Management, New Mexico. *(Photo by the author.)*

7

The Future of Public Land

Looking Forward in a Time of Peril

> There's a larger question involved here than the preferences of
> the fifteen thousand or so people who currently live in south-
> central and southeastern Utah. And that question is, who owns
> the land? . . . [W]hat right have southern Utahns to determine
> the fate of our national parks, national forests, national
> monuments and recreation areas and BLM-administered public
> lands? Most of southern Utah is the rightful property not
> of local Chambers of Commerce, but of all Americans. *All*
> Americans from California to Maine, from Alaska to Florida.
> Therefore, any decision as to the further industrial exploitation
> of these public treasures is one that should be made by the
> American people as a whole.
>
> —EDWARD ABBEY, "Letter to Mr. Williams, Utah Holiday Magazine,"
>   in David Peterson, ed., *Postcards from Ed*; emphasis original

The Political Storm Moves Ashore

ON OCTOBER 27, 2016, a federal jury in Oregon acquitted seven defendants of all conspiracy and weapons charges stemming from the Bundy militia's armed
takeover and occupation of the Malheur Refuge nearly a year
earlier (see Chapter 1).[1] Given the fact that federal prosecutors
had carefully constructed what seemed to many to be an airtight
case against the defendants (who had widely publicized all of
their illegal acts), this shocking verdict could be seen as transmit-
ting a fairly ominous message about the public's mood in rural
America.[2] The successful argument deployed by the defense was
that this storming with automatic weapons of a public facility
was all simply a matter of free speech necessitated by government
tyranny and overreach.

In retrospect, this verdict was to be a potent harbinger of the second, much-larger, political earthquake that struck less than two weeks later as real estate mogul Donald Trump won the presidency in a tremendous upset. Trump lost the popular contest by nearly three million votes, yet he managed to build a slender seventy-seven-thousand-vote margin across three key Democratic-leaning states and thereby prevail in the Electoral College. This political convulsion delivered to the Republican Party unified control of the federal government at precisely the moment when the privatization and land-transfer movements were reaching new heights of influence and relevance. As a consequence, an already clouded outlook for public lands has turned even darker, as they now face a political environment more overtly hostile than anything that has been seen since at least the Sagebrush Rebellion.

Prospects for Radical Change

Once a realm of broad bipartisan support in Congress and in most state legislatures, the environment generally and public lands specifically have become deeply polarized issues. Like waves battering a shore, the Republican-controlled House of Representatives has repeatedly passed increasingly bold measures to weaken Wilderness Act protections, eliminate the Antiquities Act, close low-visitation national park units, and transfer federal land to states (see Chapter 1); in 2015, the GOP finally managed to gain a one-vote Senate majority for a transfer provision attached to a budget bill.[3] Only a presidential veto stood in the way, and now that backstop will very possibly be removed.

The prognosis for this new era of Republican political dominance is not entirely clear. A previous era of unified Republican control (from 2003 to 2007), while certainly deregulatory and heavily geared toward ramped-up commodity production, did not have nearly as dramatic an effect on land management agencies or the basic legal underpinnings of federal land management as many feared. The central question will be whether the ensuing decade of GOP radicalization will have made the difference. The first indications available seem to suggest that this indeed is the case. On the very first day of the 115th Congress in January 2017, the House inserted a change into the budget-rules framework for the coming session. Under the old Congressional Budget Office accounting rules, budget calculations for any transfer or sale of federal land had to include the cost to the Department of the Treasury of lost revenue from fees and sales or royalties from extractive activities. Under the new rule, giving away federal land will incur no cost on the balance sheets, and thus losing them will have no officially recognized financial impact.[4]

One limiting factor on the Republican agenda and its platform-sanctioned goal of land transfer is that the 2016 elections brought about a tightly divided Senate, with only a fifty-two-seat Republican majority, which further decreased to fifty-one seats following a special-election upset in Alabama in December 2017. With such a narrow margin, especially with the filibuster available for nonbudgetary votes, it would seem that more radical measures might run into quite some difficulty clearing the Senate.[5] Furthermore, President Trump's relatively low approval ratings and a brewing grassroots mobilization on the left that, in some ways, mirrors the Tea Party movement in 2009, might make this unified Republican control of the government short-lived.

Of course, the executive branch is the other realm that needs to be considered when sizing up what the future holds for public lands. And on this issue, Trump has been something of a cipher, with little apparent interest in or knowledge of public land issues. During the campaign, Trump made vague statements both in support of and in opposition to the land transfer movement.[6] And although his transition team and cabinet picks have drawn very heavily from the libertarian orbit of the American Legislative Exchange Council (ALEC) and Koch-affiliated groups, Trump's own brand of nationalist populism would also seem to leave room for a position more amenable to national lands' staying that way. Most of Trump's cabinet choices for departments and agencies touching on environmental issues have been stridently antiregulatory and deeply committed climate denial-ists, and although his choice for interior secretary, Representa-tive Ryan Zinke (R–MT), fits this bill to some extent as an un-abashed proponent of fossil fuel and timber production on federal land, he is one of the few western Republicans who has staked out a clear position against privatization and transfer.[7] Still, the more this deeply polarizing and extremely unorthodox president loses popular support, the more he seems likely to fall back on a strategy of going all out to please the base, which, in the case of public lands, might ultimately lead to some radical changes.

Whatever its ultimate position on transfer or privatization, the Trump administration has, at the very least, begun to ush-er in an era of heavy energy development on public lands and intensified logging and mining, as political appointees bring enormous pressure to bear on unit managers to pull back from environmentally restrictive practices to facilitate maximum commodity production.[8] Yet if basic land management laws (such as the National Forest Management Act [NFMA] or the Federal Land Policy and Management Act [FLPMA]) remain in place and unaltered by Congress—and this is a big *if*—one can expect just as furious a legal counterattack by environmental groups using their well-honed skills in this last realm where they still have access, and at least some influence. They can be expected to lean on the courts in an effort to play for time and possibly block the more-egregious proposals that come forward in violation of existing statutes.

The Move against National Monuments

The first major push by the Trump administration in the realm of public lands involved not privatization or transfer but rather a major initiative ordered in April 2017 to review and possibly rescind or alter all national monument designations made since 1996. Although twenty-seven monuments in total were covered by this executive order, two in particular—Utah's Grand Stair-case–Escalante and Bears Ears—were, for political reasons, the most vulnerable. Totaling 3.1 million acres of protected land designated by Democratic presidents (Bill Clinton and Barack Obama), they have each engendered bitter opposition from Utah politicians as prime examples of a federal "lock-up" of local resources, which has put them in the political crosshairs like few other tracts of federal land. To no one's surprise, President Trump accepted the recommendations of Secretary Zinke and issued an executive order on December 4, 2017, that cut the acreage of Bears Ears by 85 percent and Grand Staircase–Escalante by half in what, at roughly 2 million acres, would be the largest rollback of protection on federal land in American history.[9] Although the 2 million declassified acres are no longer to be highly protected national monuments, they will stay federally owned and revert to their previous status as ordinary Bureau of Land Management (BLM) tracts managed under multiple-use doctrines—most likely for energy production. In fact, some evidence suggests that the Bears Ears boundaries were specifically redrawn to accommodate the desire of a Colorado company to develop uranium mines, while Grand Staircase–Escalante's new boundaries were carefully set to leave out land containing massive coal deposits.[10]

One day after the president's executive order was signed, Secretary Zinke's final report on the monument review was released. In addition to the two sites in Utah, two other national monuments—Oregon's Cascade-Siskiyou and Nevada's Gold Butte—were slated for as-yet-undetermined acreage reductions, while six more national monuments (three of those being huge marine monuments in the Atlantic and Pacific Oceans) were to face profound changes in management rules.[11] These unprecedented changes include allowing logging in Maine's new Katahdin Woods and Waters National Monument and commercial trawling in the marine monuments.[12]

During the course of this review, the Department of the Interior received more than 2.5 million public comments, of which 99.2 percent opposed reductions or changes to any monuments. "I don't yield to public pressure," was Secretary Zinke's response in the face of this massive and unified outcry.[13] Not surprisingly, within days of this announcement, at least five separate lawsuits were either filed or being prepared by environmental groups, Indian tribes, paleontologists, and the outdoor apparel company Patagonia, while Oregon is poised to sue as soon as the Cascade-Siskiyou reductions are finalized.[14] The fierce pushback that this policy move has engendered is due not in small part to the fact that national parks and monuments, among all categories of public land, have long enjoyed with the public something approaching sacrosanct status. Not surprisingly, no previous president ever moved so aggressively against national monuments.

In the long run, this move to strip national monument protections from millions of acres of federal land is by no means a sure thing. On the one hand, supporters of Trump's decision argue that the president's powers in this regard are broad and implied by the Antiquities Act, which has granted the president monument-designating power since 1906. For Utah senator Mike Lee, then, it is the quite simple matter of recognizing that "what can be done with a stroke of the executive pen can also be undone with a stroke of the executive pen."[15] A number of legal experts, however, vigorously challenge this notion and raise serious doubts about the legality of abolishing or substantially altering national monuments by simple executive decree.[16] Their arguments center on the fact that federal land management powers stem from the Constitution's Property Clause, which exclusively grants such power to Congress. The Antiquities Act, they contend, narrowly delegates a small portion of this power to the president under specific circumstances—to "reserve" federal land as national monuments to protect an imminently endangered resource of historic or scientific importance—and unless the power to rescind or diminish previous declarations is explicitly stated in the act (which it is not), then it does not exist.[17]

The first real test of this law came in 1938, when President Franklin Roosevelt asked Attorney General Homer Cummings to examine the full extent of his powers under the act and whether they included the powers to abolish or alter existing monuments. In his legal analysis, Cummings found no such power; subsequently, when writing the FLPMA in 1976, Congress used this analysis to reiterate in the text of the law that the president has no implied authority to modify or revoke monument designations.[18] The 1976 House Natural Resource Committee report clearly states that the FLPMA

> would also specifically reserve to the Congress the authority to modify and revoke withdrawals for national monuments created under the Antiquities Act.[19]

The Trump administration's efforts to roll back previous national monument designations has provoked and will continue to provoke a ferocious backlash, legal and political, from public land advocates. Zinke's final recommendations are guaranteed to be tangled up in the federal courts for quite some time. Still, they are a clear measure of how bold and once even unthinkable changes have swiftly come about in this drastically changed policy realm. If allowed to stand, it would mean that any president could, by fiat, undo the status of any national monument going back to the law's origin in 1906. Conversely, if presidents clearly have this executive power, what would stop a future president who is favorably inclined toward preservation from restoring the previous boundaries to the diminished monuments, thereby setting off an unstable game of ping-pong with once-permanent boundaries?

The Prospects for Transfer

Although much of the attention in the early part of the Trump administration has been on national monuments and the deregulation of land use, the movement to transfer the federal lands to the states still simmers in the background. Should a comprehensive land transfer bill somehow come to pass Congress, it would be only the start of a messy, complicated, and likely ferocious political conflict involving fusillades of lawsuits (including constitutional challenges), pitched battles over exactly which lands would be transferred, and the even greater complications presented by the very nature of federalism itself. As of 2017, only four of the twelve western states presumably the target of such transfer legislation have unified Republican control of state government (Utah, Idaho, Arizona, and Wyoming; Alaska has an Independent governor). The very strong possibility must be considered that Democratic governors or Democratic-controlled legislative chambers would want federal land in their states to stay federal because they would be unwilling to take on the considerable expense and responsibility of good management and fire suppression and/or would be ideologically opposed to the very concept. Could they be forced to take it anyway? Real-world politics will become a lot stickier than smooth platitudes about local control.

The Obama years will be fondly remembered by groups committed to a more environmentally protective stance on federal lands. President Obama put in place a moratorium on new coal leases, blocked drilling and mining in many sensitive areas, and added tens of millions of acres of new national monuments in Utah, New Mexico, Washington, California, Nevada, and Maine.[20] Meanwhile, under sympathetic leadership, land management agencies were largely free to move forward with initiatives and procedures aimed at incorporating the ecosystem management and ecosystem services frameworks in policy-making and valuation decisions.

The flipside of this unapologetic commitment to environmental protection was the continuing mobilization of a seething movement of opposition in parts of the rural West. As shown in Chapter 1, this movement has antecedents going far back in American history. What is most clear is that the worst flare-ups of rural anger in the past half century have tended to occur during Democratic administrations that move policy in a direction of consolidated federal control and regulation. So we see the Sagebrush Rebellion of the Jimmy Carter years, the Wise Use and county sovereignty movements during the Clinton years, and, most recently, the land transfer movement and Bundy-like militias of the Obama years. It remains to be seen whether the current anger and momentum will dissipate under a friendlier

Republican administration as it previously did under Ronald Reagan, and in both Bush presidencies.

These movements share the dubious notion that any federal ownership of land is a constitutionally prohibited activity, an idea that only recently has been mainstreamed. Numerous court rulings and most serious legal analyses find in the Constitution's Property Clause clear and indisputable constitutional authority for the federal government to own and control land, but opponents insist, through a rather tortured interpretation, that the Constitution obligates the federal government to surrender all public land to the states.[21] The opponents of transfer clearly have the much-stronger legal argument on the grounds of the disclaimer clauses built into all the enabling acts that established the western states. Utah's, for example, requires that inhabitants of the "proposed state so agree and declare that they forever disclaim all right and title to the unappropriated public lands lying within the boundaries thereof."[22] Writing about the county supremacy movement of the 1990s, William Chaloupka takes note of this stubborn insistence on upholding an imaginary constitutional principle to undermine the achievements that the real Constitution has made possible: "It is as if the originating document is somehow sacred, while the history it made possible is profane."[23] In a chillingly prescient passage written more than twenty years ago, Chaloupka could have easily been talking about the Bundy family or even the 2016 presidential race:

> It should at least give pause that the available forms of elite leadership, media interpretation, and other methods of policing the boundaries of governmental and social legitimacy seem so ill equipped to deal with this kind of criticism.
>
> As significant as these movements may become to the future of federalism, their implications for our national politics may be even more important. The county movement and militias practice, at their most radical moments, an odd mixture of antigovernment hysteria and an unusual application of civic moralism and historical precedent,

in an often paranoid, conspiratorial framework. American politics, which for so long dismissed outbreaks of populist radicalism with ease, may now be forced to deal with a more durable and vituperative variation of such activity.[24]

Defending Public Land in This New Era

The one thing that public lands have going for them in this politically hostile environment is that broad sectors of the American public still love them and care deeply about them. Although defense of public lands usually does not qualify as a top-level concern of voters, this lack of attention might be partly because public lands have never really faced so direct an existential threat before. If the supporters of public land are to rally a movement to defend them, it will have to be a broad, passionate, articulate, and nimble effort. The communication theorist George Lakoff reminds us of the importance of language and the framing of arguments,[25] and the successful defense of public lands will be no exception. Elements of an effective strategy might include the following:

- **Frame public lands as a patriotic imperative.** Turn tangible places into potent symbols and speak of the federal lands with the same reverence as one would speak of any other profound and sacred national symbol. Make the protection of these endowments a measure of true love of country; this approach would suggest that there is no better way to show this love than to actually protect its physical integrity. Let the despoilers be seen as selfish and indifferent and let privatization seem more akin to flag-burning than the "freedom" of libertarians' privatization arguments. As far as populism is concerned, what is more populist than every American together owning our valuable inheritance and being assured of access? Try as they might to associate public lands with an elite, nothing is less true, and this point needs to be hammered home at every opportunity; it is every person's hunting ground, hiking place, picnic spot, and place for repose and solace that no developer or resource conglomerate can take from them.

- **Seize the historical narrative.** Public lands desperately need a bold and effective narrative that describes the story of how they came to be. The county supremacy and militia movements and their political allies have created a mythological past that bears no resemblance to historical facts. For example, during both Bundy standoffs and in all subsequent discussions of transfer, opponents of public lands managed to get all sorts of media, even the most responsible outlets, to routinely parrot the line that local communities very reasonably want an overreaching federal government to *return* the land to them. But you cannot, of course, have returned to you what was never yours in the first place, as was laid out in Chapter 1. Native American tribes are the one and only group who can legitimately make that argument.

- **Make the argument that state transfer likely means no more truly public land.** On paper, the transfer movement's aims might sound fairly responsible: keep land public, but devolve control to a level more responsive to local concerns. In all likelihood, though, the transfer movement is apt to be a stalking horse for either outright privatization or the quasi-privatization of the trust model. In the best-case scenario, former national forests, BLM lands, and possibly wildlife refuges would be transferred to states, but the management model employed would likely be that of state-trust lands, not regular state parks or state wildlife areas. This distinction is crucial, because trust lands are not truly public in terms of access—they have a largely closed-off decision-making and management apparatus, and they have a fiduciary duty to raise revenue, with few or no mandated responsibilities for biodiversity protection, recreation, hunting, or any other form of public interest. As such, federal lands, now managed for a multiplicity of uses, are pretty much guaranteed to be managed strictly for oil, gas, and coal production if transferred. Indeed, a study commissioned by the Utah Legislature concluded that the only way the state could afford the management of all the transferred federal land it was demanding would be through aggressive energy production.[26] Lest there be any doubt about intentions, a Utah Resolution (SCR 4) passed in 2015 declared oil and gas production to be "the highest and best-use" of the land.[27]

Trust lands can also be sold at any time to generate revenue, and indeed, for this very reason, many western states have much smaller trust-land portfolios than they started with at statehood. In fact, Idaho has sold 1.76 million acres, or 41.4 percent, of its granted trust lands. And this figure is not just the result of misguided policy from long ago, as 100,434 acres of that total has been privatized just since 2000, with an additional 13,500 acres, on average, sold each year.[28] Although it was narrowly averted in the eleventh hour, the rather shocking proposal by Oregon to sell the entire Elliott State Forest, a trust property that became Oregon's first state forest in 1930, should dispel any illusions as to what the future holds for much transferred land (see Preface, note 3). Thus, the worst-case scenario for the transferred federal lands is that this whole initiative might very well be a clever, two-stage form of privatization advanced by powerful commodity interests that could never achieve anything as controversial as the direct privatization of the federal domain. But in this way, once out of the spotlight, it can happen slowly at the state level with much less attention. Modern-day transfer advocates complain that they are being unfairly accused of having a hidden privatization agenda, but the record would seem to suggest otherwise. As the prominent transfer advocate and Utah state representative Ken

Ivory puts it, "It's like having your hands on the lever of a modern-day Louisiana Purchase."[29] Even if we were to take them at their word, though, no guarantees hold for a new generation of state officials thirty years down the road. Certainly the Wisconsin conservation officials who many decades ago purchased various tracts for the public did not foresee the day in 2017 when some of those tracts would be sold.

- **Build as broad a coalition as possible.** Environmental groups have long been at the forefront of battles over public land, and although they have resources, political savvy, and legal expertise to put up quite a fight, changes in the political landscape have made them less-effective messengers than they used to be. Given the radical polarization of the times, they are too closely identified with one side of a huge cultural and partisan divide. The movement to protect public lands needs a grand coalition that can cut across class, cultural, and political boundaries and raise a clamorous and unified roar of disapproval over any plans to separate the public from its lands. For example, Iraq and Afghanistan War veterans have been emerging as powerfully effective messengers on behalf of public lands and wilderness, which have been, for many, some of the only places they could find healing and solace after the shattering experiences of war.[30] Likewise, organized groups of backcountry hunters (such as the Backcountry Hunters & Anglers Association) can articulate what public wilderness means to them in ways that mainstream environmentalists cannot, as they and veterans have a legitimacy in certain arenas and with certain rural audiences that environmental groups often lack.

A good example of this dynamic could be seen when Representative Jason Chaffetz (R–UT) introduced H.R. 621 in the opening days of the 115th Congress in 2017. This bill, which would have authorized the federal government to privatize 3.3 million acres of federal land, engendered such a fierce backlash among outdoor and hunting groups in Utah and nationally that Chaffetz quickly withdrew his bill via an Instagram message in which he made sure to extol his love of hunting and the outdoors.[31] If solely Sierra Club members were raising this uproar, it is probably safe to assume that the bill would not have been withdrawn.

Another key ally in this fight will be Native American groups, whose voice has a special moral authority regarding this issue. Despite losing their ancestral homes to the establishment of the public domain, many Native Americans are steadfast opponents of privatization, as public lands, at their best, can act to protect sacred sites, resources, and landscapes, with at least some accountability and accessibility for tribes.[32]

As we have seen in Chapter 4, public lands spread their wealth and value far and wide, and groups that have come to depend on them—such as the outdoor industry, gateway communities, tourism-related industries, local chambers of commerce, outfitters, and guides—need to become loud advocates in this coalition as well. As it stands now, no family gets in their car in Ohio and drives to a management unit of Montana state-trust land for a two-week vacation, and if this is the fate of federal land, then many livelihoods will be endangered. Even many resource users, such as ranchers or small logging operations, very well might prefer their stable, predictable, and inexpensive access to federal resources over the "Wild West" of private markets. Indeed, the first Sagebrush Rebellion fizzled out, in part, for this very reason. Bringing such order and access to all users was one of the main reasons for the shift from a policy of disposal to retention in the late nineteenth century. Patricia Limerick quotes the president of the Delta County Stock Grower's Association speaking in 1909 regarding the advent of forest reserves available for grazing, where he and his fellow ranchers enjoy "peace, protection, and prosperity, instead of suffering the pangs of friction, bloodshed, and criminality. . . . We know today what we may expect tomorrow."[33]

Public Lands over the Long Term:
Trends and Challenges

If we are to assume that our system of public lands emerges from the Trump era and the corresponding ascendance of Republican power in some recognizably intact form, then it becomes equally important to assess challenges and opportunities that public lands face over the long run.

More People, Less Space

According to U.S. Census projections, America in 2060 will have 416 million inhabitants,[34] and if current development patterns that favor low-density sprawl continue to persist, then we can expect the consumption of land for urbanization to accelerate. If the period between 2000 and 2010 is any indication, high-growth metro areas will spread over two to four times more land each decade. Approximately 5.6 percent of the overall U.S. landmass is currently developed,[35] but this figure is a bit misleading, because the places where about 80 percent of the public lives (metro counties) are considerably more developed and will only continue to become more so. For this reason, public lands might acquire enhanced importance as (1) reservoirs of biodiversity, ecological coherence, and other public goods in an increasingly fragmented landscape; and (2) assets ever more necessary for securing quality of life in growing metro areas. To be sure, these pressures will be felt differently across disparate regions and jurisdictions, with state and local public lands being especially important in this regard. However, the West is one of the fastest-growing regions of the country, and there, the outer edge of urban sprawl is increasingly butting up against federal lands.

In response to these trends, some state and local governments have become quite proactive in securing additional open space in high-growth areas, with some even going to referendum to secure bonds for land acquisition, as Minnesota did in 2008 with a historic $5.5-billion authorization and New Jersey did in 1998 through a Constitutional Amendment, which dedicated $2.94 billion in sales tax to the Garden State Preservation Trust.[36] In fact, nationwide, more than 75 percent of open space referenda are successful.[37]

The Blurring of Public and Private Conservation

Although this expansion of conservation initiatives in some localities involves the outright acquisition of more public land, it is no longer the only model available, as the traditional lines between public and private conservation are beginning to blur. Purchase of development rights (PDR), for example, is increasingly becoming a tool for governments to meet conservation goals while leaving the land in private hands. And private conservation organizations, such as land trusts and conservancies, are also becoming important players. By 2005, more than seventeen hundred private conservation groups protected 37 million acres through ownership or easement.[38]

Perhaps none of these groups is as large or well known as The Nature Conservancy (TNC), which owns or holds easements on 5 million acres in the United States (although it has acquired a total of 21 million acres at one time or another).[39] In fact, TNC is so well established that privatizers often single it out as an example of how private conservation can and should work after the federal domain is liquidated. Given that three-quarters of the land that TNC has acquired over the years have eventually been transferred over to some unit of government, perhaps this organization is not the model that privatizers make it out to be. TNC passes off the bulk of its acquisitions because, despite its impressive size, it simply does not have the wherewithal to manage an enormous system of protected land in the way that governments can. As a nonprofit, TNC operates on donations, and its holdings do not generate revenue, so how could this approach be scaled up to hundreds of millions of acres? Indeed, as earlier chapters showed, for all sorts of reasons, governments are the only entities capable of this scale of management.

TNC has become such an important player in the conservation realm because it is nimble, quick, and overloaded with scientific talent. As such, it can work to promptly identify threats, efficiently leverage significant resources, and move in to protect fragile and threatened sites of great biodiversity with a rapidity that lumbering government institutions may not be able to replicate. TNC eventually passes most of these sites on to governments for safekeeping while moving on to the next troubled hotspot. That pattern makes it the perfect partner for government, not its replacement.

Another public-private model that is beginning to appear is for the management of public land units to be given over to private trustees. Some units within California's Golden Gate National Recreation Area, including the famed Presidio, are already managed this way. The boldest experiment using this model came about in 2000, when Senator Pete Domenici (R-NM) reluctantly acquiesced to mounting pressure for the federal government to buy the Baca Ranch in New Mexico's spectacular Valles Caldera. But he did so only on the condition that this quasi-private management model be tried out. Consequently, special arrangements were built into the legislation authorizing the creation of the Valles Caldera National Preserve, which provided for a presidentially appointed board of trustees representing various stakeholders and a fiduciary duty to be financially self-sustaining.[40] Ultimately, though, the best this preserve could achieve toward this end while still fulfilling its mission and legal environmental mandates was to generate 28 percent of its budget; the plug was pulled on this experiment in 2014, and management was transferred by Congress to the National Park Service (NPS).[41] According to Melinda Benson, the board may have failed in its goal of economic self-sufficiency, but it actually performed its management duties quite well, with a collaborative scientific management approach. Ultimately, the board failed because it saw financial return as only one of its many mandated responsibilities, and, as Benson reminds us, "making money is not what public lands do best."[42]

PDRs, easements, and collaboration groups can be seen

as positive developments that give governments more tools to achieve conservation in times of scarce resources. Likewise, private conservation organizations can be seen as like-minded partners and collaborators working toward the same goals. Other aspects of this blurring line, however, are not necessarily so positive. For example, the privatizing of park operations is a growing trend that has some ominous portents. As previous chapters showed, many states have moved to outsource traditionally public functions, such as campground management, maintenance, and facilities operation. In some places, conservation functions are all that remain public, and even these are now in doubt.[43] In this upside-down world, the concessionaires call the shots, as we caught a glimpse of when a private company (Delaware North) trademarked the historic Yosemite place names of Ahwahnee (Lodge), Curry Village, and even the name Yosemite itself. When the concessionaire lost its contract, it tried to charge the NPS to continue to use the Ahwahnee and Curry Village names. Consequently, the NPS has had to drop those venerable names while it pursues the matter in the courts.[44]

Frozen, declining, or even disappearing budgets have also led park agencies to explore other versions of private-sector collaboration—most often some form of partnership whereby companies "adopt" or sponsor parks, park systems, or certain park functions in exchange for advertising displays, publicity, naming rights, or exclusive product placement in facilities. Given the trajectory of budget politics in the last decade, this trend is likely to intensify in coming years, as impossibly squeezed park managers have to turn to whomever they can to patch together the resources necessary to keep the bare minimum of services and operations afloat.

A corollary to private partnerships will likely be increases of existing user fees and the implementation of new ones for park entrance, parking, camping, and many other activities. In the face of declining or canceled general revenue support, fees become one of the few tools left for revenue generation, but agencies risk cutting off park access to vast chunks of the population should the prices rise too high. This trend is not just limited to state park systems, as in October 2017, the NPS announced it was raising entry fees to the most-visited parks in the system to $70.[45] Speaking of all these soft privatization trends, Leigh Raymond and Sally Fairfax worry that the shift will harm equal access to public lands and remove decision making from the reach of the public.[46]

Changing Lifestyles and Demographics

If public lands' greatest asset is the fact they are treasured by the public, then perhaps one of the more serious long-term threats would be if that support were to ever turn into indifference. This issue is relevant in terms of generational and other demographic changes that the country faces. By 2060, the Census Bureau projects that the United States will be a minority-majority country, with the share of non-Hispanic whites down to 43.6 percent of the population.[47] This fact is salient because a racial and ethnic gap currently exists regarding park usage, with only 21 percent of park visitors being people of color, according to 2011 NPS surveys.[48] African Americans constitute 14 percent of the U.S. population,[49] yet they make up only 7 percent of national park visitors.[50] For the U.S. Forest Service (USFS), the statistics are even more dire. Nonwhites in general account for only 12.6 percent of national forest visitors, and African Americans constitute only 1.2 percent of all forest visitors and 0.7 percent of wilderness visitors.[51] Former NPS Director Jonathan Jarvis explains why this distinction matters:

> Some of the things we are seeing now are symptoms of waning relevancy[: t]he flattening of our budget, sequestration cuts, the political pressures on the Park Service. . . . [W]e need to . . . make that connection with all people.[52]

The African American superintendent of Mesa Verde National Park, meanwhile, echoes his boss's notion:

> We can't allow millions of people, generations of people,
> to not experience parks and have no connection to them.
> When those people get into positions where they'll influ-
> ence policy and hold purse strings, they won't understand
> what parks are and how important they are.[53]

Jarvis and the superintendent suggest that if the American public circa 2060 does not have the same positive attitudes toward and experiences with public land that have bound past generations to it, the parks' vast constituency will weaken and possibly disintegrate, leaving public lands even more vulnerable than they are today. Because of this concern, the NPS and other agencies have begun to take this issue very seriously.

Analyses attempting to explain this demographic disconnect identify barriers ranging from geographic to economic to cultural, yet one thing is clear: an undeniable racial construction around outdoor recreation and federal parklands strongly sends the message that this is all a "white" activity most properly done by white people. This notion gets reinforced in countless ways, from past discrimination to advertising to the racial makeup of park rangers to the stories that are told about public lands and their heroes in popular culture, books, movies, and classrooms. But such observers as Carolyn Finney, Wayne Hare, and James Mills remind us that African Americans have been intimately tied to the land and have a rich, varied, and glorious history as conservationists, explorers, adventurers, and frontier soldiers— much of which, at least until recently, had been lost to what Hare calls an "un-coloring" of frontier history.[54] Finney argues that as parks and the outdoors were being culturally constructed as "white spaces" in a time of vicious segregation, African Americans became "psychologically divorced" from the natural world, and the alienation that exists today is a legacy of the "cognitive maps" drawn at that time.[55]

A cultural shift away from the outdoors may be driven not just by race or ethnicity but also by generational differences. In his seminal work *Last Child in the Woods*, psychologist Richard Louv finds that America's children, obsessed and distracted by technology and hemmed in by their parents' fears of traffic, strangers, and crime, suffer from what he coins *Nature Deficit Disorder*, leaving a generation of young people profoundly out of touch with the natural world.[56] Louv argues that this alienation from nature comes at severe social, psychic, spiritual, and physical costs, as children desperately need to play and explore in the natural world for healthy development.

Perhaps the most significant wedge in generational preferences, lifestyles, and mental habits has been the advent of the 24/7 digital world, which seems to offer nothing less than a portal into a virtual world separate from the physical, natural one. The journalist Timothy Egan worries that many of these young people in the millennial generation, with their short attention spans, need for constant connection, and altered perceptions of what is worthy of awe, might end up ultimately robbing public lands of their mass constituency.[57] The former NPS director Jarvis shares these concerns:

> Young people are more separated from the natural world than perhaps any generation before them. . . . There are times when it seems as if the national parks have never been more passé than in the age of the iPhone. The national parks risk obsolescence in the eyes of an increasingly diverse and distracted demographic.[58]

And despite record-breaking attendance for the national parks in recent years, NPS data show that millennials visit them at only two-thirds of their proportion of the overall population—the exact inverse of the baby boomers' visitation numbers.[59]

The irony of this situation is that millennials, as a generation, tend to show some of the strongest levels of support for environmental protection for any demographic category. For example, among eighteen- to twenty-nine-year-olds, 70 percent think stricter environmental laws and regulations are worth the cost, versus only 53 percent of fifty- to sixty-four-year-olds and 47 percent of those over sixty-five.[60] Furthermore, millennials support a strong government role in handling policy problems (62 percent versus 46 percent for nonmillennials), and, notably, their specific support for the *federal* government's fulfilling this role stands at 47 percent versus 30 percent for nonmillennials. Even conservative millennials report less-intense antipathy toward the federal government than do their older counterparts (26 percent supportive versus 10 percent).[61] What this generational data seem to suggest is that millennials' enhanced support for the environment and the government's role in protecting it might serve as a countervailing factor of sorts, balancing out whatever lifestyle preferences might keep younger people indoors.

Not everyone, however, is willing to concede that young people are a lost cause as an ardent future constituency of our public lands. Louv himself professes to be quite heartened by the incredible proliferation of initiatives and projects to get children outdoors that have sprung up in the decade since his book first caught notice.[62] These efforts, many quite tech-savvy, are organized at every level, from towns and school districts all the way up to federal agencies and even President Obama and the First Lady, who made this goal a personal priority through their "Every Kid in a Park" initiative. Speaking of this initiative, former Interior Secretary Sally Jewell expressed hope that "we'll have a whole generation of students whose love for public lands was sparked in fourth grade."[63]

Although these demographic gaps can seem daunting, a look at park visitation data since 1904 offers some wider perspective. In 1904, far less than 1 percent of the American public visited a national park, and it was not until the 1950s that the figure hit 10 percent. Since the 1980s, the figure has wavered between 20 percent and 30 percent, peaking in 1995.[64] If public lands have persevered through eras with far less visitation, then future drop-offs, if they occur and stay relatively modest, may not necessarily prove to sound the death knell. Meanwhile, state and local preserves, which exist much closer to where most people live and work, feature visitation figures that dwarf even the most popular federal lands. In fact, the fifty most-visited city parks have roughly the same annual visitation as the entire national park system,[65] while Busse Woods, a fairly ordinary

2,000-acre unit of the Cook County Forest Preserve District outside Chicago, receives 2.5 million annual visits, about the same as Glacier National Park.[66]

Climate Change, the 800-Pound Gorilla in the Room

A final trend that will influence the future of public land, and one that promises to have outsized impacts, is climate change. Many future scenarios of climate change focus the worst impacts on the West and the Southwest because of their already arid conditions, acute water shortages, and dependence on snowpack, and because major urban and agricultural development may have actually occurred during an unusually wet interval.[67] Climate change poses grave threats to the integrity of all public land in the West and beyond, with a possible future of cataclysmic fires, megadroughts, invasive species, floods, disease outbreaks, and rapid ecological change that will push managers and their expertise to the limits. In 2017, we caught a glimpse of how daunting these challenges will be in the brutal fire season in California and many other western states, which burned tens of millions of acres of public land and thousands of homes. Meanwhile, Hurricanes Irma and Maria, which caused catastrophic damage to the U.S. Virgin Islands and Puerto Rico, left the Virgin Islands National Park and El Yunque National Forest in Puerto Rico smashed to pieces.

In the face of such daunting challenges, federal land management agencies have had mandated adaption programs in place since at least 2001.[68] In their surveys of federal land managers, however, Kelli Archie et al. find that progress toward actually developing and implementing such climate adaptation plans has been somewhat spotty. Only 29 percent of those managers surveyed reported that their offices were currently engaged in adaptation planning or implementation.[69] Among specific agencies, the authors find that the USFS and the USFWS were doing best, with about half reporting that they were developing or carrying out plans; the USFWS was the furthest along in actual implementation. By contrast, 60 percent of BLM and 78 percent of NPS personnel were not yet developing plans, or at least not aware of any.[70] The most commonly reported barriers to adaptation were lack of relevant information and budget constraints.[71]

A 2010 Resources for the Future report on climate-change adaptation for public lands recommends an increased focus on coordination and collaboration across jurisdictions, holistic approaches to adaptive ecosystem management, and enhanced monitoring and vulnerability assessment.[72] The report's authors find that the fragmentation of federal management will likely hinder effective responses and might, therefore, require some pretty drastic rebalancing of local and national interests. Consequently, they call for greater centralization of federal environmental management, including a unified Department of Natural Resources (which would include all land management agencies, the National Oceanic and Atmospheric Administration, and the Environmental Protection Agency) as well as a new agency—the National Climate Service—to take the lead in research and coordination.[73]

As species shift by latitude and altitude, adaptive management raises all sorts of potentially fraught questions regarding the most appropriate practices, making the already difficult task of natural resource management infinitely more so.[74] For example, a major goal of land managers has been the restoration of impaired land to a healthy functioning semblance of a previous ecological community before settlement and disturbance. But what if that previous regime was based on assumptions of a static and stable climate? In other words, what does the manager restore the land to: what it was or what it is to become? And who exactly decides what it is to become? In the worst-case scenario, species might need relocation along with the replication of ecosystems on which they depend. This possibility will raise all sorts of nettlesome biological and ethical questions and will require incredible amounts of patience, humility, foresight, and creativity among land managers.

This scenario of rapid and damaging ecological change is undeniably dire, yet it also makes public lands that much more valuable. Given the ecological disruption that is inevitable, large blocks of contiguous, unfragmented landscapes will be more crucial than ever for the forces of nature to play out and organisms to adapt, whether with the help of managers or on their own. For example, flora and fauna will need to migrate to different, more-amenable climate zones or niches, and large tracts of habitat linked by corridors will be essential. Species trapped in fragmented, isolated little parcels will likely face a death sentence if confronted by rapid ecological change.[75] In this context, the size and integrity of wild landscapes will determine their resilience.

Also, wild landscapes will generally have much-greater carbon-storage capacities (see Chapter 3), which will become increasingly vital in ensuring no further aggravation of an already-harmful carbon balance. Those large, intact public forests that can survive a warming planet will become a critical asset, and all ecosystem services produced on public lands will take on heightened importance on a stressed planet. These large, contiguous public habitats will also provide a baseline of sorts for vital ongoing scientific research.[76] Finally, the vast tracts of public land, especially BLM range and desert lands in the sunny Southwest, provide prime and readily available sites for massive alternative-energy projects, such as the Ivanpah Solar Electric Generating System in California's Mojave Desert, which at 392 megawatts is the world's largest solar-thermal facility.[77]

Conclusion: What Are Our Public Lands For?

The purpose of this book is to make a broad and vigorous case that public lands in the United States are a unique treasure and the envy of the world, and, as such, American citizens are extraordinarily fortunate to have them. This argument has been articulated on all sorts of grounds: biological, cultural, aesthetic, economic, psychological, and political. Some of these arguments, such as the ecosystem services framework and the notion of collective moral/value preference, might even be philosophically at odds, to some extent. But all are very important to articulate for this reason: by any measure, for any one of a number of reasons, privatizing public land is a spectacularly bad and harmful policy that will enrich the few at the expense of the many.

To answer the question "What are public lands for?" is to acknowledge that one-third of our nation's landmass cannot be for any one thing or to serve any one purpose. Rather, different units of land, controlled by different agencies and jurisdictions under different mandates and procedures, social needs, and pressures are managed in a variety of ways for a variety of purposes. They provide critical and otherwise unavailable habitats for precious biodiversity. They churn out trillions of dollars of ecological services, generally unpriced yet vital to life. They provide recreation and aesthetic wonders that undergird entire regional economies. They provide stable access to such resources as timber, minerals, energy, and pasture that also support local economies. They also provide untold intangible benefits: wonder, reverence, solitude, psychological and physical health, history, national and community pride, connections to land and place, and an intergenerational continuity in an increasingly turbulent and confusing world. And the annual cost to manage the federal portion of this bounty, which spreads across nearly a third of our landmass, is approximately the cost of a hundred F-35 fighter jets.[78] Equally important, the decisions that determine and prioritize these uses, while often fraught, messy, complicated, and polarizing, are generally made by talented and committed professionals through open, accessible, and accountable processes on behalf of and in dialogue with the people of the nation, state, county, or municipality that owns the land. Despite privatizers' fanciful promises of economic growth, better decision making, and more environmental productivity, the only real guarantee that we can extrapolate from their demands is that something infinitely precious and invaluable will be taken from the many and given to a privileged and well-connected few to use however they see fit, without any say from the rest of us. One more guarantee: any society that gives up such an endowment, which can never again be reassembled, is certain to profoundly regret it and curse the day it was lost.

FOLLOWING PAGE: Moses Creek Conservation Area, Florida. *(Photo by the author.)*

Notes

PREFACE

1. Steven Davis, "The Politics of Urban Natural Management at the Local Level: A Case Study," *Kentucky Journal of Equine, Agricultural, and Natural Resources Law* 2, no. 2 (2010): 136nn58, 63.

2. U.S. Census Bureau, *Largest Urbanized Areas with Selected Cities and Metro Areas*, available at https://www.census.gov/dataviz/visualizations/026/508.php

3. For example, in 2012, Wisconsin's budget under Governor Scott Walker required the state Department of Natural Resources (DNR) to identify and sell 10,000 acres of state land by 2017; also in 2017, Oregon came within inches of privatizing the 82,500-acre Elliott State Forest. Only after massive public outcry did the state reverse course. Lisa Speckhard, "Wisconsin DNR Identifies 128 Properties to Sell, 12 in Dane County," *Wisconsin State Journal*, June 27, 2016; Rob Davis, "Oregon Takes Big Step toward Privatizing Elliott State Forest," *The Oregonian*, February 15, 2017; Anna Smith, "Oregon Keeps the Elliott State Forest Public," *High Country News*, May 11, 2017.

4. Charles Goodsell, *The Case for Bureaucracy* (Washington, DC: CQ Press, 2004).

CHAPTER 1

1. Wallace Stegner, "The Best Idea We Ever Had," in *Marking the Sparrow's Fall: The Making of the American West*, ed. Page Stegner (New York: Henry Holt, 1998), p. 137.

2. Scott Lehmann, *Privatizing Public Land* (New York: Oxford University Press, 1995), p. 31.

3. Ibid., pp. 31–32.

4. Ibid., pp. 32–33.

5. Ibid., p. 33.

6. Ibid.; Jodi Stemler, "Our Public Lands: Not for Sale," *Backcountry Hunters and Anglers Report*, November 2014, p. 9.

7. Peter W. Culp et al., *State Trust Lands in the West* (Lincoln Institute of Land Policy Report, 2015), pp. 7–12, available at http://www.lincolninst.edu/sites/default/files/pubfiles/state-trust-lands-in-the-west-updated-full.pdf.

8. Paul Frymer, "A Rush and a Push and the Land Is Ours: Territorial Expansion, Land Policy, and U.S. State Formation," *Perspectives on Politics* 12, no. 1 (March 2014): 119–147.

9. For some examples of how important publicity was in solidifying support for the national parks, see Dayton Duncan and Ken Burns, eds., *The National Parks: America's Best Idea* (New York: Knopf, 2011), pp. 139–144, 147–148, 161–163.

10. Lehmann, *Privatizing Public Land*, p. 36.

11. For a good overview of this period, see Douglas MacCleery, *American Forests: A History of Resiliency and Recovery* (Durham, NC: Forest History Society, 2011), pp. 13–28.

12. Ibid., p. 38.

13. David M. Wrobel, "The Closing Gates of Democracy: Frontier Anxiety before the Official End of the Frontier," *American Studies* 32 (Spring 1991): 50.

14. An interesting and important footnote to this period in federal land history is the crucial role played by African American cavalry (the famed "Buffalo Soldiers") in patrolling and protecting some of the early national park units before any federal agency had been created to formally oversee them. James Mills, *The Adventure Gap* (Seattle: Mountaineers Books, 2014), pp. 65–68.

15. Patricia Nelson Limerick, "A History of the Public Lands Debate," in *Challenging Federal Ownership and Management: Public Lands and Public Benefits* (University of Colorado Law School, Boulder, October 11–13, 1995), pp. 12–15, available at http://scholar.law.colorado.edu/challenging-federal-ownership-management/2.

16. William Shands, "The Lands Nobody Wanted: The Legacy of the Eastern National Forests," in *The Origins of the National Forests*, ed. Harold Steen (Durham, NC: Duke University Press, 1992), p. 23.

17. Sarah Saetre, "Chequamegon National Forest: The Making of a Forest" (unpublished manuscript, 1983), on file at the Supervisor's Office of the Chequamegon-Nicolet National Forest, Rhinelander, WI.

18. Shands, "The Lands Nobody Wanted," pp. 24–25. The most infamous of these fires started after a hot and droughty summer and autumn, on October 8, 1871, near the town of Peshtigo, Wisconsin, on the same day as the Great Chicago Fire. It soon flared into the largest and deadliest fire in North American history, consuming an estimated 1.2 million acres and

completely destroying the town of Peshtigo and several others. The death toll was estimated at between 1,200 and 2,400 people. Kim Estep, "Tales of Heroism and Tragedy Swirl around Fire," *Green Bay Press Gazette*, November 2, 1999; Deana C. Hipke, *The Great Peshtigo Fire of 1871* (2001), available at www.peshtigofire.info/.

19. Samuel Hayes, *Conservation and the Gospel of Efficiency* (Cambridge, MA: Harvard University Press, 1959).

20. John Loomis, *Integrated Public Lands Management* (New York: Columbia University Press, 1993), pp. 26–27.

21. Ibid.

22. Thomas More, "Privatization of Public Lands," in *Proceedings of the 2006 Northeastern Recreation Research Symposium* (U.S. Department of Agriculture, Forest Service Report, GTR-NRS-P-14, 2006), p. 136.

23. Mark Spence, *Dispossessing the Wilderness: Indian Removal and the Making of the National Parks* (New York: Oxford University Press, 1999), p. 139.

24. Leigh Raymond and Sally Fairfax, "The 'Shift to Privatization' in Land Conservation: A Cautionary Essay," *Natural Resources Journal* 42 (Summer 2002): 602.

25. In particular, the naturalist and explorer John Muir and the industrialist Stephen Mather, who went on to become the agency's first director. For a good review of the NPS's formative years, see Duncan and Burns, *The National Parks*.

26. It was not until the passage of the Federal Land Policy Management Act of 1976, however, that Congress finally cast permanent retention as the official policy for the remaining federal domain. Joseph Sax, "The Legitimacy of Collective Values: The Case of the Public Lands," *University of Colorado Law Review* 56 (1984): 538. For further discussion of the New Deal era's effect on public land policy, see Randall Wilson, *America's Public Lands* (Lanham, MD: Rowman and Littlefield, 2014), pp. 50–51.

27. Jeanne Nienaber Clarke and Daniel McCool, *Staking Out the Terrain* (Albany: State University of New York Press, 1996), p. 191.

28. Ross Gorte et al., *Federal Land Ownership: Overview and Data* (Congressional Research Service Report R42346, February 8, 2012), p. 19.

29. For an overview of this process, see Shands, "The Lands Nobody Wanted."

30. Steven Davis, "The Forests Nobody Wanted: The Politics of Land Management in the County Forests of the Upper Midwest," *Journal of Land Use and Environmental Law* 28, no. 2 (Spring 2013): 201–203.

31. Limerick, "A History of the Public Lands Debate," p. 10.

32. Wilson, *America's Public Lands*, pp. 3–4.

33. Steven Davis, "Preservation, Resource Extraction, and Recreation on Public Lands: A View from the States," *Natural Resources Journal* 48 (Spring 2008): 305.

34. Gerald Williams, *The USDA Forest Service—the First Century* (U.S. Department of Agriculture, Forest Service Report FS-650, April 2005), p. 31.

35. Regarding rising postwar demand and federal timber production, see MacCleery, *American Forests*, pp. 41–47; for data on reductions in south-

ern timber production, see John Fedkiw, *Managing Multiple Use on National Forests 1905–1995* (U.S. Department of Agriculture, Forest Service Report FS-628, 1998), pp. 45–70.

36. U.S. Department of Agriculture, Forest Service, *FY 1905–2014 National Summary Cut and Sold Data and Graphs*, November 2014, available at http://www.fs.fed.us/forestmanagement/documents/sold-harvest/docu ments/1905-2014_Natl_Summary_Graph.pdf.

37. This argument is made, most prominently, in the classic Phillip O. Foss, *Politics and Grass* (Seattle: University of Washington Press, 1960).

38. Elise Jones and Cameron Taylor, "Litigating Agency Change: The Impact of the Courts and the Administrative Appeals Process on the Forest Service," *Policy Studies Journal* 23, no. 3 (Summer 1995): 311–314.

39. Ibid., pp. 329–331.

40. Ibid., pp. 331–334.

41. See, for example, Steven L. Yaffee et al., *Ecosystem Management in the United States* (University of Michigan School of Natural Resources Report, November 15, 1995); Craig W. Thomas, *Bureaucratic Landscapes* (Boston: Massachusetts Institute of Technology Press, 2003); Hanna Cortner and Margaret Moote, *The Politics of Ecosystem Management* (Washington, DC: Island Press, 1998).

42. In fact, in Pennsylvania's state forests alone, 1,020 natural wells and accompanying infrastructure have been approved, and 608 of those were drilled on leases totaling 132,000 acres of state forest land. In 2015, Governor Tom Wolf declared a moratorium on all new wells on public land. Jon Hurdle, "Marcellus Producers on State Land Pulled Back Again in 2014, Data Show," *State Impact Pennsylvania* (National Public Radio Special Reporting Project, July 23, 2015), available at https://stateimpact.npr.org/ pennsylvania/2015/07/23/marcellus-producers-on-state-land-pulled-back- again-in-2014-data-show/; Susan Phillips, "Gov. Wolf Bans New Drill- ing in State Parks and Forests," *State Impact Pennsylvania*, January 29, 2015, available at https://stateimpact.npr.org/pennsylvania/2015/01/29/gov-wolf- bans-new-drilling-in-state-parks-and-forests/.

43. The figures for federal acreage are from Gorte et al., *Federal Land Ownership*, p. 3; state acreage figures are from Davis, "Preservation, Resource Extraction, and Recreation on Public Lands," p. 307.

44. It is important to note that these numbers are somewhat fluid. Although the federal government's policy of large-scale disposal has ended, it sometimes stills occurs on a smaller scale, such as when a military base closes or the BLM transfers some lands to the state of Alaska, as required by law. Furthermore, exact acreage controlled by the four main federal land management agencies is fluid, as land is sometimes transferred by Congress or, more often, by executive order between jurisdictions (for example, BLM or USFS land becoming national monuments in the NPS).

45. Gorte et al., *Federal Land Ownership*, pp. 3, 13.

46. U.S. Department of the Interior, Bureau of Indian Affairs, *About Us*, available at https://www.bia.gov/about-us.

47. Gorte et al., *Federal Land Ownership*, p. 19.

48. Timothy Egan, *The Big Burn* (Boston: Mariner, 2009), p. 79.

49. Most monuments are administered by the NPS, but in 1996, President Clinton invoked the Antiquities Act to create the 1.9-million-acre Grand Staircase–Escalante National Monument out of BLM lands. However, for the first time, instead of being transferred to the NPS for management, a new national monument stayed under the BLM's control. This model has been used subsequently, so that the BLM now also manages its own portfolio of national monuments.

50. Gorte et al., *Federal Land Ownership*, p. 9.

51. Clarke and McCool, *Staking Out the Terrain*, p. 109.

52. Robert Fischman, "The Significance of National Wildlife Refuges in the Development of U.S. Conservation Policy," *Journal of Land Use and Environmental Law* 21, no. 1 (Fall 2005): 3–4.

53. Gorte et al., *Federal Land Ownership*, p. 8. The agency also oversees an additional 418 million acres of national marine monuments, which, as areas of open ocean, generally are not considered part of America's public land domain. U.S. Department of the Interior, U.S. Fish and Wildlife Service webpage, available at www.fws.gov/refuges/.

54. Fischman, "The Significance of National Wildlife Refuges," pp. 15–22.

55. In fact, only 388,054 acres, or 0.1 percent of BLM land, exist outside the twelve states of the West. Gorte et al., *Federal Land Ownership*, pp. 10, 19.

56. Lehmann, *Privatizing Public Land*, pp. 43–44.

57. Ibid.

58. The Wilderness Act, Public Law 88-577 (16 U.S. C. 1131–1136) 88th Cong., 2nd Sess. (September 3, 1964), available at http://wilderness.nps.gov/document/wildernessAct.pdf.

59. Gorte et al., *Federal Land Ownership*, pp. 13–14.

60. Ibid.

61. James Morton Turner, *The Promise of Wilderness* (Seattle: University of Washington Press, 2012), p. 1.

62. U.S. Department of Agriculture, Forest Service, *RARE II Final Environmental Statement Roadless Area Review and Evaluation* (Report FS-325, January 1979).

63. Turner, *The Promise of Wilderness*, p. 31.

64. See, for example, Joan Nice, "RARE II Tables Turn; Conservationists Enraged," *High Country News*, June 30, 1978.

65. Michael Anderson, *The Roadless Rule: A Tenth Anniversary Assessment* (Wilderness Society, 2011), available at https://wilderness.org/sites/default/files/Roadless-Rule-paper-10th-anniversary.pdf.

66. Ibid., pp. 4–6.

67. Clarke and McCool, *Staking Out the Terrain*, chaps. 1, 3, 6.

68. Davis, "Preservation, Resource Extraction, and Recreation on Public Lands," p. 307.

69. Stephanie Bertainta et al., *Collaborative Planning on State Trust Lands* (master's thesis, University of Michigan, School of Natural Resources and Environment, 2006), pp. 9–10. In fact, Alabama, with 45,000 acres; Wis-

consin, with 78,000; Mississippi, with 642,000; and Minnesota, with 2.5 million acres are the only eastern states with any school-trust land remaining. Davis, "Preservation, Resource Extraction, and Recreation on Public Lands," p. 307.

70. Montana, for example, has 5.2 million acres of state-trust land splintered among 16,000 individual parcels. Melinda Bruce and Teresa Rice, "Controlling the Blue Rash: Issues and Trends in State Land Management," *Land and Water Law Review* 29, no. 1 (1994): 6–7. For reasons of cost and efficiency, states often try to swap comparable land tracts with neighboring owners, public and private, to consolidate some of these fragments.

71. See Davis, "Preservation, Resource Extraction, and Recreation on Public Lands," for a fuller description of this framework.

72. Ibid.

73. Ibid., pp. 310–311.

74. U.S. Census Bureau, *Local Governments and Public School Systems by Type and State: 2007*, October 26, 2012, available at http://www.census.gov/govs/cog/GovOrgTab03ss.html.

75. This overall figure, however, does include some county lands located within city limits. Peter Harnik, Abby Martin, and Tim O'Grady, *2014 City Park Facts* (Trust for Public Land, February 2014), pp. 2–8.

76. Ibid. p. 9.

77. Davis, "The Politics of Urban Natural Management at the Local Level," p. 130.

78. These would include Harris County, Texas; Santa Clara, California; Montgomery, Maryland; King, Washington; Hillsborough, Florida; San Diego, California; Riverside, California; and Jackson, Missouri. Ibid.

79. Davis, "The Forests Nobody Wanted," pp. 197–199.

80. This "guesstimate" is largely drawn from the acreage of the one hundred largest urban park systems from the Trust for Public Land report by Harnik, Martin, and O'Grady, *2014 City Park Facts*, plus the acreage for the largest county park systems (see Davis, "The Politics of Urban Natural Management at the Local Level"), plus 5.4 million acres of county forests (see Davis, "The Forests Nobody Wanted").

81. Limerick, "A History of the Public Lands Debate," pp. 12–13.

82. Ibid.

83. Ibid., p. 3.

84. Bernard DeVoto, quoted in Christopher Ketcham, "The Great Republican Land Heist," *Harper's*, February 2015, p. 24.

85. Bernard DeVoto, "The West against Itself," *Harper's*, January 1947, p. 10.

86. Robert Nelson, *Public Land and Private Rights: The Failure of Scientific Management* (Lanham, MD: Rowman and Littlefield, 1995), p. xviii.

87. Ronald Reagan, quoted in R. McGreggor Cawley, *Federal Land and Western Anger: The Sagebrush Rebellion and Environmental Politics* (Lawrence: University of Kansas Press, 1993), p. 3.

88. More, "Privatization of Public Lands," p. 135.

89. Cawley, *Federal Land and Western Anger*, chap. 6.

90. Lehmann, *Privatizing Public Land*, p. 45.

91. For a manifesto of the Wise Use movement, see Ron Arnold, "Overcoming Ideology," in *A Wolf in the Garden: The Land Rights Movement and the New Environmental Debate*, ed. Philip Brick and R. McGreggor Cawley (Lanham, MD: Rowman and Littlefield, 1996), pp. 15–26. For a fuller accounting of how Wise Use and Property Rights Movements politics played out across many realms, see John Echeverria and Raymond Eby, *Let the People Judge: Wise Use and the Private Property Rights Movement* (Washington, DC: Island Press, 1995).

92. Such incidences would include the firebombing of a USFS rangers' district office in Nevada in 1995, the firebombing of a USFS employee's van in the driveway of his home, and county officials' illegal bulldozing of a road into a restricted federal area. See, for example, Ketcham, "The Great Republican Land Heist"; David Helvarg, *The War against the Greens* (San Francisco: Sierra Club Books, 1997); Ray Ring and Marshall Swearingen, "Reports from the Front Lines: Excerpts from Official Accounts of Threats against U.S. Forest Service and BLM Employees," *High Country News*, October 27, 2014; Florence Williams, "The Shovel Rebellion," *Mother Jones*, January/February 2001.

93. Helvarg, *The War against the Greens*, pp. 185–187.

94. "I don't know why," said presidential candidate Mitt Romney on the campaign trail in Nevada in 2012, "the government owns so much of this land." Joel Bleifuss, "GOP Land Grab," *In These Times*, August 25, 2012.

95. Jodi Peterson, "This Year's GOP Platform Pushes Federal Land Transfers," *High Country News*, July 14, 2016.

96. Cliven Bundy acted on the grounds that neither the federal courts nor the federal government had any authority over him or the authority to own the BLM land his cattle grazed on. For five years, Bundy routinely and illegally grazed his cattle on protected desert tortoise habitat. When the standoff occurred in April 2014, many militants took up positions on an overpass bridge and blocked Interstate 15, training their sniper rifles and automatic weapons on the federal agents below. Jaime Fuller, "The Long Fight between the Bundys and the Federal Government, from 1989 to Today," *Washington Post*, January 4, 2016. Because of this standoff, Bundy emerged a hero of the right, lionized on Fox News, hailed by Nevada's Republican governor and U.S. senator, and even visited by Senator Rand Paul (R-KY). All this support and adoration continued until Bundy suggested in a news interview that maybe slavery was not so bad and that "the Negro" today might be better off in slavery. As quickly as he had been hailed as a hero, he became radioactive. Adam Nagourney, "A Defiant Rancher Savors the Audience That Rallied to His Side," *New York Times*, April 23, 2014; Fuller, "The Long Fight between the Bundys and the Federal Government." There is an even darker side to this already sordid tale. Two participants in the April 14, 2014, standoff, Jerad and Amanda Miller, later died in a shootout with police after fatally ambushing two Las Vegas police

officers and a bystander while they ate lunch in a restaurant. A Gadsden flag ("Don't Tread on Me") was left draped over the officers' bodies. J. J. McNab, "What Las Vegas Police Killings Show about Evolving Sovereign Movement," *Forbes*, June 13, 2014. Assaults on and threats of violence toward BLM and USFS rangers are now common enough that the agencies require rangers to travel in pairs at all times in certain districts. Ketcham, "The Great Republican Land Heist," p. 24.

97. Carissa Wolf, Peter Holley, and Wesley Lowery, "Armed Men, Led by Bundy Brothers, Take Over Federal Building in Rural Oregon," *Washington Post*, January 3, 2016. A month into the standoff, most of the militants were intercepted on the highway by law enforcement officers on their way to a meeting in a neighboring county. One of them was killed in that encounter. The rest were arrested after long negotiations with the Federal Bureau of Investigation (FBI) within the next few weeks. Bundy, meanwhile, was arrested upon his arrival in Portland. Sarah Kaplan, Adam Goldman, and Mark Berman, "FBI Blockades Oregon Wildlife Refuge after Arrests; Authorities, Occupation Leader Urge Group to Leave," *Washington Post*, January 27, 2016. Subsequently, in their federal trials, one group of occupiers was acquitted in October 2016. In a separate trial, several others were found guilty of conspiracy in March 2017. See Chapter 7, note 1. In December 2017, Bundy and his sons went free after a mistrial in the Nevada case.

98. Bill Willers, "Charter Forests: Privatizing the Public Domain," *Milwaukee Business Journal*, April 14, 2002.

99. More, "Privatization of Public Lands," p. 1.

100. Ibid.

101. Jenny Rowland, *The Rise to Power of the Congressional Anti-parks Caucus* (Center for American Progress Report, April 11, 2016).

102. List of legislation from Sarah Pizzo, *Valuing Our Western Public Lands* (National Wildlife Federation Report, July 2013), pp. 20–23; League of Conservation Voters, *2015 National Environmental Scorecard*, 2016; *Public Land Watch*, News Blog, available at http://www.publiclandwatch .org/news-blog.html; The Mountaineers, *2017 Public Lands Bills: A Legislative Trail Map*, available at https://www.mountaineers.org/conserve/ Hot-Button-Issues/2017-public-lands-bills/2017-public-land-bills#legisla tion-targeting—the-antiquities-act; Western Environmental Law Center, "House Logging Bill (HR 2936) Guts Federal Environmental Laws, Literally Privatizes Public Lands, Creates Logging Free-for-All" (press release, June 21, 2017), available at https://www.westernlaw.org/article/house-log ging-bill-hr-2936-guts-federal-environmental-laws-literally-privatizes- public-lands; Center for Biological Diversity, "Republicans Advance Bill to Lock In Trump's Elimination of Grand Staircase–Escalante National Monument" (press release, December 13, 2017), available at http://www .biologicaldiversity.org/news/press_releases/2017/grand-staircase-escalan te-house-bill-12-13-2017.php; Center for Biological Diversity, "Republicans to Advance Four Bills Attacking Climate, Public Lands" (press release, November 29, 2017), available at http://www.biologicaldiversity.org/news/ press_releases/2017/public-lands-11-29-2017.php.

103. Phil Taylor, "Federal Land? Some Westerners Say There's No Such Thing," *E & E News*, March 2, 2016.

104. Ibid., p. 21.

105. Eric Johnson, "Conservatives Split over U.S. Land Transfers to Western States," *Reuters*, August 20, 2016.

106. Jeff Mapes, "GOP Platform Supports Transferring Western Public Lands to States," Oregon Public Broadcasting, July 19, 2016, available at http://www.opb.org/news/series/election-2016/republican-platform-public-land-privatization/.

107. More, "Privatization of Public Lands," p. 2.

108. Margaret Walls, *Paying for State Parks: Evaluating Alternative Approaches for the 21st Century* (Resources for the Future Report, January 2013), pp. 4–10.

109. Holly Fretwell and Kimberly Frost, "State Parks' Progress toward Self-Sufficiency," (Property and Environment Research Center Report, October 2006); Linda Baker, "State Parks Seek Corporate Donors to Stay Open," *Governing*, August 2011.

110. Thomas More, "From Public to Private: Five Concepts of Park Management and Their Consequences," *George Wright Forum* 22, no. 2 (2005): 18.

111. Phillip Foss, quoted in Lehmann, *Privatizing Public Land*, p. 8.

CHAPTER 2

1. Richard Stroup and John Baden, *Natural Resources: Bureaucratic Myths and Environmental Management* (Cambridge, MA: Ballinger, 1983), p. xv.

2. Terry Anderson, Vernon Smith, and Emily Simmons, "How and Why to Privatize Federal Lands," *Policy Analysis* (CATO publication, No. 363, November 9, 1999), p. 2.

3. Joe Klein, quoted in Scott Lehmann, *Privatizing Public Land* (New York: Oxford University Press, 1995), p. 15.

4. Steve Hanke, "On Privatizing the Public Domain," in *Private Rights and Public Lands*, ed. Phillip Truluck (Washington, DC: Heritage Foundation, 1983), p. 88.

5. B. Delworth Gardner, "The Political Economy of Public Land Use," *Journal of Agricultural and Resource Economics* 22, no. 1 (1997): 13.

6. Stroup and Baden, *Natural Resources*, p. 3.

7. Thomas More, "Privatization of Public Lands," in *Proceedings of the 2006 Northeastern Recreation Research Symposium* (U.S. Department of Agriculture, Forest Service Report, GTR-NRS-P-14, 2006), p. 137.

8. Stroup and Baden, *Natural Resources*, pp. 4–5.

9. Terry Anderson and Donald Leal, "Free Market Environmentalism," in *Thinking about the Environment: Readings on Politics, Property and the Physical World*, ed. Matthew Cahn and Rory O'Brien (New York: Routledge, 1996), p. 243.

10. Robert Nelson, *Public Land and Private Rights: The Failure of Scientific Management* (Lanham, MD: Rowman and Littlefield, 1995), p. 97.

11. Richard Stroup, "Privatizing Public Lands: Market Solutions to Economic and Environmental Problems," *Public Land and Resources Review* 19 (1998): 90.

12. Holly Fretwell, *Federal Estate: Is Bigger Better?* (Property and Environment Research Center Report, Bozeman, MT, 2000), p. 7.

13. Anderson and Leal, "Free Market Environmentalism," p. 244.

14. Stroup, "Privatizing Public Lands," p. 92.

15. Garrett Hardin, "The Tragedy of the Commons," *Science* 162, no. 3859 (December 13, 1968): 1245.

16. Stroup and Baden, *Natural Resources*, pp. 42–43.

17. Ibid., p. 37.

18. Anderson and Leal, "Free Market Environmentalism," p. 245.

19. Stroup and Baden, *Natural Resources*, p. 125.

20. Anderson and Leal, "Free Market Environmentalism," p. 246.

21. Ibid.

22. Terry Anderson, "Back to the Future: Privatizing the Federal Estate," in *Challenging Federal Ownership and Management: Public Lands and Public Benefits* (University of Colorado Law School, Boulder, October 11–13, 1995), p. 4, available at http://scholar.law.colorado.edu/challenging-federal-ownership-management/9.

23. For an overview of this debate and some empirical evidence, see Sander M. de Bruyn, *Economic Growth and the Environment: An Empirical Analysis* (Dordrecht, Netherlands: Springer, 2000).

24. Matthew Kahn, *Green Cities: Urban Growth and the Environment* (Washington, DC: Brookings Institution Press, 2007).

25. Ben Twight, *Organization Values and Political Power: The Forest Service vs. Olympic National Park* (University Park: Pennsylvania State University Press, 1983).

26. Nelson, *Public Land and Private Rights*, pp. 50–51.

27. Ibid., p. xviii.

28. Ibid., p. 92.

29. Anderson and Leal, "Free Market Environmentalism," p. 246.

30. Nelson, *Public Land and Private Rights*, p. 35.

31. Ibid., p. 235.

32. Ibid., pp. 231–232; Theodore Lowi, *The End of Liberalism* (New York: W. W. Norton, 1979).

33. Nelson, *Public Land and Private Rights*, pp. 171–172.

34. Gardner, "The Political Economy of Public Land Use," p. 14.

35. Nelson, *Public Land and Private Rights*, p. xix.

36. Ibid., p. xx.

37. Gardner, "The Political Economy of Public Land Use," p. 12.

38. See, for example, David Truman, *The Governmental Process* (New York: Knopf, 1960); Robert Dahl, *Who Governs? Democracy and Power in an American City* (New Haven, CT: Yale University Press, 1961).

39. Terry Anderson and Donald Leal, "Rethinking the Way We Think," in *Debating the Earth*, ed. John Dryzek and David Schlosberg (Oxford: Oxford University Press, 2005), pp. 220–221.

40. Lehmann, *Privatizing Public Land*, pp. 190–191.

41. Stroup, "Privatizing Public Lands," p. 85

42. Joseph Sax, quoted in Lehmann, *Privatizing Public Land*, p. 156.

43. Stroup and Baden, *Natural Resources*, p. 40

44. Ibid., p. 2.

45. Ibid., p. 22.

46. Anderson, Smith, and Simmons, "How and Why to Privatize Federal Lands," p. 17.

47. Nelson, *Public Land and Private Rights*, p. 84.

48. Anderson, Smith, and Simmons, "How and Why to Privatize Federal Lands," p. 9.

49. Lehmann, *Privatizing Public Land*, p. 15.

50. Holly Fretwell and Shawn Regan, *Divided Lands* (Property and Environment Research Center Report, Bozeman, MT, March 2015), p. 13. There are actually some big differences between the BLM and the USFS in these budget figures. The BLM, with a lot more mineral and energy production on its land, actually has a five-year annual average net revenue of $3.18 billion (or $3.11 for every dollar spent), while the USFS has net expenses of $5.14 billion (or $0.10 for every dollar spent).

51. U.S. Department of the Interior, National Park Service, *Budget Justifications and Performance Information Fiscal Year 2015*, 2014, pp. Overview-37–38; Rec Fee-1.

52. Fretwell and Regan, *Divided Lands*, p. 12.

53. Ibid., pp. 9–10.

54. Stroup and Baden, *Natural Resources*, pp. 43–44.

55. Anderson, Smith, and Simmons, "How and Why to Privatize Federal Lands," p. 11.

56. Randall O'Toole, "Reforming Public Land Management with New Incentives," in *Challenging Federal Ownership and Management: Public Lands and Public Benefits* (University of Colorado Law School, Boulder, October 11–13, 1995), p. 1, available at http://scholar.law.colorado.edu/challenging-federal-ownership-management/13/.

57. Ibid., p. 2.

58. Stroup and Baden, *Natural Resources*, pp. 12–13.

59. Nelson, *Public Land and Private Rights*, p. 35.

60. Sally Fairfax, quoted in Robert Nelson, "Free the American West," *Los Angeles Times*, March 7, 2012.

61. Dale Oesterle, "Public Land: How Much Is Enough," *Ecological Law Quarterly* 23, no. 3 (June 1996): 524.

62. Nelson, *Public Land and Private Rights*, p. 209.

63. This includes 50 percent of soft wood timber, 30 percent of coal, 80 percent of silver, 12 percent of forage, and nearly 100 percent of nickel. Oesterle, "Public Land," p. 525.

64. Ibid., pp. 525–526.

65. John Loomis, *Integrated Public Lands Management* (New York: Columbia University Press, 1993), pp. 91, 98.

66. Anderson and Leal, "Free Market Environmentalism," p. 245.

67. Anderson, Smith, and Simmons, "How and Why to Privatize Federal Lands," pp. 13–14.

68. Ibid., p. 16.

69. Hanke, "On Privatizing the Public Domain," p. 86.

70. John Baden and Richard Stroup, "Saving the Wilderness: A Radical Proposal," *Reason*, July 1981, pp. 35–36.

71. Ibid. It is important to note that Baden and Stroup offer no real scientifically rooted definition of *compatible* resource development; instead, they use the term in a rather loose and offhand way.

72. Anderson, Smith, and Simmons, "How and Why to Privatize Federal Lands," p. 18.

73. Oesterle, "Public Land," pp. 563–570.

74. Nelson, *Public Land and Private Rights*, pp. 319–328.

75. Meghan Cornwall, *How Could Your Recreational Access Change if Federal Lands Were Controlled by the States?* (National Wildlife Federation Report, 2015), p. 7, available at http://www.ourpubliclands.org/sites/default/files/files/Access_Sheets_final.pdf

76. Oesterle, "Public Land," p. 559.

77. Anderson, Smith, and Simmons, "How and Why to Privatize Federal Lands," p. 12; Stroup and Baden, *Natural Resources*, p. 99.

78. Stroup and Baden, *Natural Resources*, p. 101.

79. O'Toole, "Reforming Public Land Management with New Incentives," pp. 4–5.

80. Nelson, *Public Land and Private Rights*, p. 86.

81. Ibid., p. 183.

82. There are a few exceptions, though. For example, as mentioned in the Preface, in Wisconsin, a 2013 state budget measure put in place by a stridently anti-public-sector legislature and governor required the state's Department of Natural Resources to identify and sell 10,000 acres of public land. Lee Bergquist, "DNR Move to Sell Prime Spring Ponds Outrages Trout Anglers," *Milwaukee Journal Sentinel*, August 19, 2015.

83. Nelson, *Public Land and Private Rights*, p. 242.

84. Marion Clawson, *The Federal Lands Revisited* (Baltimore: Resources for the Future, 1983), pp. 200–224.

85. If any wildlife would dare to live in stands of productive timber, as they sometimes have the habit of doing, the result, one would presume, would be a bidding war between well-capitalized corporate entities and nonprofit environmental organizations. The biological perspective on whether privatizers' ultratidy compartmentalization of uses is truly realistic is explored more fully in the next chapter.

86. Anderson, Smith, and Simmons, "How and Why to Privatize Federal Lands," p. 10. Apparently, bargaining and accommodation in the context of the market are good, but they are bad in the political context.

87. Ibid.

88. Holly Fretwell, *Do We Get What We Pay For?* (Property and Environment Research Center Report, Bozeman, MT, 1999), pp. 9–10.

89. Ibid., p. 16.

CHAPTER 3

1. Holly Fretwell, *Federal Estate: Is Bigger Better?* (Property and Environment Research Center Report, Bozeman, MT, 2000), p. 1.

2. Terry Anderson, Vernon Smith, and Emily Simmons, "How and Why to Privatize Federal Lands," *Policy Analysis* (CATO publication, No. 363, November 9, 1999), p. 2.

3. Deborah Moeller, *Privatize the Public Lands* (Nevada Policy Research Institute Bulletin, March 17, 2002).

4. Dale Oesterle, "Public Land: How Much Is Enough," *Ecological Law Quarterly* 23, no. 3 (June 1996), pp. 555, 568.

5. Robert Nelson, *Public Land and Private Rights: The Failure of Scientific Management* (Lanham, MD: Rowman and Littlefield, 1995), p. 76.

6. Steve Hanke and Barney Dowdle, "Privatizing the Public Domain," *Proceedings of the Academy of Political Science* 36, no. 3 (1987): 115.

7. This recalls the late economist Julian Simon, who, in the debate that followed the 1972 release of the Club of Rome's gloomy *Limits to Growth* report, insisted on measuring the health of the planet in terms of the price and output levels of strategic metals and minerals and human life span. Julian Simon, *The Ultimate Resource* (Princeton, NJ: Princeton University Press, 1981).

8. Cynthia Nickerson et al., *Major Uses of Land in the United States, 2007* (U.S. Department of Agriculture, Economic Research Service, ERS Report Summary, December 2011), available at https://www.ers.usda.gov/webdocs/publications/44625/11159_eib89_2_.pdf?v=41055.

9. For an accounting of some the environmental costs of U.S. agriculture, see Erin Tegtmeier and Michael Duffy, "External Costs of Agricultural Production in the United States," *International Journal of Agricultural Sustainability* 2, no. 1 (2004); Leo Horrigan, Robert Lawrence, and Polly Walker, "How Sustainable Agriculture Can Address the Environmental and Human Health Harms of Industrial Agriculture," *Environmental Health Perspectives* 110, no. 5 (May 2002); Doug Gurian-Sherman, *CAFOs Uncovered: The Untold Costs of Confined Animal Feeding Operations* (Cambridge, MA: Union of Concerned Scientists, 2008); Timothy Meehan et al., "Agricultural Landscape Simplification and Insecticide Use in the Midwestern United States," *Proceedings of the National Academy of Sciences* 108, no. 28 (2011): 11500–11505; Jennifer Blesh and Laurie Drinkwater, "The Impact of Nitrogen Source and Crop Rotation on Nitrogen Mass Balances in the Mississippi River Basin," *Ecological Applications* 23, no. 5 (July 2013): 1017–1035; Aaron Blair and Sheila Hoar Zahm, "Agricultural Exposures and Cancer," *Environmental Health Perspectives* 103, Suppl. (November 8, 1995): 205–208.

10. Tim Reiterman, "Farmers Finding It Harder to Let Valuable Land Lie Fallow," *Los Angeles Times*, April 1, 2007; John M. Pleasants and Karen S. Oberhauser, "Milkweed Loss in Agricultural Fields Because of Herbicide Use: Effect on the Monarch Butterfly Population," *Insect Conservation and Diversity* 6, no. 2 March 2013: 135–144; Josephine Marcotty, "Plowing Away the Prairie, at a Price," *Minneapolis Star Tribune*, September 24, 2012.

11. I am not necessarily saying this to indict farmers or to demand a less-productive agriculture; I am saying it merely to refute this central argument of the privatizers, which is that productivity is a sign of good health and that private owners, given the competitive market environment they face, can always be counted on to protect the natural resources on the land.

12. Richard Stroup and John Baden, *Natural Resources: Bureaucratic Myths and Environmental Management* (Cambridge, MA: Ballinger, 1983), p. 36.

13. Sylvia LeRoy, "Beyond the Public Park Paradigm," *George Wright Forum* 22, no. 2 (2005): 39.

14. Holly Fretwell et al., *Breaking the Backlog: 7 Ideas to Address the National Park Deferred Maintenance Problem* (Property and Environmental Research Center Report, Bozeman, MT, February 2016), pp. 5–6; LeRoy, "Beyond the Public Park Paradigm," p. 34.

15. LeRoy, "Beyond the Public Park Paradigm," p. 35.

16. Terry Anderson and Donald Leal, "Rethinking the Way We Think," in *Debating the Earth*, ed. John Dryzek and David Schlosberg (Oxford: Oxford University Press, 2005), p. 225.

17. For a discussion of some of these ecological injuries visited on public lands, see Fretwell, *Federal Estate*, pp. 6–7. Anderson, Smith, and Simmons go even further, seemingly blaming the NPS for the pollution that drifts into Great Smoky Mountains National Park and for development threats to the Spotsylvania National Battlefield. How exactly privatization would ameliorate either threat or, for that matter, how public ownership is responsible is never revealed. Anderson, Smith, and Simmons, "How and Why to Privatize Federal Lands," p. 6.

18. To a remarkable degree, privatizers rely on not only anecdotes over comparative data but also often some of the very same relatively tiny-scale anecdotes. For example, the case of Rosalie Edge, a Depression-era conservationist who founded a fairly small 2,500-acre bird refuge, Hawk Mountain Sanctuary, is repeatedly lauded as a case study of private conservation in pro-privatization literature, including the following: Fretwell, *Federal Estate*, p. 12; Anderson, Smith, and Simmons, "How and Why to Privatize Federal Lands," p. 7; Jonathan Alder, "Free and Green: A New Approach to Environmental Protection," *Harvard Journal of Law and Public Policy* 24, no. 2 (Spring 2001): 685; and Robert Smith, *Hawk Mountain Sanctuary Association* (Competitive Enterprise Institute, Private Conservation Case Study, April 1999). Similarly, it seems that almost every article Richard Stroup has ever written warrants a mention of the privately owned 26,000-acre Rainey Preserve in Louisiana, where the Audubon Society, which owns it, allows for limited oil drilling (making it an irresistible anecdote). See, for example, Stroup and Baden, *Natural Resources*, p. 29; Richard Stroup, "Privatizing Public Lands: Market Solutions to Economic and Environmental Problems," *Public Land and Resources Review* 19 (1998): 85.

19. For instance, the only hard data Stroup offers on this question is research on the relative rates of depreciation of public versus private buses. Stroup, "Privatizing Public Lands," p. 98.

20. Reed Noss and Allen Cooperrider, *Saving Nature's Legacy Island: Protecting and Restoring Biodiversity* (Washington, DC: Island Press, 1994), p. 5.

21. Bruce Stein et al., "State of the States," in *Precious Heritage: The Status of Biodiversity in the United States*, ed. Bruce Stein, Lynn Kutner, and Jonathan Adams (Oxford: Oxford University Press, 2000), p. 124.

22. Stephen Chaplin et al., "The Geography of Imperilment," in *Precious Heritage: The Status of Biodiversity in the United States*, ed. Bruce Stein, Lynn Kutner, and Jonathan Adams (Oxford: Oxford University Press, 2000).

23. None of this is to suggest that deserts or montane habitats do not have extremely valuable, even rich, biodiversity worth preserving, as they certainly do. It is just that when one measures relative biodiversity in terms of overall species density, certain areas, regardless of ownership, have relatively more or less.

24. David Wilcove et al., "Leading Threats to Biodiversity," in *Precious Heritage: The Status of Biodiversity in the United States*, ed. Bruce Stein, Lynn Kutner, and Jonathan Adams (Oxford: Oxford University Press, 2000).

25. Bruce Stein et al., "A Remarkable Array: Species Diversity in the United States," in *Precious Heritage: The Status of Biodiversity in the United States*, ed. Bruce Stein, Lynn Kutner, and Jonathan Adams (Oxford: Oxford University Press, 2000), p. 61.

26. Lawrence Master et al., "Vanishing Assets," in *Precious Heritage: The Status of Biodiversity in the United States*, ed. Bruce Stein, Lynn Kutner, and Jonathan Adams (Oxford: Oxford University Press, 2000), p. 101.

27. Wilcove et al., "Leading Threats to Biodiversity," p. 245.

28. These would be endangered status, threatened status, proposed species, and candidate species. Craig Groves et al., "Owning Up to Our Responsibilities: Who Owns the Lands Important for Biodiversity?" in *Precious Heritage: The Status of Biodiversity in the United States*, ed. Bruce Stein, Lynn Kutner, and Jonathan Adams (Oxford: Oxford University Press, 2000), pp. 275–300.

29. For federally listed species, 62 percent have a presence on private land, 59 percent on public land, and 58 percent on state land. Ibid., p. 281.

30. Ibid., p. 280.

31. Ibid., p. 282. This study, sponsored by The Nature Conservancy (TNC), separated TNC land from all other private land. TNC lands, which account for only 0.1 percent of U.S. land, contain an astonishing 3 percent of all imperiled species population occurrences. The missing quarter of occurrences in the overall distribution is due to indeterminate data.

32. Interestingly, Groves et al. find that, adjusted for overall acreage, the federal jurisdiction with the highest concentration of imperiled species is the U.S. Department of Defense (DOD; not even one of the big four land management agencies), followed by the USFS, the NPS, the U.S. Fish and Wildlife Service (USFWS), and last, the BLM. Much of this probably has to do with geography, hydrology, and topography. For example, almost all BLM lands are in arid parts of the West; 86 percent of USFWS acreage is in Alaska, with relatively few imperiled species; and the USFS and the DOD

tend to have much more acreage than the others in biodiverse regions like the Southeast, and in the DOD's case, Hawaii. Groves et al., "Owning Up to Our Responsibilities," p. 283.

33. Ibid., p. 281.

34. Ibid.

35. Ibid., p. 285.

36. Bradley Karkkainen, "Biodiversity and Land," *Cornell Law Review* 83, no. 1 (1997): 46.

37. Bruce A. Stein, Cameron Scott, and Nancy Benton, "Federal Lands and Endangered Species: The Role of Military and Other Federal Lands in Sustaining Biodiversity," *Bioscience* 58, no. 4 (April 2008): 346.

38. Karkkainen, "Biodiversity and Land," p. 53.

39. Jeremy Higgins, Gary Larson, and Kenneth Higgins, "Floristic Comparisons of Tallgrass Prairie Remnants Managed by Different Land Stewardships in Eastern South Dakota," in *Proceedings of 17th North American Prairie Conference* (Mason City, IA, 2001), pp. 23–24. Although the private sites had a slightly higher mean number of species (82 versus 79), this figure includes weed species and destructive invasives.

40. According to Gerould Wilhelm, a score of 35 or below does not meet the threshold for being considered a native prairie worth preservation efforts, while an FQI of 45 is considered the threshold for a "good" representative prairie, and a score of 60 and above marks "excellent" sites. Ibid., p. 24.

41. Ibid.

42. Jeremy Higgins, Gary Larson, and Kenneth Higgins, "Managing Tallgrass Prairie Remnants: The Effects of Different Types of Land Stewardship on Grassland Bird Habitat," *Ecological Restoration* 20, no. 1 (March 2002): 21.

43. Ibid., p. 20.

44. Michael Loring and John Workman, "The Relationship between Land Ownership and Range Condition in Rich County, Utah," *Journal of Range Management* 40, no. 4 (July 1987): 291–293.

45. Thomas Spies et al., "Potential Effects of Forest Policies on Terrestrial Biodiversity in a Multi-ownership Province," *Ecological Applications* 17, no. 1 (2007): 48–65.

46. The authors credit dramatic changes in federal forest policy in the 1990s for the trajectory toward enhanced biodiversity that these forests are headed for. The decades-long political battle over the spotted owl led to court injunctions on logging federal forests in the Pacific Northwest and eventually, in 1994, to the Northwest Forest Plan, which served to reduce annual harvests in federal forests in the Pacific Northwest by 80 to 90 percent. Ibid., pp. 50, 53.

47. Ibid., p. 57.

48. Thomas Eichner and Ruediger Pethig, "Economic Land Use, Ecosystem Services and Microfounded Species Dynamics," *Journal of Environmental Economics and Management* 52, no. 3 (November 2006): 707.

49. Denis White et al., "Assessing Risks to Biodiversity from Future Landscape Change," *Conservation Biology* 11, no. 2 (April 1997): 352.

50. Ibid., pp. 355–356.

51. Mark Bryer, "More than a Sum of the Parts," in Stein, Kutner, and Adams, *Precious Heritage*, p. 203.

52. Stein et al., "A Remarkable Array," pp. 80–81.

53. Bryer, "More Than a Sum of the Parts," p. 234.

54. Groves et al., "Owning Up to Our Responsibilities," p. 288.

55. David W. Crumpacker et al., "A Preliminary Assessment of the Status of Major Terrestrial and Wetland Ecosystems on Federal and Indian Lands in the United States," *Conservation Biology*, March 1988, p. 111.

56. Groves et al., "Owning Up to Our Responsibilities," p. 290.

57. Ibid., p. 292.

58. Karkkainen, "Biodiversity and Land," p. 45.

59. Bryer, "More Than a Sum of the Parts," p. 235.

60. This might be because these lands were not the post-homesteading leftovers of the vast western domain; instead, they were pieced together through targeted purchases and acquisitions. As such, they zeroed in on places where one could get more "bang" for the conservation "buck."

61. Karkkainen, "Biodiversity and Land," pp. 44–45.

62. Savanna Oak Foundation, "Geography of Oak Savannas," *Oak Savannas: Characteristics, Restoration and Long-Term Management*, available at http://oaksavannas.org/geography.html.

63. For old-growth acreage estimates, see Eliot Norse, *Ancient Forests of the Pacific Northwest* (Washington, DC: Island Press, 1990), pp. 245–248; National Commission on Science for Sustainable Forestry (NCSSF), *Beyond Old Growth: Older Forests in a Changing World* (NCSSF, 2008), pp. 12, 36.

64. NCSSF, *Beyond Old Growth*, p. 26.

65. Janet Ohmann, Matthew Gregory, and Thomas Spies, "Influence of Environment, Disturbance, and Ownership on Forest Vegetation of Coastal Oregon," *Ecological Applications* 17, no. 1 (2007): 26.

66. The lower estimate is from Whit Bronaugh, "Congaree: Where the Trees Are Still Tall," *American Forests* 115, no. 2 (Summer 2009); the higher one is from Mary Davis (ed.), "Extent and Location," in *Eastern Old-Growth Forests: Prospects for Rediscovery and Recovery* (Washington, DC: Island Press, 1996), p. 21.

67. Robert Leverett, "Definitions and History," in *Eastern Old-Growth Forests: Prospects for Rediscovery and Recovery*, ed. Mary Davis (Washington, DC: Island Press, 1996), p. 8.

68. Reed F. Noss, Edward T. LaRoe III, and J. Michael Scott, *Endangered Ecosystems of the United States: A Preliminary Assessment of Loss and Degradation* (U.S. Department of the Interior, National Biological Service Report 28, February 1995), p. 69.

69. Estimates of remaining Wisconsin savanna and original savanna acreage are found in Wisconsin Department of Natural Resources, *Ecological Landscapes of Wisconsin* (Handbook 1805.1, Madison, WI, 2012), chap. 2,

pp. 17–19; David Sample and Michael Mossman, "Birds of Wisconsin Oak Savannas: Past, Present, Future," *Proceedings of the North American Conference on Savannas and Barrens* (Bloomington-Normal, IL, 1994).

70. World Wildlife Fund, *Upper Midwest Forest-Savanna Transition*, Ecoregion Inventory, available at http://www.worldwildlife.org/ecoregions/na 0415.

71. Heather Maldegen-Long, "Sand Dune Protection vs. Private Property Rights," *Michigan Green Law* (blog post, September 12, 2012), available at http://michigangreenlaw.com/sand-dune-protection-vs-private-proper ty-rights.

72. Wilcove et al., "Leading Threats to Biodiversity," p. 242

73. Karkkainen, "Biodiversity and Land," p. 7.

74. Frank Casey et al., *Incentives for Biodiversity Conservation: An Ecological and Economic Assessment* (Defenders of Wildlife Report, Washington, DC, 2006), p. 13.

75. Ralph Alig, "Society's Choices: Land Use Changes, Forest Fragmentation, and Conservation," *Science Findings* (U.S. Department of Agriculture, Forest Service, Pacific Northwest Research Station), no. 88 (November 2006): 2–3.

76. Sara Vickerman, *National Stewardship Initiatives: Conservation Strategies for U.S. Land Owners* (Defenders of Wildlife Report, Washington, DC, 1998), p. 8.

77. Much of this is drawn from island biogeography theory, which looks at how populations of species function on small islands under conditions of isolation and constraint. Robert H. MacArthur and Edward O. Wilson, *The Theory of Island Biogeography* (Princeton, NJ: Princeton University Press, 1967). Other studies finding various negative ecological impacts of fragmentation include Almo Farina, *Principles and Methods in Landscape Ecology: Towards a Science of the Landscape* (Dordrecht, Netherlands: Kluwer Academic Press, 2006); Christer Nilsson and Gunnell Grelsson, "The Fragility of Ecosystems: A Review," *Journal of Applied Ecology* 32, no. 4 (November 1995): 677–692; Lluis Brotons and Sergio Herrando, "Factors Affecting Bird Communities in Fragments of Secondary Pine Forests in the Northwestern Mediterranean Basin," *Acta Oecologica* 22 (2001): 1–11; William Laurance et al., "Rainforest Fragmentation Kills Big Trees," *Nature* 404 (April 20, 2001): 836.

78. Nick Haddad et al., "Habitat Fragmentation and Its Lasting Impact on Earth's Ecosystems," *Science Advances* 1, no. 2 (March 20, 2015): 5.

79. Ibid.

80. Ibid., p. 4.

81. For a fuller examination of *edge effects*, see Eben Broadbent et al., "Forest Fragmentation and Edge Effects from Deforestation and Selective Logging in the Brazilian Amazon," *Biological Conservation* 141 (2008): 1745–1757.

82. See, for example, Scott Robinson et al., "Management Implications of Cowbird Parasitism on Neotropical Migrant Songbirds," in *Sta-*

tus and Management of Neotropical Migratory Birds, General Technical Report RM-229, ed. Deborah Finch and Peter Stangel (Fort Collins, CO: U.S. Department of Agriculture, Forest Service, Rocky Mountain Forest and Range Experiment Station, 1993), pp. 93–102; Eric Gustafson et al., "Evaluation of Spatial Models to Predict Vulnerability of Forest Birds to Brood Parasitism by Cowbirds," *Ecological Applications* 12, no. 2 (April 2002): 412–426.

83. For more on this relationship between climate change and habitat fragmentation, see Paul Opdam and Dirk Wascher, "Climate Change Meets Habitat Fragmentation: Linking Landscape and Biogeographical Scale Levels in Research and Conservation," *Biological Conservation* 117, no. 3 (May 2004): 285–297.

84. Karkkainen, "Biodiversity and Land," p. 47.

85. Ibid., pp. 50–51n274.

86. Bill Cook, *Public Forest Ownership Has Many Implications* (Michigan State University Extension, blog post, June 5, 2012), available at http://msue.anr.msu.edu/news/public_forest_ownership_has_many_implications.

87. Wisconsin Department of Natural Resources, *Ecological Landscapes of Wisconsin*, p. C-73.

88. Kurt Riitters et al., "Fragmentation of Continental United States Forests," *Ecosystems* 5 (2002): 819, 821.

89. Kurt Riitters, John Coulston, and James Wickham, "Fragmentation of Forest Communities in the Eastern United States," in *Forest Ecology and Management* 263 (2012): 90.

90. Moeller, *Privatize the Public Lands*.

91. Karkkainen, "Biodiversity and Land," pp. 26–27.

92. Adrian Wydeven et al., "GIS Evaluation of Wolf Habitat and Potential Population in the Great Lakes States," in *Wisconsin Wolf Management Plan* (Madison: Wisconsin Department of Natural Resources, 1999), app. C, pp. 46–49.

93. "Meet Oregon's New Wolves: 77 Animals, 9 Packs, 26 New Pups" (KVAL TV news website, Eugene, OR, February 25, 2015), available at http://kval.com/news/local/meet-oregons-wolves-77-animals-9-packs-26-new-pups-11-12-2015.

94. Brenda McComb, Thomas Spies, and Keith Olsen, "Sustaining Biodiversity in the Oregon Coast Range: Potential Effects of Forest Policies in a Multi-ownership Province," *Ecology and Society* 12, no. 2 (2007): 9.

95. Ibid.

96. Robert Inman, "Wolverine Ecology and Conservation in the Western United States" (Ph.D. diss., Swedish University of Agricultural Sciences, Uppsala, 2013), pp. v, 11, available at https://www.nps.gov/grte/learn/nature/upload/2013-Wolveirne-Ecology-Conservation-in-Western-US-RM-Inman-Dissertation-cmprsd-opt.pdf.

97. Jodi Stemler, "Our Public Lands: Not for Sale," *Backcountry Hunters and Anglers Report*, November 2014, p. 10.

98. Cook, *Public Forest Ownership Has Many Implications*.

99. Scott Pearson, Monica Turner, and Jason Drake, "Landscape Change and Habitat Availability in the Southern Appalachian Highlands and Olympic Peninsula," *Ecological Applications* 9, no. 4 (November 1999): 1302.

100. Ibid.

101. John Sprankling, "The Antiwilderness Bias in American Property Law," *University of Chicago Law Review* 63, no. 2 (1996): 520.

102. This is to such an extent that it is nearly impossible to create a "nuisance" on wild land because any such nuisance is liable to be the sort of productive activity that the law privileges. Ibid., pp. 555–556.

103. U.S. Department of Agriculture, Forest Service, *Who Owns America's Forests?* (Northern Research Station, NRS-INF-06-08, May 2008), pp. 2–3.

104. It is reported, for example, that by 1890, only 80 acres of virgin timber remained standing in the entire state of Wisconsin. Gordon Robinson, *The Forest and the Trees* (Washington, DC: Island Press, 1988), p. 12.

105. Quoted in William Shands, "The Lands Nobody Wanted: The Legacy of the Eastern National Forests," in *The Origins of the National Forests*, ed. Harold Steen (Durham, NC: Duke University Press, 1992), p. 25. These lands, wrecked, abandoned, and tax delinquent, would go on to form the national, state, and county forests that dominate Wisconsin's North Woods today. USFS data show these New Deal–era eastern national forests more than doubling their standing timber volume between 1952 and 1986 as the restored forests began to take off.

106. For an epic and sweeping account of this transformation of the North American forest under white settlement, see Annie Proulx, *Barkskins* (New York: Simon and Schuster, 2016). Although this volume is a work of fiction, it presents a meticulously researched and very accurate history of North American logging and the timber industry across a four-hundred-year span.

107. See Douglas MacCleery, *American Forests: A History of Resiliency and Recovery* (Forest History Society, 2011), p. 41.

108. Nelson, *Public Land and Private Rights*, p. 58.

109. Terry Anderson, "Back to the Future: Privatizing the Federal Estate," in *Challenging Federal Ownership and Management: Public Lands and Public Benefits* (University of Colorado Law School, Boulder, October 11–13, 1995), p. 3, available at http://scholar.law.colorado.edu/challenging-federal-ownership-management/9; Stroup and Baden, *Natural Resources*, p. 111.

110. Robert Lindsey, "Ancient Redwoods Fall to a Wall St. Takeover," *New York Times*, March 2, 1988. MAXXAM's logging in the Headwaters forest prompted such a furious backlash, including activists' extensive and extended campaigns of tree sitting on wooden platforms high in the redwoods, that the federal government soon became involved. And after nearly a decade of negotiations, the government bought 7,500 acres of the oldest redwoods and allowed cutting, under sharp restrictions, on the remaining 220,000 acres of MAXXAM's land. Kathryn Jones, "Charles Hurwitz Is a Greedy Clear-Cutter, Charles Hurwitz Is a Caring Environmentalist," *Texas Monthly*, June 1999.

111. Colin Clark, quoted in Zachary Smith, *Environmental Policy Paradox*, 6th ed. (Upper Saddle River, NJ: Pearson, 2013), p. 10.

112. Stroup and Baden, *Natural Resources*, p. 45.

113. Nelson, *Public Land and Private Rights*, p. 221.

114. NCSSF, *Beyond Old Growth*, p. 12; Leverett, "Definitions and History," p. 4. The NCSSF, however, reminds us that forests do not exist in a simple old-growth/not-old-growth dichotomy; rather, they are arrayed along a continuum of complexity and maturity, with many forests that contain hundred-plus-year-old trees having some of the same biodiversity characteristics as true old growth (which they are on their way to becoming if left intact). Ibid., pp. 7–8. According to a federal interagency task force mandated to develop old-growth policy in the early 1990s, the term "old growth" refers to "a forest stand usually at least 180–220 years old with moderate to high canopy closure; a multilayered, multispecies canopy dominated by large overstory trees; [a] high incidence of large trees, some with broken tops and other indications of old and decaying wood (decadence); numerous large snags; and heavy accumulations of wood, including large logs on the ground." Jack Ward Thomas et al., *Forest Ecosystem Management: An Ecological, Economic, and Social Assessment Report of the Forest Ecosystem Management Assessment Team* (Forest Ecosystem Management Team Report, 1993), pp. ix-24.

115. NCSSF, *Beyond Old Growth*, pp. 9–11. For more specific studies on biodiversity regarding the herbaceous layer, amphibians, carnivores, and birds, see Albert Meier et al., "Biodiversity in the Herbaceous Layer and Salamanders in Appalachian Primary Forests," in *Eastern Old-Growth Forests: Prospects for Rediscovery and Recovery*, ed. Mary Davis (Washington, DC: Island Press, 1996), pp. 49–64; Michael Pelton, "The Importance of Old Growth to Carnivores in Eastern Deciduous Forests," in *Eastern Old-Growth Forests: Prospects for Rediscovery and Recovery*, ed. Mary Davis (Washington, DC: Island Press, 1996), pp. 65–75; J. Christopher Haney and Charles Schaadt, "Functional Roles of Eastern Old Growth in Promoting Forest Bird Diversity," in *Eastern Old-Growth Forests: Prospects for Rediscovery and Recovery*, ed. Mary Davis (Washington, DC: Island Press, 1996), pp. 76–88.

116. Ibid., p. 5.

117. Eric White and Ralph Alig, *Public and Private Forest Ownership in the Context of Carbon Sequestration and Bioenergy Feedstock Production* (U.S. Department of Agriculture, Forest Service, General Technical Report PNW-GTR-833, March 2010), pp. 149–151.

118. Holly Fretwell, *Do We Get What We Pay For?* (Property and Environment Research Center Report, Bozeman, MT, 1999), available at https://www.perc.org/articles/do-we-get-what-we-pay.

119. Fretwell, *Federal Estate*, p. 12; Holly Fretwell, *Is No Use Good Use?* (Property and Environment Research Center Report, Bozeman, MT, 2001), p. 19.

120. Stroup and Baden, *Natural Resources*, p. 116.

121. It should be noted, however, that climate change and punishing multiyear droughts in the West are also creating megafires that burn so hot and so wildly that not even ancient forests can escape their destruction.

122. For a fuller discussion of USFS fire policy, see Scott Stephens and Lawrence Ruth, "Federal Forest Fire Policy in the United States," *George Wright Forum* 22, no. 4 (2005): 57–77.

123. Sonja N. Oswalt et al., *Forest Resources of the United States, 2012: A Technical Document Supporting the Forest Service Update of the 2010 RPA Assessment* (U.S. Department of Agriculture, Forest Service, General Technical Report WO-91, October 2014), pp. 6, 153–156.

124. See for example, Robert Nelson, *A Burning Issue: A Case for Abolishing the U.S. Forest Service* (Lanham, MD: Rowman and Littlefield, 2000), or Fretwell, *Do We Get What We Pay For?*

125. It should be noted, however, that state forests and state-owned multiple-use lands, state-trust lands, and county forests actually tend to produce considerably more timber than national forests. See Steven Davis, "The Forests Nobody Wanted: The Politics of Land Management in the County Forests of the Upper Midwest," *Journal of Land Use and Environmental Law* 28, no. 2 (Spring 2013): 206–208.

126. Oswalt et al., *Forest Resources of the United States, 2012*, p. 52.

127. Oregon Wild, *BLM Practices vs. Oregon Forest Practices Act*, February 2012, available at http://static1.1.sqspcdn.com/static/f/797309/20751305/1351133236050/Oregon+Wild+BLM+Practices+VS+OFPA.pdf?token=ai5UBLoDNk7e3hYRVRZhzUNBWPs%3D.

128. U.S. Department of Agriculture, Forest Service, *Who Owns America's Forests?* p. 2.

129. A study of privatized county forests in Minnesota found that 78 percent of them have no management whatsoever. Ross Brown and Michael Kilgore, *Evaluating the Economic Impacts of Retention and Disposal Policies for County Tax–Forfeited Land in Northern Minnesota* (University of Minnesota Department of Forest Resources, Staff Paper Series No. 196, July 2008), p. 222.

130. Wisconsin Department of Natural Resources, *Ecological Landscapes of Wisconsin*, p. C-53.

131. See, for example, Peter Smallidge and Michael Greason, *Forestry Practices to Avoid: Just Say No to High-Grading, Selective Cutting, and Diameter-Limit Cutting* (Cornell Cooperative Extension, Ithaca, NY, January 29, 2003), available at https://blogs.cornell.edu/ccednrpublications/files/2015/03/Just-say-no-o3sws4.pdf.

132. There is a vigorous debate among environmentalists about whether to emphasize the restoration or preservation of nature and what the proper role of humans should be in relation to nature. Preservationism stresses the hubris and general destructiveness of human dominance over nature. Its dualistic way of seeing humans and the natural world is well reflected in the Wilderness Act of 1964 and in wilderness preservation in general. Most wholeheartedly support wilderness and the preservation of large intact

ecosystems, but restorationists find this philosophy ill-suited to the goal of caring for the land in the places closer to where most people live. To them, this requires nondualistic notions of humans as a part of nature as well as an intense hands-on, "interventionist" commitment to the active stewardship of natural areas that are less than pristine. This, they argue, is important not only to promote the ecological health of the land being managed but also to teach people to live more harmoniously in the natural world. For a good articulation of the restorationist ethos, see William Jordan III, "Restoration, Community and Wilderness," in *Restoring Nature: Perspectives from the Social Sciences and Humanities*, ed. Paul Gobster and R. Bruce Hull (Washington, DC: Island Press, 2000), pp. 21–36; Michael Pollan, *Second Nature: A Gardener's Education* (New York: Grove Press, 1991); and William Cronon (ed.), "The Trouble with Wilderness; or, Getting Back to the Wrong Nature," in *Uncommon Ground: Rethinking the Human Place in Nature* (New York: W. W. Norton, 1995), pp. 69–90. For a good counterargument, see Eric Katz, "Another Look at Restoration: Technology and Artificial Nature," in *Restoring Nature: Perspectives from the Social Sciences and Humanities*, ed. Paul Gobster and R. Bruce Hull (Washington, DC: Island Press, 2000), pp. 37–48.

133. Actually, there are probably only a few spots in all the United States that can still truly operate as fully functioning, integrated ecosystems: Alaska, central Idaho and adjacent parts of Montana, the Greater Yellowstone area, the Grand Staircase of Utah/Arizona, and possibly parts of the Cascades and Sierra Nevada.

134. Robert Keiter, *Keeping Faith with Nature: Ecosystems, Democracy, and America's Public Lands* (New Haven, CT: Yale University Press, 2003), pp. 127–130.

135. U.S. Department of Agriculture, Forest Service, *Fiscal Year 2016 Budget Overview*, February 2015, pp. 9–13.

136. See, for example, William Stevens, *Miracle under the Oaks* (New York: Pocket Books, 1995); Andrew Light, *The Humane Metropolis* (Amherst: University of Massachusetts Press, 2005).

137. Mark Sagoff, "Market versus Libertarian Environmentalism," *Critical Review* 6, nos. 2–3 (1992): 214.

138. Anderson and Leal, "Rethinking the Way We Think," p. 225.

139. Sandy Anderson, quoted in Oesterle, "Public Land," p. 563n203.

140. Anderson and Leal, "Rethinking the Way We Think," pp. 212–213.

141. Oesterle, "Public Land," p. 563.

142. Robert Pahre, "Privatizing Isle Royale? The Limits of Free Market Environmentalism," *George Wright Forum* 25, no. 3 (2008): 26.

143. Ibid., pp. 27–31.

144. Ibid., p. 29.

145. Ibid., p. 31.

146. Ibid., p. 36.

147. There is one very notable exception regarding private land: the relatively limited acreage of private land owned or leased and managed by

private conservation organizations and land trusts, such as TNC. For example, TNC owns a mere 0.1 percent of U.S. land, yet these tiny but extraordinarily rich fragments host 20 percent of federal-listed species (Groves et al., "Owning Up to Our Responsibilities, p. 284). Private conservation organizations are an intriguing alternative to public ownership and figure into the policy ideas and proposals of many privatizers. For a fuller discussion, see Chapter 7.

148. The Wilderness Society, *Forest FAQs*, available at www.wilder ness.org/article/forest-faqs; U.S. Department of Transportation, Federal Highway Administration, *Interstate Frequently Asked Questions*, November 18, 2015, available at www.fhwa.dot.gov/interstate/faq.cfm.

149. The era of megawater projects finally petered out in the 1960s, as a newly empowered environmental movement successfully mobilized to beat back projects that would, among other things, have drowned the Grand Canyon and Dinosaur Monument. The price for saving that last place was acquiescence to the building of the Glen Canyon Dam, which, to this day, many environmental groups consider to be among their most epic blunders, as the rarely visited canyon rivaled, and to some even exceeded, the Grand Canyon in its sublimity.

150. Edward Abbey, *Desert Solitaire* (New York: Ballantine, 1968), pp. 48–73.

151. Elinor Ostrom, *Governing the Commons: The Evolution of Institutions for Collective Action* (Cambridge: Cambridge University Press, 1990).

CHAPTER 4

1. John Loomis, *Integrated Public Lands Management* (New York: Columbia University Press, 1993), p. 90.

2. Ibid., p. 96.

3. Bradley Karkainnen, "Biodiversity and Land," *Cornell Law Review* 83, no. 1 (1997): 95.

4. Loomis, *Integrated Public Lands Management*, p. 90.

5. Although if that coal seam happened to be on national forest land, it remains to be seen whether *all* the costs have indeed been internalized.

6. Loomis, *Integrated Public Lands Management*, pp. 95, 97.

7. Richard Stroup and John Baden, *Natural Resources: Bureaucratic Myths and Environmental Management* (Cambridge, MA: Ballinger, 1983), p. 18.

8. Mark Sagoff, "Market versus Libertarian Environmentalism," *Critical Review* 6, nos. 2–3 (1992): 220.

9. Loomis, *Integrated Public Lands Management*, p. 97.

10. See, for example, Daniel Chiras, *Environmental Science*, 9th ed. (Burlington, MA: Jones and Barlett Learning, 2012), p. 616.

11. See, for example, Holly Fretwell and Shawn Regan, *Divided Lands* (Property and Environment Research Center Report, Bozeman, MT, March 2015).

12. Scott Lehmann, *Privatizing Public Land* (New York: Oxford University Press, 1995), pp. 116–117.

13. Joseph Krutilla, "Conservation Reconsidered," *American Economic Review* 57, no. 4 (September 1967): 777–786.

14. Ibid., p. 779.

15. See for example, George Peterson and Alan Randall (eds.), *Valuation of Wildland Resource Benefits* (Boulder, CO: Westview Press, 1984); George Peterson, Beverly Driver, and Robin Scott Gregory, *Amenity Resource Valuation* (State College, PA: Venture Publishing, 1988); Patricia Champ, Kevin Boyle, and Thomas Brown (eds.), *A Primer on Nonmarket Valuation* (Dordrecht, Netherlands: Kluwer Academic Publishers, 2003).

16. Pete Morton, "Wildlands Economics: Theory and Practice," in *Wilderness Science in a Time of Change Conference Proceedings*, vol. 2 (U.S. Department of Agriculture, Forest Service, RMRS-P-15-VOL-2, September 2000), p. 240.

17. Jeffrey Kline et al., "Applying the Ecosystem Services Concept to Public Land Management," *Agricultural and Resource Economics Review* 42, no. 1 (April 2013): 145.

18. See, for example, Mark Sagoff, *Price, Principle, and the Environment* (Cambridge: Cambridge University Press, 2004); Yaoqi Zhang and Yiqing Li, "Valuing or Pricing Natural and Environmental Resources?" *Environmental Science and Policy* 8 (2005): 179–186.

19. Morton, "Wildlands Economics," p. 239.

20. See note 18 for just a small sample.

21. U.S. Department of Agriculture, Forest Service, "Contribution of National Forest and Grassland Resource Management to the U.S. Economy," in *National Forest System Land Management Planning Final Programmatic Environment Impact Statement*, January 2012, App. M, p. M-3.

22. Ibid.

23. U.S. Department of the Interior, Office of Policy Analysis, *U.S. Department of the Interior Economic Report FY 2015*, June 17, 2016, p. 22, available at https://www.doi.gov/sites/doi.gov/files/uploads/fy2015_doi_econ_report_2016-06-20.pdf.

24. Ibid.

25. Ibid., pp. 22–23.

26. Trust for Public Land, *Return on Investment from the Land and Water Conservation Fund*, November 2010, p. 14, available at https://www.tpl.org/sites/default/files/cloud.tpl.org/pubs/benefits-LWCF-ROI%20Report-11-2010.pdf.

27. Francis Choi and Tim Marlowe, *The Value of America's Greatest Idea: Framework for Total Economic Valuation of National Park Service Operations and Assets and Joshua Tree National Park Total Economic Value Case Study* (Harvard Kennedy School of Government Report prepared for the National Park Service, March 20, 2012), p. 50; Jeffrey Prey, David Marcouiller, and Danya Kim, *Economic Impacts of the Wisconsin State Park System: Connections to Gateway Communities* (Wisconsin Department of Natural Resources, November 2013), p. v; Pamela Kaval and John Loomis, *Updated Outdoor Recreation Use Values with Emphasis on National Park Recreation* (Report prepared for the National Park Service, Project Number IMDE-02-0070, 2003); John Loomis, "Economic

Values of Wilderness Recreation and Passive Use: What We Think We Know at the Beginning of the 21st Century," in *Wilderness Science in a Time of Change Conference Proceedings*, vol. 2 (U.S. Department of Agriculture, Forest Service, RMRS-P-15-VOL-2, September 2000), pp. 8–9.

28. John Bergstrom et al., "Economic Impacts of State Parks on State Economies in the South," *Southern Journal of Agricultural Economics*, December 1990, p. 75.

29. Ibid.

30. Prey, Marcouiller, and Kim, *Economic Impacts of the Wisconsin State Park System*, p. 1.

31. Ibid. The actual figures for total output were $626.9 million, of which $379 million was direct, $119.5 million was indirect, and $128.4 million was induced.

32. Jason Yohannan, "There's a Substantial Federal Presence in Eastern Oregon's Economy," *State of Oregon Employment Department Newsletter*, November 27, 2013.

33. Dylan Darling, "The Federal Footprint in Harney County," *Bend Bulletin*, January 14, 2016.

34. Ibid.

35. Outdoor Industry Association, *The Outdoor Recreation Economy*, 2012, pp. 3, 8.

36. Ibid., p. 15. Just for wildlife-related activities alone, Sarah Pizzo reports $145 billion in direct spending, including $89 billion for fishing and hunting and $55 billion for wildlife watching. Sarah Pizzo, *Valuing Our Western Public Lands* (National Wildlife Federation Report, July 2013), p. 9.

37. Trout Unlimited, *The Economic Impact of Recreational Trout Angling in the Driftless Area*, April 2008, p. 2, available at http://namekagon.org/wp-content/uploads/2013/07/Trout-Unlimited-EconStudy-Summary-Final.pdf.

38. Pizzo, *Valuing Our Western Public Lands*, p. 11.

39. Niall Garrahan, *Open Land Utility: A Study of Conservation, Ecosystem Services, and Recreation in Boise, Idaho* (James Monroe Scholar Program, College of William and Mary, Summer 2012), pp. 18–19.

40. Spencer R. Phillips, "Windfalls for Wilderness: Land Protection and Land Value in the Green Mountains" (Ph.D. diss., Virginia Polytechnic Institute and State University, Blacksburg, 2004), available at https://theses.lib.vt.edu/theses/available/etd-02042004-141616/unrestricted/Phillips-Spencer_VPISU-AAEC_PHD-Dissertation_2004-02-10.pdf.

41. It should be noted, though, that the federal government and many states have some sort of annual *payment in lieu of taxes* (PILT) and/or revenue sharing (for commodity lands) for local governments to offset this.

42. See, for example, Ted Sweeney, *More Extensive Is More Expensive: How Sprawl Infrastructure Bankrupts Oregon Communities, and What We Can Do about It* (1000 Friends of Oregon Report, January 2013).

43. Trust for Public Land, *Return on Investment from the Land and Water Conservation Fund*, TPL Report, November 2010.

44. Ibid.

45. Figures calculated from individual national wildlife refuge system unit data from Erin Carver and James Caudill, *Banking on Nature: The Economic Benefits to Local Communities of National Wildlife Refuge Visitation* (Division of Economics, U.S. Fish and Wildlife Service, Washington, DC, October 2013). Some units in the sample had negative returns, but most were positive, and a few were hugely so (one popular East Coast unit had a 15,500 percent ROI). The median ROI was 227 percent.

46. U.S. Department of the Interior, National Park Service, *Fiscal Year 2016 Budget Justifications* (2015), Overview, p. 1; Trust for Public Land, *North Carolina's Return on the Investment in Land Conservation*, February 2011, p. 15.

47. Headwaters Economics, *Economists Urge President Obama to Protect Federal Public Lands* (Headwaters Economics press release, November 2011), available at http://headwaterseconomics.org/public-lands/protected-lands/economists-president-public-lands/.

48. Headwaters Economics, *West Is Best: How Public Lands in the West Create a Competitive Economic Advantage* (Headwaters Economics Report, November 2012), pp. 6–10.

49. Gundars Rudzitis and Rebecca Johnson, "The Impact of Wilderness and Other Wildlands on Local Economies and Regional Development Trends," in *Wilderness Science in a Time of Change Conference Proceedings*, vol. 2 (U.S. Department of Agriculture, Forest Service, RMRS-P-15-VOL-2, September 2000), p. 23.

50. Ibid.

51. See, for example, Kevin T. Duffy-Deno, "The Effect of Federal Wilderness on County Growth in the Intermountain Western United States," *Journal of Regional Science* 38, no. 1 (February 1998): 109–136; F. Patrick Holmes and Walter Hecox, "Does Wilderness Impoverish Rural Regions?" *International Journal of Wilderness* 10, no. 3 (December 2004): 34–39; Megan Lawson, *Federal Lands in the West: Liability or Asset?* (Headwaters Economics Report, February 2016); Ray Rasker, "An Exploration into the Economic Impact of Industrial Development versus Conservation on Western Public Lands," *Society and Natural Resources* 19, no. 3 (February 2006): 191–207; Ray Rasker, Patricia H. Gude, and Mark Delorey, "The Effect of Protected Federal Lands on Economic Prosperity in the Non-metropolitan West," *Journal of Regional Analysis and Policy* 43, no. 2 (2013): 110–122; Rudzitis and Johnson, "The Impact of Wilderness and Other Wildlands."

52. Headwaters Economics, *West Is Best*, p. 19.

53. Rasker, Gude, and Delorey, "The Effect of Protected Federal Lands on Economic Prosperity," p. 119.

54. See, for example, Richard Reeder and Dennis Brown, *Recreation, Tourism, and Rural Well-Being* (U.S. Department of Agriculture, Forest Service, Economic Research Report No. 7, August 2005), p. 14; Rudzitis and Johnson, "The Impact of Wilderness and Other Wildlands," p. 15; Rasker, "An Exploration into the Economic Impact of Industrial Development," p. 191.

55. Lawson, *Federal Lands in the West*, p. 1.

56. Reeder and Brown, *Recreation, Tourism, and Rural Well-Being*, p. iii.

57. Rasker, "An Exploration into the Economic Impact of Industrial Development," p. 191.

58. Robert Costanza et al., "The Value of the World's Ecosystem Services and Natural Capital," *Nature* 387 (May 15, 1997): 253–260; Gretchen Daily (ed.), *Nature's Services: Societal Dependence on Natural Ecosystems* (Washington, DC: Island Press, 1997); Paul Hawken, Amory Lovins, and L. Hunter Lovins, *Natural Capitalism: The Next Industrial Revolution* (Boston: Little, Brown, 1999).

59. Robert Smail and David Lewis, *Forest Land Conversion, Ecosystem Services, and Economic Issues* (U.S. Department of Agriculture, Forest Service, Pacific Northwest Research Station, General Technical Report PNW-GTR-797, August 2009), p. 4.

60. Rudolf de Groot, Matthew Wilson, and Roelof Boumans, "A Typology for the Classification, Description and Valuation of Ecosystem Functions, Goods and Services," *Ecological Economics* 41, no. 3 (2002): 393–408. As for item 10, habitat and biodiversity, there is some debate in the literature as to whether biodiversity per se should be considered an ecosystem service. Sara Vickerman strongly argues that it should, as it serves a crucial role as a genetic library or "bank account." Sara Vickerman, *Nature's Benefits: The Importance of Addressing Biodiversity in Ecosystem Service Programs* (Defenders of Wildlife Report, Washington, DC, 2013), p. 3.

61. Actually, classical economics did include land as an element of production until the first half of the twentieth century, when, according to Thomas Brown, John Bergstrom, and John Loomis, neoclassical economists began to deemphasize land and all its natural processes, treating them as a given. Thomas Brown, John Bergstrom, and John Loomis, "Defining, Valuing and Providing Ecosystem Goods and Services," *Natural Resources Journal* 47, no. 2 (Spring 2007): 336.

62. Margaret Walls and Anne Riddle, *Biodiversity, Ecosystem Services, and Land Use: Comparing Three Federal Policies* (Resources for the Future Report, RFF DP 12-08, Washington, DC, February 2012), p. 12. It should be noted that Mark Sagoff claims that this famous case is exaggerated and a bit misleading. Mark Sagoff, "On the Value of Natural Ecosystems: The Catskills Parable," *Politics and the Life Sciences* 21, no. 1 (March 2002): 16–21.

63. Robert Nelson, "Free the American West," *Los Angeles Times*, March 7, 2012.

64. Costanza et al., "The Value of the World's Ecosystem Services and Natural Capital," p. 253. This figure is roughly the mid-point of the $16-trillion to $54-trillion range they posit.

65. David Holzman, "Accounting for Nature's Benefits: The Dollar Value of Ecosystem Services," *Environmental Health Perspectives* 120, no. 4 (April 2012): 153.

66. Rebecca Moore et al., *Quantifying the Value of Non-timber Ecosystem Services from Georgia's Private Forests* (Georgia Forestry Foundation Report, June 2011), p. 34.

67. Rowan Schmidt, David Batker, and Jennifer Harrison-Cox, *Nature's Value in the Skykomish Watershed: A Rapid Ecosystem Service Valuation* (Earth Economics Report, Tacoma, WA, December 2011), p. 7.

68. The Office of Management and Budget figure comes from Carol Vincent, Laura Hanson, and Jerome Bjelopera, *Federal Land Ownership: Overview and Data* (Congressional Research Service Report, Washington, DC, December 29, 2014), p. 12.

69. Brown, Bergstrom, and Loomis differentiate between ES exchanges with private buyers and government sellers (such as a timber contract), government buyers and private sellers (such as a conservation easement), government buyers and sellers (such as a state wildlife area lease on BLM land), and private buyers and sellers (carbon credit markets). Brown, Bergstrom, and Loomis, "Defining, Valuing and Providing Ecosystem Goods and Services," pp. 363–367.

70. James Salzman, "A Field of Green? The Past and Future of Ecosystem Services," *Journal of Land Use and Environmental Law* 21, no. 2 (Spring 2006): 136.

71. Brown, Bergstrom, and Loomis, "Defining, Valuing and Providing Ecosystem Goods and Services," p. 375.

72. Kent Redford and William Adams, "Payment for Ecosystem Services and the Challenge of Saving Nature," *Conservation Biology* 23, no. 4 (August 2009): 786.

73. Brown, Bergstrom, and Loomis, "Defining, Valuing and Providing Ecosystem Goods and Services," p. 374.

74. Frank Casey et al., *Incentives for Biodiversity Conservation: An Ecological and Economic Assessment* (Defenders of Wildlife Report, Washington, DC, 2006).

75. Salzman, "A Field of Green?" p. 141.

76. Vickerman, *Nature's Benefits*, p. 1.

77. Kline et al., "Applying the Ecosystem Services Concept to Public Land Management," p. 140.

78. Ibid., p. 146. This move was the culmination, perhaps, of a long evolution in the bureaucratic culture of the USFS and the resulting paradigm shift that accompanied it. It is related to many factors, including the demographic and professional diversification of the agency over the past few decades and the pressures introduced by the successful environmental court challenges over the spotted owl in the late 1980s, which led to the Northwest Forest Plan and dramatically reduced logging volumes in some national forests. See Chapter 6 for a fuller discussion.

79. Ibid., pp. 146–152.

80. J. B. Ruhl raises a host of good questions that probe the nitty-gritty of federal management from this paradigm. For example, how does one manage competing ecosystem services in an area governed by a single-use mandate, such as wilderness? The agency could not really prioritize or trade off between specific ecosystem services as it could on multiple-use land. J. B. Ruhl, "Ecosystem Services and Federal Public Lands: Start-up Policy

Questions and Research Needs," *Duke Environmental Law and Policy Forum* 20, no. 2 (Summer 2010): 286.

81. Douglas McCauley, "Selling Out Nature," *Nature* 443 (September 7, 2006): 27–28.

82. Ibid., p. 28.

83. Belinda Reyers et al., "Finding Common Ground for Biodiversity and Ecosystem Services," *BioScience* 62, no. 5 (2012): 505.

84. Along these lines, Ruhl ("Ecosystem Services and Federal Public Lands," p. 289) notes that carbon sequestration, among commonly identified ecosystem services, might have the best market potential, but it conflicts with so many other land management priorities that it could "swamp" these other ES flows.

85. McCauley, "Selling Out Nature," p. 27.

86. Redford and Adams, "Payment for Ecosystem Services and the Challenge of Saving Nature," p. 786.

87. Mark Sagoff, "The Allocation and Distribution of Resources," in *Debating the Earth*, ed. John Dryzek and David Schlosberg (Oxford: Oxford University Press, 2005), p. 157.

88. Mark Sagoff, "The Rise and Fall of Ecological Economics: A Cautionary Tale," *Breakthrough Journal*, no. 2 (Fall 2011): 58.

89. Ibid.

90. Sagoff, "The Allocation and Distribution of Resources," p. 157.

91. Ibid., p. 158; emphasis original.

92. McCauley, "Selling Out Nature," p. 28.

93. Lynn Maguire and James Justus, "Why Intrinsic Value Is a Poor Basis for Conservation Decisions," *BioScience* 58, no. 10 (November 2008): 910.

94. Ibid.

95. Robert Costanza, "Nature: Ecosystems without Commodifying Them," Letters to the Editor, *Nature* 443 (October 19, 2006): 749.

96. Walter Reid, "Nature: The Many Benefits of Ecosystem Services," Letters to the Editor, *Nature* 443 (October 19, 2006): 749.

97. Costanza, "Nature: Ecosystems without Commodifying Them," p. 749.

98. Choi and Marlowe, *The Value of America's Greatest Idea*, p. 3.

99. For a free-market critique of the ES framework, see R. David Simpson, "Are Ecosystem Services Really Valuable Enough to Justify Conservation?" *PERC Report* 35, no. 1 (June 8, 2016).

100. Choi and Marlowe, *The Value of America's Greatest Idea*, pp. 39–40.

101. Sagoff, *Price, Principle, and the Environment*.

102. Holly Fretwell, *Federal Estate: Is Bigger Better?* (Property and Environment Research Center Report, Bozeman, MT, 2000), p. 6.

103. Headwaters Economics, *National Forest Gross Receipts from Commercial Activities, FY 1986–2015* (Headwaters Economics Report, June 2016), available at http://headwaterseconomics.org/dataviz/national-forests-gross-receipts/.

104. Privatizers admiringly point to the state-trust lands, which are entirely oriented toward commodity production and exist solely to generate revenue for given state public schools. See, for example, Fretwell and Regan, *Divided Lands*. This is one of the few areas of public land management in the United States to operate at a surplus, given its aggressive (and, critics would say, destructive) management approach.

105. Lehmann, *Privatizing Public Land*, p. 115.

106. "Making State Parks Self-Sustaining a Recipe for Disaster," Editorial, *Racine Journal Times*, May 13, 2015.

107. Rita Beamish, "National and State Parks Suffering from Budget Cuts," *Stateline*, Pew Charitable Trusts, May 24, 2013.

108. Vincent, Hanson, and Bjelopera, *Federal Land Ownership*, 21.

109. Ney Landrum, "Entrepreneurialism in America's State Parks," *George Wright Forum* 22, no. 2 (2005); Steven Davis, "Preservation, Resource Extraction, and Recreation on Public Lands: A View from the States," *Natural Resources Journal* 48 (Spring 2008), pp. 332–338.

110. Monte Burke, "Why We Need More—and Not Less—Conservation Funding in the Federal Budget," *Forbes*, November 22, 2013.

111. D. Andrew Austin, *Discretionary Budget Authority by Subfunction: An Overview* (Congressional Research Service Report, Washington, DC, February 5, 2015), p. 20.

112. Dale Oesterle, "Public Land: How Much Is Enough," *Ecological Law Quarterly* 23, no. 3 (June 1996), p. 546.

113. Randall O'Toole, "Reforming Public Land Management with New Incentives," in *Challenging Federal Ownership and Management: Public Lands and Public Benefits* (University of Colorado Law School, Boulder, October 11–13, 1995), pp. 3–4.

114. Linda Bilmes, *The Financial Legacy of Iraq and Afghanistan: How Wartime Spending Decisions Will Constrain Future National Security Budgets* (Harvard Kennedy School Faculty Working Paper Series, March 2013).

115. Michael Kelley and Geoffrey Ingersoll, "The Staggering Cost of the Last Decade's US War in Iraq—in Numbers," *Business Insider*, June 20, 2014.

CHAPTER 5

1. Terry Anderson and Donald Leal, "Rethinking the Way We Think," in *Debating the Earth*, ed. John Dryzek and David Schlosberg (Oxford: Oxford University Press, 2005), p. 217.

2. Dale Oesterle, "Public Land: How Much Is Enough," *Ecological Law Quarterly* 23, no. 3 (June 1996): 575.

3. Terry Anderson, Vernon Smith, and Emily Simmons, "How and Why to Privatize Federal Lands," *Policy Analysis* (CATO publication, No. 363, November 9, 1999), p. 21.

4. Richard Stroup and John Baden, *Natural Resources: Bureaucratic Myths and Environmental Management* (Cambridge, MA: Ballinger, 1983), p. 7.

5. Hal Herring, "Return of the Public-Land Privatizers," *Field and Stream*, May 20, 2015.

6. Scott Lehmann, *Privatizing Public Land* (New York: Oxford University Press, 1995), p. 47.

7. Jodi Stemler, "Our Public Lands: Not for Sale," *Backcountry Hunters and Anglers Report*, November 2014, p. 7.

8. George Cameron Coggins, "Abdication Can Be Fun, Join the Orgy, Everyone: A Simpleton's Perspective on Abdication of Federal Land Management Responsibilities," in *Challenging Federal Ownership and Management: Public Lands and Public Benefits* (University of Colorado Law School, Boulder, October 11–13, 1995), p. 4.

9. Lehmann, *Privatizing Public Land*, p. 48.

10. What is interesting is that in calling for "commodity lands" to be sold and for noncommodity lands to be retained, even Dale Oesterle, the privatization advocate, suggests that the government would need to develop criteria and negotiate between long-standing antagonists in what might become a very contentious process ("Public Land," p. 564)—all of which sounds suspiciously similar to the "politics" and scientific management decisions that privatizers profess to abhor. Why is this a recommended and necessary process only when the end result is disposal, but not when it is long-term management?

11. Joseph Sax, "The Legitimacy of Collective Values: The Case of the Public Lands," *University of Colorado Law Review* 56 (1984): 542.

12. Ibid., pp. 549–550.

13. Mark Sagoff, "The Allocation and Distribution of Resources," in *Debating the Earth*, ed. John Dryzek and David Schlosberg (Oxford: Oxford University Press, 2005), p. 150.

14. Mark Sagoff, "Market versus Libertarian Environmentalism," *Critical Review* 6, nos. 2–3 (1992): 222.

15. Sagoff, "The Allocation and Distribution of Resources," p. 157

16. Ibid., pp. 159–160. After this episode, the Mineral King area was subsequently transferred to Sequoia National Park and control of the NPS.

17. Sagoff, "Market versus Libertarian Environmentalism," p. 213.

18. Ibid.

19. Lehmann, *Privatizing Public Land*, p. 156; emphasis original.

20. Sagoff, "The Allocation and Distribution of Resources," p. 160.

21. Sax, "The Legitimacy of Collective Values," p. 546.

22. Lehmann, *Privatizing Public Land*, p. 18.

23. Sax, "The Legitimacy of Collective Values," p. 544.

24. Oesterle, "Public Land," p. 549.

25. Stroup and Baden, *Natural Resources*, p. 40.

26. Lehmann, *Privatizing Public Land*, p. 133.

27. Ibid., p. 134; emphasis original.

28. Sagoff, "Market versus Libertarian Environmentalism," p. 221.

29. Ibid., p. 213.

30. Lehmann, *Privatizing Public Land*, p. 172.

31. Sagoff, "Market versus Libertarian Environmentalism," pp. 211, 221.

32. Ibid., p. 215.

33. Lehmann, *Privatizing Public Land*, p. 20.

34. Sax, "The Legitimacy of Collective Values," p. 543.

35. Sagoff, "Market versus Libertarian Environmentalism," p. 222; emphasis original.

36. Lehmann, *Privatizing Public Land*, p. 156.

37. For a good overview of the grassroots nature of the environmental movement, see Benjamin Kline, *First along the River: A Brief History of the U.S. Environmental Movement* (San Francisco: Acada Books, 2000).

38. Terry Tempest Williams, "Covenant," in *The National Parks: America's Best Idea*, ed. Dayton Duncan and Ken Burns (New York: Knopf, 2011), p. 376.

39. Ibid.

40. William Cronon, quoted in Sarah Pizzo, *Valuing Our Western Public Lands* (National Wildlife Federation Report, July 2013), p. 14.

41. Michael Frome, quoted in Bill Wade, "A New Tragedy for the Commons: The Threat of Privatization to National Parks (and Other Public Lands)," *George Wright Forum* 22, no. 2 (2005): 66.

42. Sagoff, "The Allocation and Distribution of Resources," p. 155; emphasis original.

43. These estimates are based on extrapolations from some very limited available data. William Stevens estimates 5,000 volunteers working on 200 restoration sites in the Chicago metropolitan area, while a 2011 study reports 2,774 volunteers in the Boulder, Colorado, area. The proportion of those two citizen efforts to their larger metro-area populations ranges from .0005 to .0009. Extrapolating that ratio to the entire U.S. population gives us a figure of between 162,000 and 292,000 volunteers. The Colorado report accounts for 1.3 million hours of volunteer labor on environmental restoration work in the state in 2010. The Boulder area alone logged 34,362 hours, while the Pikes Peak area saw 23,879 hours in 2013. These figures seem to suggest total hours at least in the tens of millions, as Colorado is ranked right in the middle of population among states (22nd). William Stevens, *Miracle under the Oaks* (New York: Pocket Books, 1995), p. 11; Emily Jerman, Ann Baker Easley, and Sue Anderson, *Colorado's Public Lands: Engaging Our Communities in Their Care and Protection Report on the Impact of Volunteer Stewardship in 2010* (Volunteers for Outdoor Colorado Report, April 2011), pp. 9–10; Rocky Mountain Field Institute, *2015 Volunteer Report*, December 18, 2015, p. 2.

44. Stevens, *Miracle under the Oaks*, chaps. 1–2, 7.

45. David Bollier, quoted in Wade, "A New Tragedy for the Commons," p. 67.

46. Armond Acri, quoted in Pizzo, *Valuing Our Western Public Lands*, p. 15.

47. Stemler, "Our Public Lands," p. 3.

48. Thomas More, "Privatization of Public Lands," in *Proceedings of the 2006 Northeastern Recreation Research Symposium* (U.S. Department of Agriculture, Forest Service Report, GTR-NRS-P-14, 2006), p. 139.

49. Stemler, "Our Public Lands," p. 4.

50. Arthur Okun, *Equality and Efficiency: The Big Tradeoff* (Washington, DC: Brookings Institution, 1975).

51. Sylvia LeRoy, "Beyond the Public Park Paradigm," *George Wright Forum* 22, no. 2 (2005): 34.

52. Edward Abbey, *Desert Solitaire* (New York: Ballantine, 1968), p. 211.

53. Ibid., p. 163.

54. Colorado College, *Western States Survey*, 2015, p. 15, available at https://www.coloradocollege.edu/dotAsset/f8b242ee-17a7-426d-8c5f-a970bde80f74.pdf.

55. It is not unreasonable to speculate that attitudes in California, the Pacific Northwest, the Upper Great Lakes, and New England might be even more protective of public lands. Even 2016 survey research from the considerably less-progressive state of Ohio finds that 84 percent of respondents think it is "very important" to keep federal lands open to the public and that 83 percent oppose "the U.S. Congress passing laws that allow national public lands to be sold for private uses such as housing developments, resorts, mining and oil and gas drilling." Casey Skeens, *New NWF Poll Findings on Public Lands in Ohio* (National Wildlife Federation press release, May 26, 2016), available at https://www.nwf.org/en/Latest-News/Press-Releases/2016/5-26-16-New-NWF-Poll-Findings-On-Public-Lands-In-Ohio.

56. See, for example, Benjamin Spillman, "Poll: Trump and Non-Trump Voters Agree on Public Lands," *Reno Gazette-Journal*, January 31, 2017.

57. Charles Goodsell, *The New Case for Bureaucracy* (Washington, DC: CQ Press, 2014), p. 199.

58. Matthew Daley, "Federal Government Agrees to Let States Pay to Reopen National Parks," *Albuquerque Journal*, October 11, 2013.

CHAPTER 6

1. Dale Oesterle, "Public Land: How Much Is Enough," *Ecological Law Quarterly* 23, no. 3 (June 1996): 555.

2. Mark Sagoff, "Market versus Libertarian Environmentalism," *Critical Review* 6, nos. 2–3 (1992): 224.

3. Scott Lehmann, *Privatizing Public Land* (New York: Oxford University Press, 1995), p. 17.

4. See, for example, Paul Culhane, *Public Lands Politics* (Baltimore: Johns Hopkins University Press for Resources for the Future, 1981); Terence Tipple and J. Douglas Wellman, "Herbert Kaufman's Forest Ranger Thirty Years Later: From Simplicity and Homogeneity to Complexity and Diversity," *Public Administration Review* 51, no. 5 (September/October 1991): 421–428; Paul Mohai, "Public Participation and Natural Resource Decision-Making:

The Case of the RARE II Decisions," *Natural Resources Journal* 27 (Winter 1987): 123–155.

5. See, for example, Herbert Kaufman, *The Forest Ranger: A Study in Administrative Behavior* (Baltimore: Johns Hopkins University Press for Resources for the Future, 1967); Ben Twight, *Organization Values and Political Power: The Forest Service vs. Olympic National Park* (University Park: Pennsylvania State University Press, 1983).

6. See, for example, Tomas Koontz, *Federalism in the Forest: National versus State Natural Resource Policy* (Washington, DC: Georgetown University Press, 2002); Steven Davis, "The Politics of Urban Natural Management at the Local Level: A Case Study," *Kentucky Journal of Equine, Agricultural, and Natural Resources Law* 2, no. 2 (2010); Steven Davis, "The Forests Nobody Wanted: The Politics of Land Management in the County Forests of the Upper Midwest," *Journal of Land Use and Environmental Law* 28, no. 2 (Spring 2013).

7. S. Davis, "The Forests Nobody Wanted," p. 220.

8. Elizabeth Estill, "The Benefits of Professional Public Land Management," in *Challenging Federal Ownership and Management: Public Lands and Public Benefits* (University of Colorado Law School, Boulder, October 11–13, 1995), p. 2.

9. Kaufman, *The Forest Ranger*, chap. 2.

10. Craig W. Thomas, *Bureaucratic Landscapes* (Boston: Massachusetts Institute of Technology Press, 2003), p. 59.

11. Jeanne Nienaber Clarke and Daniel McCool, *Staking Out the Terrain* (Albany: State University of New York Press, 1996), pp. 200–201.

12. Thomas, *Bureaucratic Landscapes*, pp. 45–46.

13. Charles Goodsell, *The Case for Bureaucracy* (Washington, DC: CQ Press, 2004), p. 104.

14. David Boaz, ed., *CATO Handbook for Policymakers*, 7th ed. (Washington, DC: CATO Institute, 2009), p. 250.

15. William Niskanen, *Bureaucracy—Servant or Master?* (London: Institute of Economic Affairs, 1973); Richard Stroup and John Baden, *Natural Resources: Bureaucratic Myths and Environmental Management* (Cambridge, MA: Ballinger, 1983), p. 43; Randall O'Toole, "Reforming Public Land Management with New Incentives," in *Challenging Federal Ownership and Management: Public Lands and Public Benefits* (University of Colorado Law School, Boulder, October 11–13, 1995), p. 2.

16. Thomas, *Bureaucratic Landscapes*, p. 29. For an edited volume that examines this question from many angles, see Andre Blais and Stephane Dion, eds., *The Budget-Maximizing Bureaucrat: Appraisals and Evidence* (Pittsburgh: University of Pittsburgh Press, 1991). Thomas finds that even this book, which sympathetically appraises Niskanen's work, offers up "only weak or contradictory evidence at best" (p. 29).

17. This is not to say that certain reforms to budgetary incentives are not warranted. For example, the fact that USFS managers get to keep a portion of timber receipts but not recreation receipts seriously distorts management

incentives. John Loomis, *Integrated Public Lands Management* (New York: Columbia University Press, 1993), p. 103.

18. Thomas, *Bureaucratic Landscapes*, p. 30.

19. Ibid., p. 32.

20. Ibid.

21. Estill, "The Benefits of Professional Public Land Management," p. 7.

22. Lehmann, *Privatizing Public Land*, pp. 188–190.

23. See, for example, Robert Dur and Robin Zoutenbier, "Working for a Good Cause," *Public Administration Review*, February 27, 2014, pp. 144–155.

24. Goodsell, *The Case for Bureaucracy*, pp. 101–106.

25. John Brehm and Scott Gates, quoted in ibid., pp. 105–106.

26. Ibid., chap. 2.

27. Thomas, *Bureaucratic Landscapes*, p. 28.

28. Estill, "The Benefits of Professional Public Land Management," p. 8.

29. Goodsell, *The Case for Bureaucracy*, pp. 36–37.

30. Ibid., p. 30.

31. Ibid., p. 27.

32. Charles Clark, "Interior Department Tops Satisfaction Survey," *Government Executive*, January 26, 2016, available at http://cdn.govexec .com/interstitial.html?v=2.1.1&rf=http%3A%2F%2Fwww.govexec.com% 2Fmanagement%2F2016%2F01%2Finterior-department-tops-satisfaction-survey%2F125388%2F.

33. U.S. Department of Agriculture, Forest Service, Research and Development, *FY 2015 Customer Satisfaction Survey*, February 12, 2015, p. 5, available at https://www.fs.fed.us/research/docs/about/customer-satisfac tion-survey/fy-2015-results.pdf.

34. U.S. Department of Agriculture, Forest Service, *National Visitor Use Monitoring Results: National Summary Report*, May 22, 2012, p. 17, available at http://www.fs.fed.us/recreation/programs/nvum/nvum_national_sum mary_fy2011.pdf.

35. U.S. Department of the Interior, National Park Service, *National Park System 2009 Visitor Survey Card Data Report* (Report # NAPA09, 2009), available at https://www.nature.nps.gov/socialscience/docs/napa_09.pdf.

36. Robert Nelson, *Public Land and Private Rights: The Failure of Scientific Management* (Lanham, MD: Rowman and Littlefield, 1995), p. 235.

37. Stroup and Baden, *Natural Resources*, p. 117.

38. Loomis, *Integrated Public Lands Management*, p. 105.

39. Hanna Cortner, "The Governance Environment: Linking Science, Citizens, and Politics," in *Ecological Restoration of Southwestern Ponderosa Pine Forests*, ed. Peter Friederici (Washington, DC: Island Press, 2003), p. 71.

40. Thomas, *Bureaucratic Landscapes*, p. 16.

41. Ibid., pp. 22–23.

42. Bill Wade, "A New Tragedy for the Commons: The Threat of Privatization to National Parks (and Other Public Lands)," *George Wright Forum* 22, no. 2 (2005): 64.

43. Elise Jones and Cameron Taylor, "Litigating Agency Change: The Impact of the Courts and the Administrative Appeals Process on the Forest Service," *Policy Studies Journal* 23, no. 3 (Summer 1995): 310.

44. Thomas, *Bureaucratic Landscapes*, pp. 258–263.

45. Jeffrey Kline et al., "Applying the Ecosystem Services Concept to Public Land Management," *Agricultural and Resource Economics Review* 42, no. 1 (April 2013): 144.

46. See, for example, Paul Mohai, "The Forest Service since the National Forest Management Act Assessing Bureaucratic Response to External and Internal Forces for Change," *Policy Studies Journal* 23, no. 2 (Summer 1995): 247–252; Timothy Farnham and Paul Mohai, "National Forest Timber Management over the Past Decade: A Change in Emphasis for the Forest Service?" *Policy Studies Journal* 23, no. 2 (Summer 1995): 268–280; Timothy Farnham, Cameron Taylor, and Will Calloway, "A Shift in Values: Non-commodity Resource Management and the Forest Service," *Policy Studies Journal* 23, no. 2 (Summer 1995): 281–295.

47. Thomas, *Bureaucratic Landscapes*, p. 263.

48. Ibid., p. 265.

49. Koontz's data show that among twenty measurements of environmental criteria comparing federal to state forest management, federal managers were found to be more environmentally stringent in sixteen measures, roughly the same in four, and weaker than states in none. Koontz, *Federalism in the Forest*, p. 52.

50. S. Davis, "The Forests Nobody Wanted."

51. O'Toole, "Reforming Public Land Management with New Incentives," p. 2.

52. See, for example, Ben Twight and Fremont Lyden, "Measuring Forest Service Bias," *Journal of Forestry* 87, no. 5 (1989): 35–41; Ben Twight, Fremont Lyden, and E. Thomas Tuchman, "Constituency Bias in a Federal Career System? A Study of District Rangers of the U.S. Forest Service," *Administration and Society* 22 (1990): 358–389.

53. Phillip O. Foss, *Politics and Grass* (Seattle: University of Washington Press, 1960).

54. Jeffrey Berry and Clyde Wilcox, *The Interest Group Society*, 5th ed. (New York: Pearson Longman, 2009), chap. 2.

55. For works that argue that participation matters, see, for example, Culhane, *Public Lands Politics*; Paul Culhane, "Public Participation in National Forest Planning: Is It Different or Just More?" (paper presented at the annual meeting of the Western Political Science Association, Seattle, March 21, 1991); Charles Davis and Sandra Davis, "Analyzing Change in Public Lands Policymaking: From Subsystems to Advocacy Coalitions," *Policy Studies Journal* 17, no. 1 (1988): 3–24. For those who doubt its efficacy, see Twight, *Organization Values and Political Power*; Jim Britell, "When You Must Negotiate . . . Negotiate to Win," *Forest Watch*, May 1991, pp. 17–24.

56. Wendy Espeland, "Bureaucratizing Democracy, Democratizing Bureaucracy," *Law and Social Inquiry* 25, no. 4 (October 2000): 1077–1109.

57. S. Davis, "The Forests Nobody Wanted"; Koontz, *Federalism in the Forest*.

58. Berry and Wilcox, *The Interest Group Society*.

59. Robert Paehlke, "Democracy and Environmentalism: Opening a Door to the Administrative State," in *Debating the Earth*, ed. John Dryzek and David Schlosberg (Oxford: Oxford University Press, 2005), pp. 173–175.

60. Left unsaid by the Sagebrush Rebels and devolutionists is the fact that the next step in this trust model is for states to do with the land as they see fit, which could very well mean disposal.

61. Oesterle, "Public Land," pp. 552–553.

62. John Baden, quoted in B. Delworth Gardner, "The Political Economy of Public Land Use," *Journal of Agricultural and Resource Economics* 22, no. 1 (1997): 15.

63. Estill, "The Benefits of Professional Public Land Management," p. 6.

64. George Cameron Coggins, "Abdication Can Be Fun, Join the Orgy, Everyone: A Simpleton's Perspective on Abdication of Federal Land Management Responsibilities," in *Challenging Federal Ownership and Management: Public Lands and Public Benefits* (University of Colorado Law School, Boulder, October 11–13, 1995), p. 2.

65. Ibid., p. 3.

66. Different agencies have different ways of dealing with this geographic reality. According to Kaufman, the USFS response to this decentralization was to build such a strong agency culture and esprit de corps that it could largely trust district rangers to faithfully discharge the agency's mission without much oversight. But just as insurance, it also moved rangers around throughout their careers so they would not develop too many loyalties to the communities they were stationed in. The BLM, on the other hand, encouraged its unit managers to become members of their communities, and, in contrast, they were not transferred around. Clarke and McCool, *Staking Out the Terrain*, p. 163.

67. Koontz, *Federalism in the Forest*, p. 15.

68. Estill, "The Benefits of Professional Public Land Management," p. 10.

69. Randall Wilson, *America's Public Lands* (Lanham, MD: Rowman and Littlefield, 2014), p. 55.

70. For a very thorough overview of collaborative conservation, see Matthew McKinney and William Harmon, *The Western Confluence: A Guide to Governing Natural Resources* (Washington, DC: Island Press, 2004); Julia Wondolleck and Steven Yaffee, *Making Collaboration Work* (Washington, DC: Island Press, 2000); Benjamin Donatelle, "Instituting Collaborative Conservation in Federal Land Management: The BLM's Resource Advisory Councils as an Example" (master's thesis, paper #4566, University of Montana, Missoula, 2015), available at http://scholarworks.umt.edu/cgi/viewcontent.cgi?article=5599&context=etd.

71. Donatelle, "Instituting Collaborative Conservation in Federal Land Management," pp. 26–29.

72. Hal Bernton, "The Story behind the Malheur National Wildlife Refuge, Ranchers, and the Armed Anti-government Protestors," *Seattle Times*, January 9, 2016.

73. Ibid.

74. Jonathan Thompson, "Bears Ears a Go—but Here's Where Obama Drew the Line," *High Country News*, December 29, 2016.

75. Kickapoo Valley Reserve, *Home* and *About Us* pages, available at http://kvr.state.wi.us/Home.

76. Wilson, *America's Public Lands*, p. 139.

77. Donatelle, "Instituting Collaborative Conservation in Federal Land Management," pp. 25–26.

78. Ibid.

79. Mary Chapman, "Consensus Groups and Grassroots Democracy: Maybe Those Who Say It Cannot Be Done Should Get Out of the Way of Those Doing It," in *Challenging Federal Ownership and Management: Public Lands and Public Benefits* (University of Colorado Law School, Boulder, October 11–13, 1995); Sarah Parks and John Gowdy, "What Have Economists Learned about Valuing Nature? A Review Essay," *Ecosystem Services* 3 (2013): e8.

80. Elinor Ostrom, *Governing the Commons: The Evolution of Institutions for Collective Action* (Cambridge: Cambridge University Press, 1990).

CHAPTER 7

1. Courtney Sherwood and Kirk Johnson, "Bundy Brothers Acquitted in Takeover of Oregon Wildlife Refuge," *New York Times*, October 27, 2016. A subsequent trial for another set of four defendants from the same standoff found two guilty of conspiracy and acquitted two others (although the two acquitted of conspiracy were found guilty of lesser charges) in March 2017. Maxine Bernstein, "Two Convicted and Two Acquitted of Conspiracy in Oregon Occupation Trial," *Oregonian*, March 10, 2017.

2. Eleven of twelve jurors were white, and eight were from beyond the Portland area. Conrad Wilson, "Jury Selected for Refuge Occupation Trial," *Oregon Public Broadcasting*, September 9, 2016, available at http://www.opb.org/news/series/burns-oregon-standoff-bundy-militia-news-updates/jury-refuge-occupation-trial-makeup/.

3. Cally Carswell, "Federal Public Land Transfers Get a Congressional Boost," *High Country News*, March 31, 2015.

4. Juliet Eilperin, "House GOP Rules Change Will Make It Easier to Sell Off Federal Land," *Washington Post*, January 3, 2017.

5. Republicans were, however, able to achieve a decades-long goal to allow oil drilling in Alaska's pristine Arctic National Wildlife Refuge by attaching the controversial measure to their massive tax overhaul, which passed the Senate 51–48, using budget reconciliation rules that do not allow for the use of filibusters.

6. Tay Wiles, "Trump Met with a Leader of the Land Transfer Movement," *High Country News*, October 17, 2016.

7. There is some evidence that because Trump's son Donald Jr. is a big-game hunter with connections to sportsmen's groups opposed to transfer, he influenced his father to pick Zinke over the initial choice for the U.S. Department of the Interior, the strongly pro-transfer congresswoman Cathy McMorris Rogers (R-WA). Esther Whieldon and Annie Snider, "Trump's Interior Pick Lifts Outdoors Groups," *Politico*, December 15, 2016, available at http://www.politico.com/story/2016/12/trump-interior-ryan-zinke-sportsmens-group-environment-232716.

8. For a summary of some of these regulatory changes, see Ellen Gilmer, "2017 in Court: Regulations, Pipelines and Public Lands," *E&E News*, December 21, 2017, available at https://www.eenews.net/stories/1060069613.

9. Julie Turkewitz, "Trump Slashes Size of Bears Ears and Grand Staircase Monuments," *New York Times*, December 4, 2017.

10. Hal Herring, "What the Reductions to National Monuments Could Mean for Our Hunting and Fishing Access and Your Tax Dollars," *Field and Stream*, December 20, 2017.

11. Juliet Eilperin, "Zinke Backs Shrinking More National Monuments and Shifting Management of 10," *Washington Post*, December 5, 2017.

12. Ibid.

13. Ibid.; Herring, "What the Reductions to National Monuments Could Mean for Our Hunting and Fishing Access and Your Tax Dollars."

14. Todd A. Curry and Rebecca A. Reid, "Trump Is Being Sued to Stop Him from Shrinking Bears Ears National Monument by 85 Percent. Who Will Win?" *Washington Post*, December 11, 2017.

15. Ben Lockhart, "Conservative Think Tank Concludes Trump Can Rescind Bears Ears Monument," *Deseret News*, March 29, 2017.

16. See, for example, Mark Squillace et al., "Presidents Lack the Authority to Abolish or Diminish National Monuments," *Virginia Law Review* 103 (June 2017): 55–71; Alexandra Wyatt, *Antiquities Act: Scope of Authority for Modification of National Monuments* (Congressional Research Service Report R44687, November 14, 2016).

17. Squillace et al., "Presidents Lack the Authority to Abolish or Diminish National Monuments," pp. 58–59. The power to diminish is far less legally clear than full-fledged abolishment. Congress clearly can reduce monument acreage (and has, in the past), but only rarely have presidents done this, and it has never faced legal challenge. There are certainly legal grounds to consider the diminishment of a significant-enough proportion of a monument to be a sort of de facto abolishment. Wyatt, *Antiquities Act*, p. 5.

18. Ibid.

19. Robert Rosenbaum, "No, President Trump Can't Revoke National Monuments," *Washington Post*, March 29, 2017.

20. This was just for terrestrial national monuments. He also added new areas to national marine monuments in the oceans totaling in the hundreds of millions of acres and numerous historical monuments.

21. Robert B. Keiter and John C. Ruple, *A Legal Analysis of the Transfer of Public Lands Movement* (Stegner Center White Paper No. 2014-2, October 27, 2014).

22. Ibid., p. 3.

23. William Chaloupka, "The County Supremacy and Militia Movements: Federalism as an Issue on the Radical Right," *Publius: The Journal of Federalism* 26, no. 3 (Summer 1996): 175.

24. Ibid.

25. See, for example, George Lakoff, *Don't Think of an Elephant* (White River Junction, VT: Chelsea Green, 2004).

26. Bobby Magill, "America's Best Climate Defense Lies in Public Lands," *Scientific American*, March 12, 2015.

27. Brian Maffly, "Legislative Resolution: Drilling Is 'Best Use' for Cedar Mesa and San Rafael Swell," *Salt Lake Tribune*, March 10, 2015.

28. The Wilderness Society, *Idaho Lands—and Recreation Access—Lost to the Highest Bidder*, May 2016, available at http://wilderness.org/sites/default/files/Idaho%20lands%20-%20TWS%20Report%20%28May%202016%29 .pdf.

29. Representative Ken Ivory, quoted in Hal Herring, "Can We Make Sense of the Malheur Mess?" *High Country News*, February 12, 2016.

30. See, for example, Garett Reppenhagen, "A Veteran of the Iraq War Finds Healing, and a New Sense of Purpose, among America's Wildlands," *Sierra*, June 7, 2016.

31. Brad Plumer, "After a Massive Backlash, a Republican Yanks His Bill to Sell Off Public Lands," *Vox*, February 2, 2017.

32. See, for example, Ian Kullgren, "Burns Paiute Tribe: Militants Need to Get Off 'Our Land,'" *The Oregonian*, February 22, 2016.

33. Patricia Nelson Limerick, "A History of the Public Lands Debate," in *Challenging Federal Ownership and Management: Public Lands and Public Benefits* (University of Colorado Law School, Boulder, October 11–13, 1995), p. 17.

34. Sandra L. Colby and Jennifer M. Ortman, *Projections of the Size and Composition of the U.S. Population: 2014 to 2060* (U.S. Census Bureau Current Population Reports, March 2015), available at https://www.census.gov/content/dam/Census/library/publications/2015/demo/p25-1143.pdf.

35. U.S. Census Bureau, *Statistical Abstract of the United States: 2012*, August 2011, p. 227.

36. Trust for Public Land, *MN Voters Approve $5.5 Billion to Protect Land and Water*, November 6, 2008, available at https://www.tpl.org/media-room/mn-voters-approve-55-billion-protect-land-and-water#sm.000009 b5hj14gpewrye37aaw60hpr.

37. Lorna Benson, "Andover and Other Communities Ask Voters to Save Open Spaces," *MPR News*, October 15, 2006, available at http://www .mprnews.org/story/2006/10/10/openspaces.

38. Mark Clayton, "Private Land Conservation Booms in U.S.," *Christian Science Monitor*, December 14, 2006; Wendy Koch, "More U.S. Land Conserved as Parks, Farms, Nature Areas," *USA Today*, November 17, 2011.

39. The Nature Conservancy, *About Us: Private Land Conservation*, available at http://www.nature.org/about-us/private-lands-conservation/.

40. Melinda Benson, "Shifting Public Land Paradigms: Lessons from the Valles Caldera National Preserve," *Virginia Environmental Law Journal* 34, no. 1 (2016): 9–13.

41. Ibid., pp. 4, 15.

42. Ibid., p. 42.

43. Bill Wade finds this pressure to contract out scientific and archaeological assessment to be present at the U.S. Department of the Interior during the Bush administration. Bill Wade, "A New Tragedy for the Commons: The Threat of Privatization to National Parks (and Other Public Lands)," *George Wright Forum* 22, no. 2 (2005): 64.

44. Michael Hiltzik, "The Corporate Grab behind the Yosemite Trademark Clash," *Los Angeles Times*, February 29, 2016.

45. Brian Maffly and Erin Alberty, "Proposed $70 National Park Fee Would Hurt Rural Businesses, Utah Governor Tells Interior Department," *Salt Lake Tribune*, October 24, 2017.

46. Leigh Raymond and Sally Fairfax, "The 'Shift to Privatization' in Land Conservation: A Cautionary Essay," *Natural Resources Journal* 42 (Summer 2002): 637–638.

47. Colby and Ortman, *Projections of the Size and Composition of the U.S. Population*, p. 9.

48. Jodi Peterson, "Parks for All?" *High Country News*, May 19, 2014.

49. Colby and Ortman, *Projections of the Size and Composition of the U.S. Population*, p. 9.

50. Peterson, "Parks for All?"

51. U.S. Department of Agriculture, Forest Service, *National Visitor Use Monitoring Results: National Summary Report*, May 22, 2012, p. 8.

52. Peterson, "Parks for All?"

53. Ibid.

54. Wayne Hare, "Our Public Lands Should Reflect White, Black and Brown," *High Country News*, July 17, 2007; Carolyn Finney, *Black Faces, White Spaces: Reimagining the Relationship of African Americans to the Great Outdoors* (Chapel Hill: University of North Carolina Press, 2014); James Mills, "In Search of Diversity in Our National Parks," *High Country News*, July 22, 2011; James Mills, *The Adventure Gap* (Seattle: Mountaineers Books, 2014).

55. Finney, *Black Faces, White Spaces*, p. 53. It is worth noting that although racial and ethnic minorities may be less oriented toward parks and the outdoors, black and Hispanic legislators are among the most stalwart defenders of public lands, wilderness protection, and park budgets. In fact, there is probably no member of Congress with a better record on defending wilderness and public land than the Mexican American representative Raul Grijalva (D-AZ), the ranking member of the House Committee on Natural Resources. League of Conservation Voters, *2015 National Environmental Scorecard*, 2016, available at http://scorecard.lcv.org/.

56. Richard Louv, *Last Child in the Woods* (Chapel Hill, NC: Algonquin Books, 2005).

57. Timothy Egan, "Can the Selfie Generation Unplug and Get into Parks?" *National Geographic*, October 2016, available at https://www.nationalgeograph ic.com/magazine/2016/10/unplugging-the-selfie-generation-national-parks/.

58. Jonathan Jarvis, quoted in ibid.

59. Ibid.

60. Kristen Bialik, *Most Americans Favor Stricter Environmental Laws and Regulations* (Pew Research Center, Fact-Tank, December 14, 2016), available at http://www.pewresearch.org/fact-tank/2016/12/14/most-americans-favor-stricter-environmental-laws-and-regulations/.

61. Guy Molyneux and Ruy Teixeira, *The Generation Gap on Government* (Center for American Progress Report, July 2010), p. 11.

62. Richard Louv, *Children and Nature Movement*, March 2008, available at http://richardlouv.com/books/last-child/children-nature-movement/.

63. Egan, "Can the Selfie Generation Unplug?"

64. Ibid.

65. Steven Davis, "The Politics of Urban Natural Management at the Local Level: A Case Study," *Kentucky Journal of Equine, Agricultural, and Natural Resources Law* 2, no. 2 (2010): 127.

66. Stephen Christy, *The Forest Preserve District of Cook County: Study and Recommendations* (Friends of the Forest Preserves and Friends of the Parks Report, Phase I, March 2002), p. 14.

67. Robert Kunzig, "Drying of the West," *National Geographic*, February 2008.

68. Kelli Archie et al., "Climate Change and Western Public Lands: A Survey of U.S. Federal Land Managers on the Status of Adaptation Efforts," *Ecology and Society* 17, no. 4, (2012): 1.

69. Ibid., pp. 4–5.

70. Ibid., p. 5.

71. Ibid., p. 6.

72. Joel Smith and William Travis, *Adaptation to Climate Change in Public Lands Management* (Resources for the Future, Issue Brief 10-04, February 2014), p. 2.

73. Ibid., pp. 3–4.

74. Ibid., pp. 4–5.

75. For this reason, smaller and more isolated national wildlife refuges, especially those originally established for a target species and often focused on preserving a particular, narrow habitat, will be more challenged in the future than the larger interconnected complexes of federal land, especially out west.

76. Magill, "America's Best Climate Defense Lies in Public Lands."

77. Ibid. Solar-thermal facilities differ from more traditional photovoltaic solar arrays in that they use large mirrors to reflect the sun's energy to power large boilers. This setup, consequently, requires a lot of land.

78. The portion of the budget that goes to the federal land management agencies (see Table 4.7) is $11.1 billion, and the price of an F-35 as of the summer of 2016 was $109.88 million. Kyle Mizokami, "The F-35 Is about to Get a Lot Cheaper. Sort Of," *Popular Mechanics*, July 11, 2016.

Selected Bibliography

This bibliography includes only the sources more central to this book's theoretical and empirical arguments.

Abbey, Edward. *Desert Solitaire*. New York: Ballantine, 1968.

Anderson, Terry. "Back to the Future: Privatizing the Federal Estate." In *Challenging Federal Ownership and Management: Public Lands and Public Benefits*. Boulder: University of Colorado Law School, 1995.

Anderson, Terry, and Donald Leal. "Free Market Environmentalism." In *Thinking about the Environment: Readings on Politics, Property and the Physical World*, edited by Matthew Cahn and Rory O'Brien, pp. 242–249. Armonk, NY: M. E. Sharpe, 1996.

———. "Rethinking the Way We Think." In *Debating the Earth*, edited by John Dryzek and David Schlosberg, pp. 211–228. Oxford: Oxford University Press, 2005.

Anderson, Terry, Vernon Smith, and Emily Simmons. "How and Why to Privatize Federal Lands." *Policy Analysis*. CATO publication, No. 363, November 9, 1999.

Baden, John, and Richard Stroup. "Saving the Wilderness: A Radical Proposal." *Reason*, July 1981, pp. 28–35.

Benson, Melinda. "Shifting Public Land Paradigms: Lessons from the Valles Caldera National Preserve." *Virginia Environmental Law Journal* 34, no. 1 (2016): 1–51.

Berry, Jeffrey, and Clyde Wilcox. *The Interest Group Society*. 5th ed. New York: Pearson Longman, 2009.

Blais, Andre, and Stephane Dion, eds. *The Budget-Maximizing Bureaucrat: Appraisals and Evidence*. Pittsburgh: University of Pittsburgh Press, 1991.

Brown, Thomas, John Bergstrom, and John Loomis. "Defining, Valuing and Providing Ecosystem Goods and Services." *Natural Resources Journal* 47, no. 2 (Spring 2007): 329–376.

Bruce, Melinda, and Teresa Rice. "Controlling the Blue Rash: Issues and Trends in State Land Management." *Land and Water Law Review* 29, no. 1 (1994): 1–58.

Carver, Erin, and James Caudill. *Banking on Nature: The Economic Benefits to Local Communities of National Wildlife Refuge Visitation.* Washington, DC: Division of Economics, U.S. Fish and Wildlife Service, 2013.

Cawley, R. McGreggor. *Federal Land and Western Anger: The Sagebrush Rebellion and Environmental Politics.* Lawrence: University of Kansas Press, 1993.

Chaloupka, William. "The County Supremacy and Militia Movements: Federalism as an Issue on the Radical Right." *Publius: The Journal of Federalism* 26, no. 3 (Summer 1996): 161–175.

Clarke, Jeanne Nienaber, and Daniel McCool. *Staking Out the Terrain.* Albany: State University of New York Press, 1996.

Coggins, George Cameron. "Abdication Can Be Fun, Join the Orgy, Everyone: A Simpleton's Perspective on Abdication of Federal Land Management Responsibilities." In *Challenging Federal Ownership and Management: Public Lands and Public Benefits.* Boulder: University of Colorado Law School, 1995.

Cortner, Hanna. "The Governance Environment: Linking Science, Citizens, and Politics." In *Ecological Restoration of Southwestern Ponderosa Pine Forests*, edited by Peter Friederici, pp. 70–79. Washington, DC: Island Press, 2003.

Cortner, Hanna, and Margaret Moote. *The Politics of Ecosystem Management.* Washington, DC: Island Press, 1998.

Costanza, Robert. "Nature: Ecosystems without Commodifying Them." Letters to the Editor. *Nature* 443 (October 19, 2006): 749.

Costanza, Robert, Ralph d'Arge, Rudolf de Groot, Stephen Farber, Monica Grasso, Bruce Hannon, Karin Limburg, Shahid Naeem, Robert V. O'Neill, Jose Paruelo, Robert G. Raskin, Paul Sutton, and Marjan van den Belt. "The Value of the World's Ecosystem Services and Natural Capital." *Nature* 387 (May 15, 1997): 253–260.

Culhane, Paul. *Public Lands Politics.* Baltimore: Johns Hopkins University Press for Resources for the Future, 1981.

Daily, Gretchen, ed. *Nature's Services: Societal Dependence on Natural Ecosystems.* Washington, DC: Island Press, 1997.

Davis, Charles, and Sandra Davis. "Analyzing Change in Public Lands Policymaking: From Subsystems to Advocacy Coalitions." *Policy Studies Journal* 17, no. 1 (1988): 3–24.

Davis, Steven. "The Forests Nobody Wanted: The Politics of Land Management in the County Forests of the Upper Midwest." *Journal of Land Use and Environmental Law* 28, no. 2 (Spring 2013): 197–225.

———. "The Politics of Urban Natural Management at the Local Level: A

Case Study." *Kentucky Journal of Equine, Agricultural, and Natural Resources Law* 2, no. 2 (2010): 127–155.

———. "Preservation, Resource Extraction, and Recreation on Public Lands: A View from the States." *Natural Resources Journal* 48 (Spring 2008): 303–352.

Duncan, Dayton, and Ken Burns, eds. *The National Parks: America's Best Idea.* New York: Knopf, 2011.

Dur, Robert, and Robin Zoutenbier. "Working for a Good Cause." *Public Administration Review*, February 27, 2014, pp. 144–155.

Espeland, Wendy. "Bureaucratizing Democracy, Democratizing Bureaucracy." *Law and Social Inquiry* 25, no. 4 (October 2000): 1077–1109.

Estill, Elizabeth. "The Benefits of Professional Public Land Management." In *Challenging Federal Ownership and Management: Public Lands and Public Benefits.* Boulder: University of Colorado Law School, 1995.

Finney, Carolyn. *Black Faces, White Spaces: Reimagining the Relationship of African Americans to the Great Outdoors.* Chapel Hill: University of North Carolina Press, 2014.

Fischman, Robert. "The Significance of National Wildlife Refuges in the Development of U.S. Conservation Policy." *Journal of Land Use and Environmental Law* 21, no. 1 (Fall 2005): pp. 1–22.

Foss, Phillip O. *Politics and Grass.* Seattle: University of Washington Press, 1960.

Fretwell, Holly. *Do We Get What We Pay For?* Property and Environment Research Center Report, Bozeman, MT, 1999.

———. *Federal Estate: Is Bigger Better?* Property and Environment Research Center Report, Bozeman, MT, 2000.

———. *Is No Use Good Use?* Property and Environment Research Center Report, Bozeman, MT, 2001.

Fretwell, Holly, and Shawn Regan. *Divided Lands.* Property and Environment Research Center Report, Bozeman, MT, 2015.

Frymer, Paul. "A Rush and a Push and the Land Is Ours: Territorial Expansion, Land Policy, and U.S. State Formation." *Perspectives on Politics* 12, no. 1 (March 2014): 119–147.

Gardner, B. Delworth. "The Political Economy of Public Land Use." *Journal of Agricultural and Resource Economics* 22, no. 1 (1997): 12–29.

Goodsell, Charles. *The Case for Bureaucracy.* Washington, DC: CQ Press, 2004.

———. *The New Case for Bureaucracy.* Washington, DC: CQ Press, 2014.

Groves, Craig, Lynn Kutner, David Stoms, Michael Murray, J. Michael Scott, Michael Schafale, Alan Weakley, and Robert Pressey. "Owning Up to Our Responsibilities: Who Owns the Lands Important for Biodiversity?" In *Precious Heritage: The Status of Biodiversity in the United States,* edited by Bruce Stein, Lynn Kutner, and Jonathan Adams, pp. 275–300. Oxford: Oxford University Press, 2000.

Hanke, Steve. "On Privatizing the Public Domain." In *Private Rights and Public Lands,* edited by Phillip Truluck, pp. 85–94. Washington, DC: Heritage Foundation, 1983.

Hanke, Steve, and Barney Dowdle. "Privatizing the Public Domain." *Proceedings of the Academy of Political Science* 36, no. 3, (1987): 114–123.

Hardin, Garrett. "The Tragedy of the Commons." *Science* 162, no. 3859 (December 13, 1968): 1243–1248.

Hare, Wayne. "Our Public Lands Should Reflect White, Black and Brown." *High Country News*, July 17, 2007.

Hayes, Samuel. *Conservation and the Gospel of Efficiency.* Cambridge, MA: Harvard University Press, 1959.

Headwaters Economics. *West Is Best: How Public Lands in the West Create a Competitive Economic Advantage.* Headwaters Economics Report, 2012.

Jones, Elise, and Cameron Taylor. "Litigating Agency Change: The Impact of the Courts and the Administrative Appeals Process on the Forest Service." *Policy Studies Journal* 23, no. 3 (Summer 1995): 310–336.

Karkkainen, Bradley. "Biodiversity and Land." *Cornell Law Review* 83, no. 1 (1997): 1–104.

Kaufman, Herbert. *The Forest Ranger: A Study in Administrative Behavior.* Baltimore: Johns Hopkins University Press for Resources for the Future, 1967.

Keiter, Robert B., and John C. Ruple. *A Legal Analysis of the Transfer of Public Lands Movement.* Stegner Center White Paper No. 2014-2, 2014.

Kline, Benjamin. *First along the River: A Brief History of the U.S. Environmental Movement.* San Francisco: Acada Books, 2000.

Kline, Jeffrey, Marisa J. Mazzotta, Thomas A. Spies, and Mark E. Harmon. "Applying the Ecosystem Services Concept to Public Land Management." *Agricultural and Resource Economics Review* 42, no. 1 (April 2013): 139–158.

Koontz, Tomas. *Federalism in the Forest: National versus State Natural Resource Policy.* Washington, DC: Georgetown University Press, 2002.

Krutilla, Joseph. "Conservation Reconsidered." *American Economic Review* 57, no. 4 (September 1967): 777–786.

Lawson, Megan. *Federal Lands in the West: Liability or Asset?* Headwaters Economics Report, 2016.

Lehmann, Scott. *Privatizing Public Land.* New York: Oxford University Press, 1995.

LeRoy, Sylvia. "Beyond the Public Park Paradigm." *George Wright Forum* 22, no. 2 (2005): 33–42.

Limerick, Patricia Nelson. "A History of the Public Lands Debate." In *Challenging Federal Ownership and Management: Public Lands and Public Benefits.* Boulder: University of Colorado Law School, 1995.

Loomis, John. *Integrated Public Lands Management.* New York: Columbia University Press, 1993.

Louv, Richard. *Last Child in the Woods.* Chapel Hill, NC: Algonquin Books, 2005.

MacCleery, Douglas. *American Forests: A History of Resiliency and Recovery.* Durham, NC: Forest History Society, 2011.

Maguire, Lynn, and James Justus. "Why Intrinsic Value Is a Poor Basis for

Conservation Decisions." *BioScience* 58, no. 10 (November 2008): 910–911.

Master, Lawrence, Bruce Stein, Lynn Kutner, and Geoffrey Hammerson. "Vanishing Assets." In *Precious Heritage: The Status of Biodiversity in the United States*, edited by Bruce Stein, Lynn Kutner, and Jonathan Adams, pp. 93–118. Oxford: Oxford University Press, 2000.

McCauley, Douglas. "Selling Out Nature." *Nature* 443 (September 7, 2006): 27–28.

McKinney, Matthew, and William Harmon. *The Western Confluence: A Guide to Governing Natural Resources.* Washington, DC: Island Press, 2004.

Mills, James. *The Adventure Gap.* Seattle: Mountaineers Books, 2014.

———. "In Search of Diversity in Our National Parks." *High Country News*, July 22, 2011.

Mohai, Paul. "Public Participation and Natural Resource Decision-Making: The Case of the RARE II Decisions." *Natural Resources Journal* 27 (Winter 1987): 123–155.

More, Thomas. "From Public to Private: Five Concepts of Park Management and Their Consequences." *George Wright Forum* 22, no. 2 (2005): 12–20.

———. "Privatization of Public Lands." In *Proceedings of the 2006 Northeastern Recreation Research Symposium.* U.S. Department of Agriculture, Forest Service Report, GTR-NRS-P-14, 2006, pp. 135–141.

National Commission on Science for Sustainable Forestry (NCSSF). *Beyond Old Growth: Older Forests in a Changing World.* NCSSF, 2008.

Nelson, Robert. "Free the American West." *Los Angeles Times*, March 7, 2012.

———. *Public Land and Private Rights: The Failure of Scientific Management.* Lanham, MD: Rowman and Littlefield, 1995.

Niskanen, William. *Bureaucracy—Servant or Master?* London: Institute of Economic Affairs, 1973.

Noss, Reed, and Allen Cooperrider. *Saving Nature's Legacy Island: Protecting and Restoring Biodiversity.* Washington, DC: Island Press, 1994.

Noss, Reed F., Edward T. LaRoe III, and J. Michael Scott. *Endangered Ecosystems of the United States: A Preliminary Assessment of Loss and Degradation.* U.S. Department of the Interior, National Biological Service Report 28, 1995.

Oesterle, Dale. "Public Land: How Much Is Enough?" *Ecological Law Quarterly* 23, no. 3 (June 1996): 521–575.

Ostrom, Elinor. *Governing the Commons: The Evolution of Institutions for Collective Action.* Cambridge: Cambridge University Press, 1990.

O'Toole, Randall. "Reforming Public Land Management with New Incentives." In *Challenging Federal Ownership and Management: Public Lands and Public Benefits.* Boulder: University of Colorado Law School, 1995.

Paehlke, Robert. "Democracy and Environmentalism: Opening a Door to the Administrative State." In *Debating the Earth*, edited by John Dryzek and David Schlosberg, pp. 163–179. Oxford: Oxford University Press, 2005.

Pahre, Robert. "Privatizing Isle Royale? The Limits of Free Market Environmentalism." *George Wright Forum* 25, no. 3 (2008): 23–39.

Peterson, Jodi. "Parks for All?" *High Country News*, May 19, 2014.

Pizzo, Sarah. *Valuing Our Western Public Lands*. National Wildlife Federation Report, 2013.

Raymond, Leigh, and Sally Fairfax. "The 'Shift to Privatization' in Land Conservation: A Cautionary Essay." *Natural Resources Journal* 42 (Summer 2002): 599–639.

Redford, Kent, and William Adams. "Payment for Ecosystem Services and the Challenge of Saving Nature." *Conservation Biology* 23, no. 4 (August 2009): 785–787.

Riitters, Kurt, James Wickham, Robert O'Neill, K. Bruce Jones, Elizabeth Smith, John Coulston, Timothy Wade, and Jonathan Smith. "Fragmentation of Continental United States Forests." *Ecosystems* 5 (2002): 815–822.

Ruhl, J. B. "Ecosystem Services and Federal Public Lands: Start-up Policy Questions and Research Needs." *Duke Environmental Law and Policy Forum* 20, no. 2 (Summer 2010): 275–290.

Sagoff, Mark. "The Allocation and Distribution of Resources." In *Debating the Earth*, edited by John Dryzek and David Schlosberg, pp. 147–162. Oxford: Oxford University Press, 2005.

———. "Market versus Libertarian Environmentalism." *Critical Review* 6, nos. 2–3 (1992): 211–230.

———. "The Rise and Fall of Ecological Economics: A Cautionary Tale." *Breakthrough Journal*, no. 2 (Fall 2011): 45–58.

Salzman, James. "A Field of Green? The Past and Future of Ecosystem Services." *Journal of Land Use and Environmental Law* 21, no. 2 (Spring 2006): 133–151.

Sax, Joseph. "The Legitimacy of Collective Values: The Case of the Public Lands." *University of Colorado Law Review* 56 (1984): 537–557.

Shands, William. "The Lands Nobody Wanted: The Legacy of the Eastern National Forests." In *The Origins of the National Forests*, edited by Harold Steen, pp. 19–44 (Durham, NC: Duke University Press, 1992).

Spence, Mark. *Dispossessing the Wilderness: Indian Removal and the Making of the National Parks*. New York: Oxford University Press, 1999.

Squillace, Mark, Eric Biber, Nicholas Bryner, and Sean Hecht. "Presidents Lack the Authority to Abolish or Diminish National Monuments." *Virginia Law Review* 103 (June 2017): 55–71.

Stein, Bruce, Jonathan Adams, Lawrence Master, Larry Morse, and Geoffrey Hammerson. "A Remarkable Array: Species Diversity in the United States." In *Precious Heritage: The Status of Biodiversity in the United States*, edited by Bruce Stein, Lynn Kutner, and Jonathan Adams, pp. 55–92. Oxford: Oxford University Press, 2000.

Stein, Bruce, Lynn Kutner, Geoffrey Hammerson, Lawrence Master, and Larry Morse. "State of the States." In *Precious Heritage: The Status of Biodiversity in the United States*, edited by Bruce Stein, Lynn Kutner, and Jonathan Adams, pp. 119–158. Oxford: Oxford University Press, 2000.

Stemler, Jodi. "Our Public Lands: Not for Sale." *Backcountry Hunters and Anglers Report*, November 2014.

Stevens, William. *Miracle under the Oaks*. New York: Pocket Books, 1995.

Stroup, Richard. "Privatizing Public Lands: Market Solutions to Economic and Environmental Problems." *Public Land and Resources Review* 19 (1998): 79–101.

Stroup, Richard, and John Baden. *Natural Resources: Bureaucratic Myths and Environmental Management*. Cambridge, MA: Ballinger, 1983.

Thomas, Craig W. *Bureaucratic Landscapes*. Boston: Massachusetts Institute of Technology Press, 2003.

Tipple, Terence, and J. Douglas Wellman. "Herbert Kaufman's Forest Ranger Thirty Years Later: From Simplicity and Homogeneity to Complexity and Diversity." *Public Administration Review* 51, no. 5 (September/October 1991): 421–428.

Turner, James Morton. *The Promise of Wilderness*. Seattle: University of Washington Press, 2012.

Twight, Ben. *Organization Values and Political Power: The Forest Service vs. Olympic National Park*. University Park: Pennsylvania State University Press, 1983.

Twight, Ben, and Fremont Lyden. "Measuring Forest Service Bias." *Journal of Forestry* 87, no. 5 (1989): 35–41.

Twight, Ben, Fremont Lyden, and E. Thomas Tuchman. "Constituency Bias in a Federal Career System? A Study of District Rangers of the U.S. Forest Service." *Administration and Society* 22 no. 3 (1990): 358–377.

Vickerman, Sara. *Nature's Benefits: The Importance of Addressing Biodiversity in Ecosystem Service Programs*. Defenders of Wildlife Report, Washington, DC, 2013.

Wade, Bill. "A New Tragedy for the Commons: The Threat of Privatization to National Parks (and Other Public Lands)." *George Wright Forum* 22, no. 2 (2005): 61–67.

Wilson, Randall. *America's Public Lands*. Lanham, MD: Rowman and Littlefield, 2014.

Wondolleck, Julia, and Steven Yaffee. *Making Collaboration Work*. Washington, DC: Island Press, 2000.

Wrobel, David M. "The Closing Gates of Democracy: Frontier Anxiety before the Official End of the Frontier." *American Studies* 32 (Spring 1991): 49–66.

Wyatt, Alexandra. *Antiquities Act: Scope of Authority for Modification of National Monuments*. Congressional Research Service Report R44687, 2016.

Index

Steven Davis is a Professor of Political Science and Environmental Studies at Edgewood College in Madison, Wisconsin.